N·I·C·K·E·L
Dreams

N·I·C·K·E·L
Dreams

MY LIFE

TANYA TUCKER
WITH
PATSI BALE COX

HYPERION

NEW YORK

Library of Congress Cataloging-in-Publication Data

Tucker, Tanya.
  Nickel dreams : my life / by Tanya Tucker with Patsi Bale Cox.—
1st ed.
    p.   cm.
  Discography: p.
  ISBN 0-7868-6305-6
  1. Tucker, Tanya. 2. Country musicians—United States—Biography.
I. Title.
ML420.T897A3 1997
782.421642'092—dc21
[B]   96-39594
                CIP
                MN

Book design by Nicholas A. Bernini

FIRST EDITION

10 9 8 7 6 5 4 3 2 1

This book is dedicated to all
my friends I didn't mention—
and you know who you are!

ACKNOWLEDGMENTS

_S_pecial thanks to my entire family. Without all of you these nickel dreams wouldn't be worth a penny!

To Leslie Wells, for being both a great editor and great friend to this book. To Bob Miller, Kris Kliemann, Lisa Kitei, and all the wonderful people at Hyperion.

To everyone at Tanya Tucker, Inc., especially Suzanne Crowley and Colleen Chapple, who did double duty!

To the William Morris Agency: my Los Angeles agent, Hal Ray, who began encouraging me to write a book years ago; my literary agent, Mel Berger, for sticking with me throughout; and my Nashville agent, Paul Moore, for two decades of great gigs and unwavering friendship.

To my record label, Capitol Nashville, for continued support through a "Complicated" project!

To all the people who helped us with their recollections, personal insights, and professional advice, including: Shirley Porter Burns, Tudy Clymer, Roe Farone, Tracy Johnson, Barb Shipley, Pam Scoggins, T. Martin, Pam Hyatt, Becky Waymack, Brian Edwards, Stephanie Beck, Patrick Carr, Ben Reed, Billy Sherrill, Al Gallico, Jerry Crutchfield, Joanne and Elmo Morris, Cindy Morris, Chuck Olson, Lew King, Cathy Gurley, Bonnie Rasmussin Taggart, Bill Carter, Joanna Carter, T.C. Carnicello, Dixie Carter, and Nancy Nicholas.

To the Country Music Foundation: Ronnie Pugh, Kent Henderson, and Daniel Cooper, for being invaluable to this book, as well as to all who are researching country music.

Finally, to my pal Patsi: In your liner notes on my box-set collection, you said I was the person you'd want riding shotgun if you had to go through 40 miles of bad road through enemy territory. You were my shotgun rider on this.

I lay in my bed at Nashville's Vanderbilt Hospital, numbed by painkillers, watching the 1991 Country Music Association Awards on television. That afternoon I'd given birth to my second child, a son I named Beau Grayson Tucker. My parents had been with me throughout the day. My daughter, Presley, was at the hospital, as was the father of both my children, Ben Reed. But they had all gone back to my house earlier, to watch the televised show. I figured I'd be drifting in and out of it anyway, and there was no reason for them to stay. No matter who is nominated or who wins, country music awards have always been a big thing for the Tucker family.

I was a candidate for the Female Vocalist Award, but because my life had been in such a mess for the past several months, winning was the last thing on my mind. I'd been nominated for awards many times since that first time in 1973 after "Delta Dawn" became a hit. But I'd always lost. Mother and Dad say I probably got used to losing clear back when I was a kid and they were signing me up for half the talent contests in Arizona. I kept coming in second to girls twirling batons or dancing with rag dolls tied to their feet. I always told myself that winning awards from my peers was never what motivated me, anyway. Fans are the ones who buy my CDs and attend my concerts, so performing and making records keep me going. Awards would just be the icing on the cake. I used to say, "Just call me Tanya Timex. I take a lickin' and keep on kickin'."

Things got confusing when Clint Black and Roy Rogers came out to announce Female Vocalist. Clint read off the names: Patty Loveless, Reba McEntire, Kathy Mattea, Lorrie Morgan. Then he stopped and looked kind of blank. I thought, "Dang, Clint, you know I'm up for it, don't forget me!" Finally he looked over at Roy and said, "Did we mention Tanya Tucker?" He said later that the TelePrompTer went out right after Lorrie's name. Then Roy Rogers announced that I'd won.

I couldn't react at first. I'd won the Academy of Country Music's Most Promising Female Vocalist in 1972 and, as I said, not much since. I was still lying there trying to get used to the idea of coming up a winner twice in one day when the phone rang and it was Jimmy Bowen, who was president of my record label. Most of the staff of Capitol Records had been sitting in his living room when the announcement was made, and pandemonium broke out. It made me feel great to hear that—the fact that they shared in the win. Nobody gets anywhere in this business without a team, and those people made up a big part of mine.

The next call I received was from the label's publicist, Cathy Gurley, calling from the Press Room at the Grand Ole Opry House where the CMA (Country Music Association) Awards Show was taking place. She said the entire press corps gave me a standing ovation. One journalist shouted, "It's about damn time!" Then Cathy told me that backstage after the show, Reba was talking to Patty Loveless and said, "Thank God. Thank God she finally won that award."

The reaction wasn't all positive, though. Later I found out that some deejay had been angry I won and accused the CMA of making a tramp its Top Female Vocalist. He figured my wild reputation and two children born out of wedlock were all the justification he needed to label me unworthy. Lord only knows what he would have called me if he'd known everything that had been going on in my life that year.

I talked to my parents, who could barely believe I'd won, too, and when I hung up the telephone, the Postpartum & Postaward Blues hit. Two highpoints of my life, having my son and winning my first Female Vocalist Award, had come on the heels of some of the worst times I'd ever gone through. Seems like life sometimes hands you an ice cream cone with one hand and smacks a pie in your face with the other.

I used to say that if I wrote a book it would be about my dad, not me, since Beau Tucker was the one who got me wherever it is I am in this world. I couldn't imagine what I'd say about myself, anyway. Talking or thinking about myself is not among my favorite things to do. I don't sit around and analyze all the rights and wrongs I've done, and I try not to make excuses. I hope when all is said and done, my rights outweigh my wrongs, because that would make the right things I've done pretty damned heavy duty. But I always thought that if I did try to write about myself, I'd call the book *Nickel Dreams*, which is a Mac McAnally song about a little girl who dreams of becoming a singer. Once she does, she finds out it wasn't exactly what she counted on. Although I love this song, I've never recorded it. Maybe it hits a little too close to home.

About a year ago, when I was just starting to work on my memoirs, my dad turned to me and said, "I don't like this new image of yours. They're trying to make you look too slick. Too Hollywood. You need to get back to being Tanya Tucker."

He brings this up every time he sees a new photo session that he doesn't like, or when a hairdresser gives me some kind of an uptown cut or a makeup artist gets heavy-handed with the mascara. My answer is usually something like this: "Daddy, why don't you tell me how to do that? How do I get back to being Tanya Tucker when I don't know who or what a Tanya Tucker is?"

Working on the book has given me some insights, but I sure don't have all the answers. I've been standing on the midway for a long time, twenty-five of my thirty-eight years. Show business brought me and my family out of poverty. Singing brought me a personal fulfillment surpassed only by the birth of my children. I've experienced many highs and lows over these twenty-five years, on both individual and career levels, and as happened in 1991, sometimes they occurred simultaneously.

The thing is, every one of us has good and bad times in their lives. In my case, they have been to extreme. Sometimes I feel like I've been on one long bungee jump, with the cord that pulls me back safely each time being an intertwining of music and family. I still might jump once in a while, and I'll probably land in the tabloids because of it. But that's less likely these days. I wasn't even included in *People*'s Top Ten Party Girls this year. I lost out to Drew Barrymore and Sharon Stone.

I know that many people know and like my music, but I don't know if many of them really know anything about me, as a person. So I'll tell you about a few of the places I've been and some of the things that have happened to me. This book isn't a body count. I'm not going to write down a list of all the men I've slept with or every drug I've ever taken or glass of whiskey I've thrown back. But neither am I going to list every charity concert I've performed or every sick child I've visited, just to show you I'm a good-hearted good old girl. I'm not going to pretend that I haven't been in denial about some of my problems over the years, either. After thinking about my life over the past months, I came to the conclusion that the book could also be titled after my 1992 album: *Can't Run from Yourself.* I've tried it and I couldn't do it. And it could be named after my latest album, too: *Complicated.* Things in my life have never been easy to figure.

I once read that a movie historian said it was "the autobiographies of the second-tier performers—the Mary Astors, not the Bette Davises—that really told how movies were made, how the industry functioned and how an actor survived year after year" (*New York Times*, 29 December 1994). The *New York Times* reviewer who reported the historian's assessment said it applied to music books, too. She said that many years in the business leave some people with an image to worship and others with a story to tell. Well, I don't think of myself as a second-tier performer, but I don't see myself as having an image to worship, either. And the story I have to tell starts in dust bowl Oklahoma, where my dad was born.

N·I·C·K·E·L
Dreams

ONE

My father's family was living in a little shack around twelve miles southeast of Colgate, Oklahoma, during the cold winter of 1934, and Grandma Tucker tried to insulate the walls by wallpapering with newspapers. As insulation went, newspaper pasted up with flour and water wasn't the best, but it was better than nothing. It was the bottom of the Great Depression, a sorry time for crops and trapping game, when the family got some outside help. One day a man showed up at the Tuckers' door, and although he was carrying a rifle, nobody remembers feeling afraid or threatened in any way. He was a handsome and soft-spoken gentleman, who very politely asked Grandma if she had any food.

"I'm sorry," Grandma apologized. "All we've got is some turnip greens. I've got some meal that I could use to make up some cornbread. Just with water, though. And we've got no salt."

"Not much luck shooting possum these days?"

"Traps have been bare," she said, then started busying herself with the cornbread and turnip greens.

While the food was cooking, the man went outside and got to talking to my dad, Beau, who was seven, and his brother Jack, who was fifteen.

"Any of you boys a good shot with a .22?" he asked.

Jack said he was, so the man handed him the rifle.

"See if you can shoot that post over there," he said, and Jack took aim and put a hole right through the post.

"Well, that's pretty good," the fellow said, and he took an old Prince Albert can from a pile of junk in the yard and set it up against the post. He started shooting, and before he was through, he'd cut Prince Albert's face right out of the can. Then he had Jack and Dad throw some rocks and a marble up in the air and he busted them in half.

He went back inside and sat down to eat his cornbread and greens. But he didn't say anything until they'd finished. Then he nodded toward the newspapers on the wall. One upside-down page showed a picture of the FBI's Most Wanted Man.

"What would you do if that man showed up at your door?" he asked.

"Well, I expect I'd feed him," she said.

When he'd gone, Grandma picked up the pie plate he'd been eating from and found a $20 bill. It was the most cash money she'd had in over a year.

The boys followed him outside, and as he was leaving, the man handed Jack the .22 and said, "Son, now when you need a rabbit for dinner, use this rifle and remember that you've been trained by an expert." Jack and Dad ran in and showed their mother the rifle the man had given them.

"Do you know him?" Jack asked.

Grandma nodded her head. "That was Mamie Floyd's boy, Charley."

Their visitor had been the famous Pretty Boy Floyd, known in his home state of Oklahoma as much for his gifts of large amounts of cash to any farm family who fed him as he was for being the FBI's Most Wanted Man. No matter how many banks he might have robbed, he always showed respect for poor folks. He often dropped by people's farms when he was on the run. In my family he's remembered as a man who'd trade $20 and a .22 rifle for some watered-down cornbread and turnip greens.

Some months later Pretty Boy Floyd was shot and killed by government agents in an Ohio cornfield. Thousands of people gathered in Akins, Oklahoma, for his funeral. I imagine a lot of them had stories to tell that were similar to my family's experience. I guess he knew it was safer to rely on people in the Oklahoma hill country for food than to be seen dining out in public. That was the sort of environment that produced my father, a country where you barely scratched out a living, and you put your trust in common folks.

Dad's father, my Grandpa Tucker, abandoned his wife and eight kids in the Oklahoma hills in the middle of the Great Depression, leaving behind nothing but a fiest dog named Shorty and a chopping ax. For those unfamiliar with hill country talk, a fiest dog is a squirrel dog, handy only if any squirrels were able to live through the drought that caused the dust bowl.

My dad isn't even sure what sort of work his father did for a living. He thinks the old man did a little sharecropping and a lot of backwoods whiskey making. Tom Tucker wasn't a bad man, according to those who knew him, but he was weak when it came to taking care of his family. And by turning his back on them, he made his kids grow up to be strong, natural survivors. The Tuckers' strong sense of family came from my grandmother, Beatrice Vinson Tucker. She had a life that would make any woman hard, but her dignity was unshakable. My dad says that he never heard his mother utter a bad word against anyone, even the husband who left her high and dry. I guess her only failing, if you can call it that, was snuff. The kids sometimes stole a chicken or two to barter so she could indulge that little vice. She'd ask them where they got the snuff and they'd say, "Oh, we just found it out by the road. Ain't that somethin'?"

Grandma and her kids lived off the land after Grandpa left, and pickings were slim in Oklahoma during the dust bowl days. They grew what they could, and they trapped possum and rabbits, but food was always scarce. They had no cash whatsoever and wouldn't see the inside of a grocery store for six or seven months at a time. Everything in their lives revolved around finding food, and before they got that gun from Pretty Boy Floyd and could hunt squirrel, they scavenged for what they could find.

One night when Daddy was around six, Jack shook him awake in the middle of the night. The air in the room was thick with a fine, powdery dust, and the wind howled outside.

"We got to go," Jack said. "We got to go find some food."

Daddy crawled off the old mattress carefully, so as not to awaken his sleeping brothers and sisters curled up beside him. He put on his pants and followed Jack. If there was food to be had, real food, he wanted to find it. They'd been living on cornbread and turnip greens for a week. When they'd slipped out of

4 •   TANYA TUCKER

the little tar-paper shack, Jack handed Dad a gunnysack and led him out into the hills, explaining that he'd heard of a nearby farmer who had a shed full of so many potatoes that a family couldn't eat them all in a year. Jack figured that made them fair game, so to speak. Daddy followed with his gunnysack slung over his shoulder, his stomach aching with hunger at the thought of more potatoes than someone could eat in a year.

Daddy and Jack sneaked through the fields in the moonlight, toward the nearby farm, dodging tumbleweeds and praying they didn't run up on any rattlesnakes, since those hills were full of them.

"I can smell 'em, Jack," Daddy said when they crested the hill above the next farm. "I can smell potatoes."

Daddy said later that it felt like they were following their noses to heaven. When they got to the little shed, Jack tried the door. It was locked tight. They made their way around the side, looking for any weak spot, a loose board or a broken window. Suddenly, Dad spotted a hole near the ground where it looked like an animal had chewed its way through. He got down on his stomach and peered through.

"There they are, Jack," he called. "There's stacks of potatoes in there." He stuck his hand through the hole and a trap snapped down on his arm. And although the pain was agonizing, he didn't dare cry out for fear of awakening the farmer. Jack ran around to the side of the shed, found a piece of metal, and frantically whacked at the lock until he broke it off. Dad almost passed out by the time Jack pried the trap off his bloody arm. It was an old, worn-out trap, or he could never have done it. Jack ran out of the shed and hurriedly wrapped Daddy's arm in one of the gunnysacks, then pulled him to his feet and started to help him out of the farmer's barnyard.

"Did you get the potatoes?" Dad asked.

Jack bit his lip, torn between needing to get Daddy home and needing food. He ran back and filled his sack, and the two boys made their way back through the hills. They cleaned Daddy's wound at the pump and slipped back inside. Fortunately, the bone wasn't broken, and there was no infection. It was a miracle that he didn't get tetanus from that old trap. Daddy hid his wound from his mother until it was nearly healed, then made up some lie about how it had happened. Grandma Tucker had so many worries, she didn't have time to question it. When his arm ached at night, Daddy just turned over in bed and grit his teeth.

People grew up hard in dust bowl Oklahoma, especially in a family without a father. Dad says that if you got in a fight with someone and just knocked him down, you'd be facing his brothers and cousins the next night. You had to hurt him bad enough to make him back off for good. Dad learned that early on. We call it Tucker tough, and I think he's used that principle more than once when he dealt with unscrupulous show promoters.

I once jokingly told a reporter that I liked having grown up poor because it made a better story, but compared to the way Dad and his brothers and sisters grew up, I had it good. His childhood, or lack of one, made him as tough as any person I've ever known. Ask anyone who's ever negotiated a contract with him, and they'll tell you. It also made him respect a dollar. Dad hangs onto his money now, whereas mine just seems to run on down the road.

I've never stuck my arm through a shed and had a trap snap down on it, but I've been a lot of places I shouldn't be and done a lot of things I shouldn't do. And I've spent a lot of my life trying to stay Tucker tough.

My mother's family, the Cunninghams, came from around Abilene, Texas. My great-grandfather, Gid Cunningham, was Irish and Cherokee Indian, a lethal combination when it came to drinking whiskey, which he did frequently. Still, in 1937, a rancher named Roy Wasson took a liking to the family and asked Gid to bring them all and come work for him, growing everything from cotton to watermelon and running horses and cattle. Three generations of Cunninghams moved to Gaines County, Texas, to live on the ranch and help Roy Wasson. They were Gid, his son Marion, Marion's wife, Thella Hindsley Cunningham, and their eight children. The oldest of the Cunningham kids was my mother, Juanita.

Roy Wasson was such a powerful man in Gaines County that the town closest to his ranch was named after him. Mr. Wasson wanted to help the Cunninghams make a better life, and he offered a good-sized parcel of land to my great-grandpa, Gid, at 50 cents an acre. But Gid Cunningham had squandered nearly every bit of cash that crossed his palms on whiskey, so he had to turn down the deal, and somebody else bought the property.

Oil companies had been leasing drilling rights in the area since 1927, and in 1935, they struck oil. The Denver Producing and Refining Company moved in and began intensive drilling once that happened, and the original wells in that forty-five-mile area still produce approximately 250,000 barrels of crude oil a day. One-fourth of America's oil reserves were stored under the south plains of Texas, and even a few acres of that land would have made more money than ten generations could have spent. The sign that once read Wasson Ranch later read Shell Oil. So, thanks to whiskey and Great-Grandpa Cunningham, I lost the chance to be born with a silver spoon in my mouth—not that I regret it. In fact, I wonder just how much trouble I might have got myself into if I'd been a billionaire oil heiress and not had to work for a living.

It was in Wasson, Texas, that my mother and father met. Dad's family had finally made it out of the hills to work the cotton patch circuit, and between jobs my dad would try to make it to a school somewhere. He met my mother on the school bus when they were both eleven. As he tells it, "I took one look and I was a goner." His way of making her notice him was about as cool as most eleven-year-old boys' attention-getters— he started stealing cookies from her lunch sack. She couldn't stand him.

In 1939 the Denver Producing and Refining Company decided a town needed to be located closer to the drilling sites, so they picked up the buildings in Wasson and moved three miles north, naming the new town Denver City. Most of the residents worked the oil fields, living in shotgun houses and tents and using public bath houses. The Tuckers and the Cunninghams moved into the tent city and kept working the oil fields. There were two basic kinds of tents, the more temporary kind, held down with pegs hammered into the ground, and the more permanent kinds, with wooden sides and floors. The Tuckers were lower on the social scale than the Cunninghams, although not as much as if Gid Cunningham had bought that land. Their tent didn't have flooring and wooden sides, but the families worked side by side as equals. This is how Dad got to know my grandpa, Marion Cunningham, and develop a lot of respect for him.

In 1941 Dad dropped out of school to chase after some bulldozing job with his brother Jack, and when World War II broke out, he headed up to Colorado where he heard there was work hauling water to the Japanese internment camps. Somehow he scraped together enough money to buy an old truck, and he hauled water for a few months. He was fourteen when he got back to Texas.

The first person Dad went looking for in Denver City was Juanita Cunningham. He came upon her chopping wood, wearing a little tam on her head and looking like the prettiest thing he'd ever seen, right down to her little bowlegs. Mom doesn't appreciate him saying that! By then Dad was as big as any man and very handsome. This time it was Mom who took one look and was a goner.

Within a few months of Dad's return, he and Mom wanted to get married. At first, they wanted to elope. They drove Dad's old water-hauling truck over the Texas border to Lovington, New Mexico. But Mom was so obviously underage that nobody would marry them.

On the drive back to Wasson, Dad started working up the nerve to ask for Mom's hand. She was the only woman he'd ever met that measured up to his mother. He spent the next day at the oil fields following Grandpa Cunningham before springing the question. But he needn't have worried so much. Grandpa took a few minutes to think it over and said, "Well, Beau, I guess I'd just as soon you starve her as me."

They got married on January 29, 1943, when they were only fifteen years old. Mom was a month shy of seventeen when my brother Don was born. Mom had a long labor, and Dad, who'd just turned seventeen himself, wanted to help. So he ran out and bought up a pile of Mom's favorite reading material back then— romance magazines. She says she'd have got up and whipped him if she could, though she knew he meant well. I've felt the same sometimes. When my dad makes career decisions for me I always know he is making them from his heart, even if they occasionally appear a little, well, insensitive.

Dad was a hard worker, but he never stayed at one job very long. He never got fired, though. It was always his decision to move on. He's done everything from roughnecking in the oil fields to core drilling to bulldozing to piloting—anything to keep from having to chop any more cotton or steal any more potatoes. He's an expert mechanic, and that talent has helped us keep a succession of vehicles running long past their prime. His being so good with motors makes it tough for any bus drivers who work on the road with us. He knows what maintenance work is needed, and if something goes wrong that could have been prevented, watch out.

Because Dad was a good hand, he could find work anywhere, and when I started chasing after a career in country music, Daddy's ability to land on his feet in a new town was an important asset. But for the first seventeen years of their marriage, Mom and Dad stayed put in Denver City. They never had an excess of money, but times weren't all hard, either. Dad worked the oil fields and pulled in a few extra dollars as a pilot, a skill he'd originally picked up hanging around the Denver City airport. Later, he took private lessons from a friend of his.

Dad got into some trouble during his pilot days. He bought a B-13 that the army was getting ready to scrap, repaired it, and took to the skies. One of his favorite pastimes was to buzz the town—once he even flew right under the one stoplight on Main Street. Then he'd head out and buzz the cotton fields to watch the pickers scatter. He was always getting crossways with the law about it. One time he was filling up his plane and Wiley Anderson, the Denver City sheriff, pulled up beside him.

"Beau, I'm gonna have to run you in this time," Wiley said. "I've already got a dozen complaints on you this week. You're scarin' the hell out of folks."

"Well, all right," Dad said. "Just let me move this plane so somebody else can gas up." Then he got in the plane and just took off. By the time he showed up back in Denver City things had calmed down, and Wiley was on the trail of something else. So when Dad says I'm always stirring things up, I can remind him that at least I'm not running from the law in a B-13!

My sister, La Costa, was born in 1950, delivered by the same doctor who had brought Larry Gatlin into the world two years earlier. Although we were still living in Denver City, La Costa and I were born eighteen miles away, in Seminole, where the family doctor lived.

I was born on October 10, 1958, the same year they invented hula hoops. I had a close call before I was even born. When Mom was three months along, I came loose from her uterus. It was touch and go for several weeks, and Mom and Dad were scared to death that they would lose me. But somehow I settled in and all was just fine. The experience taught her something about me, though. It was just the first example of how I've been trying to bust loose my whole life.

Unlike La Costa, who was named for Mom's friend La Costa Edwards, I was given a stranger's name Mom picked out of the Denver City newspaper. There was a christening notice about the banker's new granddaughter Tanya. My middle name, though, came because Mom's friend Dorothy Ellerd had called her daughter Denise, another name my parents loved.

TWO

*M*y dad says I've always been ornery as the devil, and people who know us well say I take after him. That should come as no surprise, since he's been the single biggest influence in my life. He's always had high hopes and big dreams, and because of him, I grew up believing I could do anything.

For instance, when I was four, Dad started teaching me how to drive a Volkswagen he owned. I don't think my mother has ever gotten over the horror she felt a few weeks later when Dad sat me behind the wheel and told her to pile in, because we were going for a ride. I not only drove around the block but parked the thing when we drove back in the yard.

In spite of the fact that my nickname is the Texas Tornado, we moved from Texas to Arizona when I was about a year and a half, so I don't remember much about living in Denver City. I love Texas now, but my childhood memories are from Cochise County in Willcox, Arizona, where one of America's great singing cowboys, Rex Allen, was born in 1921. Even now, every October the city celebrates Rex Allen Days with a rodeo and a parade and concerts, and as soon as I was old enough to ride horses, I was one of the first in line to ride the parade.

The history of this area is rich and filled with amazing tales that are told and retold by locals. I think my love of the story-telling tradition in song and of all things western is rooted right there in the Sulphur Springs Valley.

We made the move to Willcox because of the strong farming industry that had developed by the late 1950s. Farmers in the Sulphur Springs Valley grew chili peppers, potatoes, soybeans, corn, and cotton. They grew so much of it that the water table dropped drastically during the war years. To counter that problem, at various times over the next several decades, people were hired to come in to drill deeper wells. Dad was always looking for a way to better our situation, so when he heard about the good job opportunity for drillers, he went for it.

Unfortunately, housing was tight. Old-timers around Willcox say there was a housing shortage even back in the town's early days, and when we moved there in 1960, it was still in short supply. The first place we lived was an old house that had been divided into several apartments, one of which had been condemned because of weak floors or something. We lived in the front and another family lived in the back. The middle apartment was the condemned one and empty. Costa and I loved sneaking around and peering through the windows into those dusty, dangerous rooms.

The house was so dark and full of dirt when we moved in, we nicknamed it Brownsville. We were always naming houses back then. Mom says it got started because we'd find some terrible old place that was just filthy, rent it as cheaply as possible, then go in and spend a lot of time cleaning and sweeping out all the bugs and spiders. Somehow giving the places names gave them a personality and made them feel a little nicer. Another reason may have been that since we lived in so many houses and trailers, it was hard to keep track of where we'd been and where we were! I was too young to have had a part in the sanitizing of Brownsville, but I made up for it later in a succession of rundown duplexes and trailers all across Arizona and Utah.

After Brownsville we moved to a duplex on the edge of town. Some of my fondest childhood memories are associated with that house. It was a wild place, and we often cooked outside, camp-style. Sometimes people came through on horseback tracking cougars that had been after someone's cattle. If riders came through at night they'd be carrying lanterns and warning people to stay inside. Man, the air would just be electric with danger, and I loved every minute of it.

We had about forty acres, and animals everywhere. Dogs, cats, ducks, and eventually cows and horses. The people who lived down the road had a big peach orchard, and they'd let us have any peaches that fell to the ground. To this day I've never eaten juicier or sweeter peaches.

We also had a wonderful garden, and I loved knowing that the vegetables we ate were ones we'd grown ourselves. When my dad was growing up, their lives often depended on what they could grow. I doubt that I was much help when it came to actually planting and growing the vegetables, but I did love my job, which was to go pick things for dinner. Mom would give me a list of what she needed—radishes, onions, okra, squash—and I'd run out after them. I have a big garden now, but it's far away from the house and feels impersonal to me. It seems to me that gardens ought to be right outside the kitchen door.

✥ ❦ ✥ ❦

Our landlady, Mrs. Lawson, lived next door, and she was afraid I wouldn't live to see the age of ten because I climbed on everything in sight. She'd come outside and walk around looking up in the trees, calling out, "Yoo-hoo, you little monkey." I'd yoo-hoo back, but she could never spot me. I loved that feeling of blending into the trees and watching things going on all around me, like I was a part of the landscape.

I still like the feeling of blending in with things, and it's gotten me into trouble more than once. Most recognizable artists don't tend to hang out in public places alone, since as sure as anything some crazy is going to hassle them. Not me. I love to hang out, and it's not like when I hid in the treetops from Mrs. Lawson. Now if I yoo-hoo back to someone, the story lands in the tabloids.

✥ ❦ ✥ ❦

Birthdays were always important at our house, and I still celebrate mine as if it were a national holiday. I remember one in particular from my early childhood. On my fifth birthday my parents gave me a big party and a present that gave me a new place to put all my excess energy. I can still remember having on a new red dress. All my friends were over, eating cake my mother made, when Daddy came around the side of the house with Pretty Boy, my first Shetland pony. Dad, of course, had named him for his childhood hero. That was the beginning of a lifelong love of horses. Pretty Boy also taught me a very important lesson about animals. They aren't toys, and children must be taught to respect them just as they would a friend. Pretty Boy was a bad-natured animal. He was a biter and a kicker, and my friends and I did nothing to settle him down. All we knew was that it was fun to pile on him, often one rider too many, and take off.

I slowly saw that he was getting out of control, but I didn't know what to do about it. Once he nipped a friend of mine on the back, and I tried to tell her it was because she was wearing an orange sweater and Pretty Boy mistook it for a pile of oats. She didn't buy it. Nor did my dad buy it when he saw Pretty Boy rear up and smack me with a hoof one afternoon. He took the bridle in his hand, walked to town, and sold the pony on the spot.

My next horse was Honey Bun, a gelding that started wild and stayed wild. Not mean, just wild. We'd go like the wind, and my parents would practically break out in hives watching us fly over the fields near the house. La Costa had a mare, Iveena, who was a good, solid riding horse, and much gentler than Honey Bun, although they looked a lot alike. She eventually foaled my first colt, Delta Dawn.

Dad had bought Iveena at a junior rodeo. Honey Bun came from a woman who made us promise we'd sell him back to her if he was too wild for kids. Well, Dad finally determined that no matter how I tried to "gentle" him, Honey Bun needed a bigger, physically stronger rider than me. By then, he'd forgotten all about his promise to the lady who'd first owned the horse, and he got a good price for him from a rancher who had a bunkhouse full of cowboys who loved wild rides.

Sure enough, one day the old woman showed up wanting to say hello to Honey Bun. She brushed past Dad and went straight to the corral, where Iveena was standing. Dad didn't know what to say, so he kept his mouth shut. The lady looked at Iveena standing there and began to shake her head. Dad figured he was busted. The fact that Honey Bun was a gelding and Iveena was a mare left little doubt they were different horses. Aside from that obvious difference, Iveena's hooves were unusually large. Finally the woman turned to leave and said, "I sure don't know what's happened to Honey Bun's hooves. They look like they're twice as big as they used to be."

Even though I didn't understand how to gentle horses at first, I instinctively knew how to ride them. The moment Dad put me on Pretty Boy's back, it was as if I'd been born on horseback and ready to run. The same with Honey Bun, even if he was so wild. I'd ride bareback hell-bent for leather, just like the Indians who used to roam those Arizona hills. It seemed like the most natural thing in the world.

Horses were an extravagance, but we always had them. I think some people are the type to pay the rent, take care of the utility and food bills, then hope there is money left over for other things the family needs or wants. My mother and dad tended to be the opposite. They'd spend money on their kids, then Dad would work overtime or whatever he had to do to pay the monthly bills. Sometimes it worked out and sometimes it didn't. More than once we moved out of a place suddenly, and we certainly had no savings or real financial security. My dad and his ability to work hard was our only security.

It was so important to my parents to see that we had things we wanted, things that middle-class kids took for granted. One Christmas Daddy pawned a tape recorder and bought me a puppy and a bicycle. Another year we were all sitting around inside the trailer and we heard a noise outside, and Daddy said, "Santa Claus must have come early!" We ran out and there on top of the trailer was a little play-by-number organ I'd been wanting. They always tried to get us nice things, and I know it's because they had so little when they were growing up.

In fact, I can think of only one thing I'd ever wanted as a child that I didn't get, and that was a Suzy Homemaker Oven. Now, who in the world would picture me pining away for a Suzy Homemaker Oven, of all things? The power of advertising and peer pressure just got to me. My friend Jackie Smith had one, after all, so why shouldn't I? It's very typical of my mother that she still feels guilty about me not having that toy stove. She swears she's going to go out and buy one just to lay it all to rest. I don't know if Suzy Homemaker Ovens still exist, but just in case someone reading this book has the idea to get one for me, please do this: Buy it and send it to the local women's shelter. I know the kids there would love to have one.

Desperately wanting "things" can be such a trap. Sometimes I'll see a piece of costly jewelry or a pair of expensive shoes and think I can't live without them. Most of the time I end up buying the thing and then practically having an anxiety attack over spending so much money on myself.

My brother Don was ready to graduate from high school when we moved to Willcox. When he did, he went off to school in Douglas, Arizona, at Cochise College, where he studied aviation. I guess he caught the flying bug from our dad. I always loved it when Don came home because he always brought presents. He'd sweep through the door, making a big entrance with an armful of gifts. I associate Don's homecomings with Christmas and birthdays—any time gifts are exchanged. Throughout our lives, Don has dropped in and out, but I still associate him with presents and holidays.

My sister La Costa was more like our mother than I was. I was a hell-raiser like Dad. And since La Costa was a mama's girl, she did more feminine things than I did. Translate that to "housework." She'd be doing the dishes and I'd be out in the garden or playing with animals. La Costa was very close to our Grandmother Tucker, who was still living in Denver City, Texas. I think she inherited two things from Grandma: her candy-making talents and her entrepreneurial spirit. Grandma was an expert candy maker, and Costa paid close enough attention to her confectioner's secrets that today she, too, is an expert.

I think the reason I wasn't as close to my Grandma Tucker as Costa was because Grandma seemed so stern to me. Now I wish I'd spent more time with her. Family was everything to Beatrice Tucker. One time when she was staying with us, Mother and Dad went out for the evening, leaving Costa and me with her. They were only going to check on a house they thought we might be able to rent, but by the time they returned, Grandma was steamed.

"You shouldn't be leaving these babies that long at a time," she scolded. "They ought to be a part of everything you do."

Dad didn't disappoint her from then on. Believe me, the Tuckers have always been a unit.

I was closer to my Cunningham grandparents. I adored my grandpa, Marion Cunningham, and I loved going back to visit the little trailer where they still lived in Denver City. There was a smell to the trailer, a musty smell that probably wasn't all that pleasant, but I remember it fondly just because it was their place. When we drove to visit them, we'd pull in late. I'd be in my pajamas sleeping in the backseat of the car, and Dad would wrap me up and carry me to the door while I was still half asleep. Being carried into that trailer wrapped in a blanket was one of the most secure, safe feelings I've ever had.

They had a little black and white pug, and he'd be barking when we knocked on the door. We'd go in, and Grandma and Grandpa would have a pot of coffee and a big pot of white beans on the stove. Everyone would be tired that first night, so we'd get to bed and get started on the real visit early the next day. By that evening, uncles and aunts would be there, and they'd be there singing songs like "Busted" and drinking whiskey. Most of the people on both sides of my family are drinkers. The notable exceptions are my mother and father. Dad says he hates to be out of control, and therefore he never drank more than a few beers. In fact, he had his wisdom teeth pulled without benefit of Novocain because he said he didn't want to end up a dope addict. You can well imagine that sort of personality was not going to look kindly on a daughter who was prone to excesses of several kinds. He never criticized his family or my mother's family, though. They were a wild bunch, but he loved every one of them. He always tried to find something good, or funny, or notable about his family members, and he taught us kids to try to see those things in them, too.

Costa and I were very close while we were growing up, even though she was eight years older than me. I was very much the nosy kid sister, too. I loved digging around in her things, reading her diary, and looking at the things she stored in her hope chest. That was back when girls saved doilies and towel sets and anything domestic in anticipation of being married. Costa always wanted to be a married woman. I don't remember wanting a hope chest myself, but I did love snooping through hers.

By the time Costa started paying attention to boys, I was eight or nine, the age when kids are thinking up bigger and better ways to needle their siblings. I remember once when Costa got interested in a boy named Fred Smith. He'd cruise up and down our street on his motorscooter in the hopes she'd invite him inside. She was very shy, and it took her months to even go out and talk to him. She was the one who really believed kids should be seen and not heard. But finally she did ask Fred if he'd like to come in for a while.

I knew that my sister hated the fact that our furniture was so shabby. Even though she wasn't ashamed of our old house, she wasn't thrilled to let just anyone come around, especially a boy who interested her. We had a rocking chair that had been left in the apartment by the former tenants, and it was in terrible shape. It only had a couple of springs left and the stuffing was completely pulled out. We just wadded up some worn-out jeans to replace the stuffing and threw a towel over it. When you don't have much money you find many ways to improvise.

Well, the minute Fred hit the door I ran over and grabbed the towel off that rocker and pointed at the jeans. "Man, can you believe this ol' chair?" I embarrassed the dog out of her and then slid right out the back door.

I'm lucky she didn't kill me.

It seems like I was always just missing getting into big trouble. Bedtime was a problem when I was growing up, and my folks and I kept butting heads over it. I liked staying up late even back then, and I hated taking naps. Mother was the disciplinarian up to a point, but when things spun out of control she'd call Dad in on it.

Things usually started spinning after the third or fourth time I refused to go to bed. Dad would end up having to spank me. I'd stomp off to bed mad. That should have been the end of it, but not for me. I'd get up the next morning and say something like: "You know I heard about a daddy who killed his little girl spanking her. You wouldn't want to do that, would you?" Or, "Daddy, you know I heard about a man who got put in jail for whipping his little girl. You wouldn't want to go to jail, would you?" I always had a comeback, was always running my mouth asking for trouble.

The other tendency I had—and to be honest, I still do—was to try to shock people. It runs in our family, but I've carried it to extremes. One of the worst things I ever did was to play a particularly horrible practical joke on the family. My brother Don found a lost Doberman pinscher out on the highway, and he brought her home and called her Lady, a name that didn't fit her personality a bit. She must have been mistreated by someone, because Lady was the meanest-tempered dog I've ever seen. Even tied up I didn't trust her. One day Mom went by the butcher shop and got Lady a bag of bones for dinner. I snuck the bones outside and rubbed some blood on my shirt and arms. Then I busted in the front door crying, "Mother! Daddy! Lady got me! Lady got me!" Lord, my dad went nuts.

"Juanita, help Tanya," he was shouting. "By God, I'll get my gun and shoot that damn dog."

Well, of course, I just cracked up laughing. Mother and Dad thought it was about as funny as a heart attack, and they whipped my butt for it. I never gave a thought to how horrified Mother and Dad would be at the sight of a bloody kid. I just wanted to stir something up, and did.

But, like I said, the whole family liked that sort of joke. One of the times I got paid back for stunts like the bloody arms and shirt happened during the time Don was waiting to find out if he'd have to go to Vietnam. He'd been drafted and had gone for his physical. All I could think about was the news I'd seen on television, and how guys were getting blown up over there. I came home from school one day and Dad said, "Tanya, bad news. Don's gone off to Vietnam." I stood there and stared at him, then dropped my books and started bawling my head off. Then Don jumped up from behind the couch and everybody started laughing. "My bad knee saved me," Don said, with a big grin. I didn't get to whip anybody for that little prank, but I should have.

I was an ornery little girl, but I was never a mean-spirited one. I was always collecting the misfits in a classroom. I'd never in a million years be the kid making fun of someone with too-thick glasses or snot all over his face. I'd be the one siding with that kid, the champion of the underdog. One of my first friends at Willcox Elementary was a little girl who had a bladder problem and wet her pants every day on the bus. The minute I saw her being teased by the other kids, she became my new best friend.

I think one reason I collected misfits is that I knew what it was to be teased mercilessly for something you can't help. When I was very young I had some discoloration on my front teeth, a couple of brown spots that I got fixed the minute I started making some money. It might not seem like a big deal, but it was at the time. Kids can be pretty cruel if you have an obvious defect. I didn't stop getting teased about those teeth until I was in the seventh grade and we moved to St. George, Utah. The Mormon kids there never even seemed to notice, or they were too kind to say a word if they did.

What I remember most about my childhood, though, is not being teased or playing practical jokes, it's how incredibly close we were as a family. I've read that Rosanne Cash says the Carter and Cash families live out of each other's pockets, and the same can be said for the Tuckers. We've always been protective of one another, and trust me, everybody knows what everybody else had for breakfast.

If I were playing a word association game, I'd probably associate Daddy with "strength" or "hard work." Even now, when I picture my dad, I think of a man dressed in green workman's clothes. I thought they were the finest looking "uniforms" in the world. I still have a tendency to admire men who do physical work for a living, and I mean hard work, the kind of work that breaks your back.

Mother I'd associate with "good" or "spiritual." She has a level of perfection I knew even as a child I'd never be able to attain myself. Another word that comes to mind when I think of Mother is "respect," because that was one of the first things my dad taught me about dealing with her. "You call her 'Mother,' not 'Ma' or 'Mama,'" he'd say. "That's the respectful way to speak about her."

Maybe it's because she's part Indian, but Mother's spiritual nature has made her something of a healer. If you tell her you have a health problem, I guarantee she'll have a home remedy or some herb tea she thinks will fix you up. The truth is, I always preferred Daddy's home remedies. His cure was the Snickers bar cure, and to this day when I feel like a scared little kid or feel down about something, a Snickers bar will go a long way toward snapping me back.

He has a psychic side, too. He tells people he can "sense" when I'm screwing up, and I'm thinking his senses must have nearly worn out several times over the years.

Maybe we know each other so well because we spent a lot of time together as a family. We never went out a lot or entertained much. We didn't have the money for either activity. When we did go somewhere it was usually to try to get La Costa or me on some stage. I look back on all the moves we made and all the different jobs Daddy held, and it seems like we spent all those years trying to get somewhere else. And we finally did.

THREE

*L*a Costa had been singing around the house for as long as I could remember. She's always had a beautiful voice. The first time she sang for the public was on a radio show in Snyder, Texas, when she was four years old. A movie theater co-sponsored a talent contest with the local radio station, and Costa practiced for days, singing some little children's song. The only trouble was that she forgot the last line of the song. So she just stopped. The judge asked, "Miss Tucker, is that it?" Costa shrugged and said, "That's it."

She didn't win, but she was in show business, which in our household meant the whole family was in it, too.

She greatly expanded her record collection in San Simone, Arizona, where we lived briefly in 1959. It was a very tiny town and had one cafe, and that cafe had a jukebox. Every time the jukebox man changed records, Costa would go down and buy up the old ones. Her favorites were Ricky Nelson and Dean Martin. Years later she would sing one of those Dean Martin songs, "I Will," for auditions. It got her a recording contract, so I guess you never know which childhood pursuit might actually come to something.

It was only natural that I'd be singing along with my big sister from the time I could talk. Unlike guitar and piano, singing came naturally, and I could have spent every minute of my time doing it. The whole family listened to music on the radio. We loved Ernest Tubb, Loretta Lynn, Wanda Jackson, Jim Reeves, Marty Robbins, Hank Williams—and Frank Sinatra. I always loved him. My dad especially loved the old Jimmie Rodgers records. He always said he felt sorry for the kids who never heard country music pure and simple, the way Jimmie played it. La Costa and I also listened to her records and watched the *Lawrence Welk Show* on television religiously and sang along with the Lennon Sisters.

When people talk about child stars and how they are robbed of their youth, I think about two things. First, I'm reminded of my dad's so-called childhood. If anybody got cheated out of being a kid, he did, along with a hell of a lot of other depression-era children. But I also think about some of my friends from back then, and I think I had a pretty typical childhood up until my teens. I sure never felt like I was missing out on anything. Elmo and Joanne Morris were two of my folks' best friends in Willcox, and their daughter Cindy and I were practically joined at the hip, especially during the summers when we were at the swimming pool from the minute it opened until the time it closed. We even had the Hong Kong flu together. One of my favorite memories of Cindy and me and those early days in Willcox is the Halloween she dyed her entire body with green food coloring. She was so spectacular that I can't remember what I wore that year. We'd run from house to house with our favorite Halloween chant: "Trick or treat, smell my feet, give me something good to eat." She was green for about a week. Most of our games involved show business in one way or another. We danced around our rooms pretending to be Fred Astaire and Ginger Rogers, taking turns at being Ginger. Cindy's older brothers had a little band called The Jokers, and we'd all gather at the Morris house and sing with them on Sunday nights.

Cindy and I went to Willcox Elementary. There was a rule against going back into the school during recess, and that rule inadvertently caused me to get the closest thing to music training that I've ever had. One day during first grade my mother needed to pick me up early from school, and when she drove up during recess, I ran in to get my lunch pail.

Just when I rounded the corner of the hall, one of the second grade teachers, Mrs. Williams, grabbed me and asked me what

I thought I was doing. I tried to explain that Mom was waiting for me, but she wouldn't listen and marched me back outside with her fingernails still dug in my neck. Mother had also seen what happened, and when she saw the red marks on my neck she went off like a firecracker. She put me in the passenger side of the car and told me to stay there. I can still picture her marching across that playground, her hands planted firmly on her swinging hips. She told Mrs. Williams if any teacher ever grabbed me by the neck again, there'd be hell to pay. Then Mom turned on her heel and marched back to the car. If you knew Juanita Tucker, you'd never expect her to get that fired up. She's one of the most gentle human beings in the world. Unless someone messes with her family. Then she's one bad lady.

It was in the cards that I'd get Mrs. Williams the following year. The way the school system worked was that kids were divided into three categories: smart, average, and dumb. It's probably not the best way to instill confidence in the kids who get stuck in the dumb classes, but it's the way it worked, anyway. Mrs. Eikenberry and Mrs. Williams both taught the smart kids, and until I got to Mrs. Williams's class I was considered smart. You'd be surprised how dumb I was by the time I finished second grade and was promoted to third. I was suddenly put into a class that was about a step ahead of Special Ed.

As horrible as that whole time was, though, it was good training for the music business. I learned not to piss off the wrong person. She (or he) can set you back quickly if she wants to.

Mrs. Kendall was my third grade teacher, and she was a wonderful woman, very patient and kind to the students. But she seldom called on me, and I wondered why. One day I had to stay in from recess because I'd been sick. I was sitting at my desk doing homework and looked up and saw that the teacher was staring at me. She came over and sat down on the desk next to me and said, "Tanya, I guess you probably wonder why I skip you so much in class." I nodded my head and didn't say anything. I was still a little afraid of teachers after the previous year's experience.

"Well, I don't have enough time for everyone, and you don't really need the special attention," she said. "You should never have been put in this class in the first place." I was so relieved I almost cried.

The good thing about being in the dumb class was that instead of advanced reading or math, you could enroll in extra music or art classes, so I signed up for music. Right away I had trouble singing with the choir, and I thought I was messing up. Singing was something I loved to do and believed I could do. So why did I sound so wrong with the group?

Mrs. Gilbert, who taught music, had me come in one day. "Tanya," she told me, "the reason you're having problems singing the melodies on some of these songs is that your voice is a lower register. That means you're an alto, and you need to sing low harmony, or we need to find songs that can be sung in your key." I hadn't had a clue that the reason I couldn't hit high notes was something that simple, and that it wasn't a problem.

I started going in after school, and Mrs. Gilbert helped me work up songs. She soon learned that the only songs I knew or liked were country songs, and she knew nothing about country music. But God love her, she went out and bought sheet music for some of my favorites—songs like Hank Williams's "Your Cheatin' Heart" and Loretta Lynn's "Woman of the World (Leave My World Alone)" and "Don't Come Home a-Drinkin'." Once I understood what my voice would and would not do, singing was as easy as shooting fish in a barrel. One of the highlights of the year was when Mrs. Gilbert asked me to sing a solo at the school's Maypole Ceremony.

Thinking back on it, I probably ought to thank Mrs. Williams for sticking me in the dumb class.

FOUR

*S*ome articles have made it seem like we burned rubber all over the western part of the United States while Dad tried to turn La Costa and me into professional singers. That wasn't how it was at all. I was dead serious about my singing. I watched entertainers on television, and heard about talent contests, and listened to the radio. I knew my sister and I could do what those people did, and I started asking Mother and Dad to take me to hear live music in the area. Usually I'd hear about some performer coming to Willcox and then beg the folks to try to get me to the show. They always tried to expose us to good country artists, people who had already made it, whose shows could teach us something. In the back of our minds was the hope that someone would take a personal interest.

The folks would take us down to the VFW, which we called the Vets' Club, or to Rix Tavern—we called it "Rixes." Sometimes we'd drive to a club in Safford, Arizona, where I got to see people like Johnny Cash, the Carter Family, Don Gibson, and Johnny Western. It was much more than a thrill to see great stars like that. It was incentive. I sang "Your Cheatin' Heart" so many times that within a couple of years people at the VFW were actually calling me "Little Miss Cheatin' Heart."

It was at Rix Tavern that I earned my first dollar, and I still have it. I wish I'd been as careful about every dollar I earned. I'd finished singing my song and was coming back over to sit down with Mom and Dad, when a man walked up and said, "Well now, that was good. I'm gonna give you a dollar for that song." My eyes about popped out of my head. People would give you money to sing? What a deal!

My brother Don was home a lot during that period of time, and he decided La Costa and I should have a band and he should manage it. Thus was born the Country Westerns, La Costa and Tanya Tucker and two of Don's friends, Jerry and Darrell Hart. We all traded vocals. I learned then how quickly a manager can separate you from your money. One time Don got us a show at the VFW. He charged $1.50 at the door, and we got a good crowd that night—good enough that my part of the take was $35.

Don came around after the show and said, "Tanya, you only sang four or five numbers. Jerry sang a lot more than you."

I should have headed out the door right then, but I kept listening, wondering where this was going. Don hedged around and finally said, "You ought to give that thirty-five dollars to Jerry." Don later said he was only trying to be fair to Jerry. I handed over the cash, but I didn't forget it. The Country Westerns were short-lived.

We always kept a careful watch for any stars that might be passing through, and when we learned that Ernest Tubb was coming to play at the VFW, we were excited. Ernest Tubb has always been Dad's favorite performer. Mother and Dad drove through a Texas blizzard to hear him play a show in 1946. Ernest recorded for Decca Records for over twenty-five years, and in 1966, when he played that show in Willcox, he had a duet on the airwaves, "Sweet Thang," with Loretta Lynn.

Mother, Dad, Joanne and Elmo Morris, and Cindy and I went down to the Vet's Club, and Daddy asked me if I wanted to try to sing on the show. He didn't have to ask twice. We went around to the back of the club and there sat a bus with the Texas Troubadours painted on the side.

Daddy knocked on the bus door and a fellow stuck his head out and asked what we wanted. He told us he was Ernest's road manager.

"I've got this little girl who wants to sing," Daddy said. It was a line he'd use over and over in the next few years.

"Well, all right," the man said. "Ernest's just getting up, and he'll be out in a few minutes."

He invited us to come on the bus, and we climbed up the stairs and waited for Ernest Tubb. I think Daddy was far more impressed by being on the bus than I was. This man was his all-time hero. When Ernest Tubb walked out it was as if we'd known him forever. He shook our hands and asked us how we were doing. When Daddy explained that I wanted to sing, Ernest grinned that big old crooked grin of his.

"What can you sing, honey?" he asked.

"I can sing 'Sweet Thang,'" I said. Ernest got a big kick out of that and said he guessed he better hear me sing it. I must have passed his audition, because when I finished he said, "Now, when I call you up onstage you'll have to do what Loretta does before we start to sing. Loretta always gives me a little kiss on the cheek."

No problem. We went back out and sat in the audience with Mother and the Morrises. When Ernest called me up, he leaned over and I gave him a peck on the cheek, and we charged right into "Sweet Thang." We visited with Ernest a while after the show, and Daddy got his picture taken with him. Then his bus pulled out of Willcox, and I didn't see Ernest Tubb again until I performed at the Grand Ole Opry in 1972. When he called me onstage that night to sing "Delta Dawn," he said, "I sang with this little lady a few years back in Willcox, Arizona, and she blew my hat off."

Another artist who was very kind to us was Mel Tillis. The first time I sang with Mel was when he was playing a show in Douglas, Arizona. Daddy had to work, so Mother and Don drove me to the fair where Mel was booked. Don had been in school in Douglas and figured he knew the ropes, so he went backstage to negotiate the deal. Yes, Mel would be happy to meet with us, and sure, I could sing. Mel Tillis talked a long time to us about the music business. He warned us how hard it would be and talked about life on the road wearing a person out.

But he never discouraged us from trying. Mel was so kind to my mother. Unlike Don or my dad, Mother found it hard to approach entertainers and ask for help or guidance. She has always been a very private person, and forcing herself on anyone or any situation is completely foreign to her. Mel Tillis made her feel as if she had every right in the world to be there talking with him, almost as if she were an old friend. There are fine entertainers and there are fine people, and Mel Tillis is both.

I sang on Mel's first set, and during the break he asked if I'd like to stick around for the second show. Mother said she was afraid to stay too late because we didn't have a spare tire, and we headed on back to Willcox. Dad about hit the fan.

"Mel Tillis asked you to stay and do a second show and you left?" He couldn't believe she'd turned down the opportunity for an encore. Mom just shook her head and told him he'd better get a spare tire next time.

We heard about a package show in Phoenix one year, and Dad drove all of us over. It was a star-studded lineup, with Mel Tillis, George Morgan, Carl Smith, and Melba Montgomery on the bill. I got to see how some entertainers handle pushy promoters up close that afternoon. There were two separate shows, and during the first one Carl Smith stayed on a few minutes over his allotted time. When he walked off the stage, the promoter jumped all over him. "You've got to shorten that set, Carl, and I mean shorten it!" He practically screamed at Carl Smith. Well, Carl was a huge star, and he obviously didn't appreciate being treated like a dog.

The way Carl always started his big hit, "Hey, Joe," was to sing the title and kick up his leg. Every time he did that the crowd went wild. So on the next set he walked out, sang two words, "Hey, Joe," kicked his leg up, and walked off the stage. Then he asked the promoter if that was short enough for him. My dad had watched it all go down, and he thought it was a very cool move on Carl's part.

Maybe it was a result of that experience, but Dad has always taught me that it's better to cut a show a little short than to stay on too long.

One show we got on had lasting repercussions. Judy Lynn was playing at the Arizona State Fair, and Dad decided to try to get me on her show. Even though she'd only had a couple of national hits, "Footsteps of a Fool" and "My Father's Voice," Judy was a major star as far as we were concerned. She was big on the casino and rodeo circuits, and she'd been on national television. Hot stuff in the Tuckers' book. Dad had decided he was doing too much of the front work and opted to let Don do the negotiating that day. Don went around to Judy's trailer and somehow got to talk to John Kelly, Judy's husband and manager. Don must have been persuasive, because John agreed to let me sing a couple of numbers. Judy was against it, and with good reason as it turned out. She told John that if they let a kid on the show, by the next day they'd have kids lined up three deep trying to audition. I did the show, we went home, and sure enough, the next afternoon the kids and their parents were lined up three deep trying to get through to Judy Lynn.

At that time, John Kelly didn't have much advice for us. But several years later, when I had a hit record on the charts, he surfaced again, for better or worse, to manage my career.

Nothing that happened in those encounters actually deterred me. In fact, getting to be on the stage with people like Ernest Tubb just made me more determined to be a professional singer. I never let my folks forget it, either. Even at that young age. But I did start to understand that country music stars were not going to be the ones to give me my break. They were just too busy with their own careers to mess with some kid wanting a record deal. I certainly can't blame them, either. Once the bus gets rolling it travels fast, and you do well just to keep up with yourself.

But if the stars weren't able to offer much help, somebody else must be in the position to do it. And what we decided was that those people were probably in Nashville.

FIVE

I'd been pushing my folks to take La Costa and me to Music City for months when Dad came home one day and told us to step outside and take a look at what was in the yard. La Costa was seventeen and I was ten. We ran out and sitting there in front of the trailer was a brand new 1968 Cadillac El Dorado, powder blue with a white vinyl top.

"You better get packing," Daddy said. "'Cause we're goin' to Nashville and we're goin' in style."

He'd made one payment on the Caddy and still had money left over from a drilling job, so he decided to show the showbiz folks that the Tuckers were high rollers. As usual, Mother didn't argue. She just packed us up and helped load the car. It took a couple of days' hard driving to get to Tennessee, the state where both my grandmothers had been born and lived until their families headed west in wagons. Now we were heading back in a new El Dorado, riding along like Philadelphia lawyers.

The first thing on my personal agenda in Music City was to see the Grand Ole Opry, but Daddy had other plans. He parked the car down on Broadway and started talking with some fellows who looked like they might be guitar pickers. Sure enough, they knew all about getting into the music business.

One thing I've since learned about Nashville, there are a lot of experts running around. If you come to Nashville and dine out in a restaurant, the first thing you might ask your waiter or waitress is what they really do. They'll probably tell you about their last demo session.

Demos? We didn't have any idea you were supposed to have demos. We thought you just walked into somebody's office and sang for them. Then they gave you a record deal. Wrong. According to these guys, people wouldn't listen to somebody right off the street. If you wanted to look like you knew what you were doing, you had to have tapes. So off we went to a place called Exit Studios on Music Row, me kicking all the way because I wanted to see the Grand Ole Opry.

The way Exit Studios operated was that they supplied one guitarist and the studio. You chose songs that the picker knew and got a final mixdown and tape that same day. Costa did two numbers, and I was impressed by her guitar player, Wade Phillips. I couldn't believe it when he walked out of the studio and someone else came in to play on my session. My picker wasn't even close to being in the same league with Wade Phillips. I sang a couple of songs but not with good grace. Not only was I unhappy about the guitar work, I still hadn't been to the Opry.

Additionally, I was in the business of seeking autographs. Sandy Posey was in the building, and one of the secretaries asked me if I wanted her autograph. I didn't know who Sandy Posey was, but I said sure. As it turned out, she'd been a session singer in Nashville who'd had several pop hits in 1966 and 1967, including "Born a Woman" and "Single Girl." She must have guessed I was unfamiliar with her work, because she asked me if I knew who she was. I had to say I didn't, and she said she didn't see any reason I'd need her autograph, then. The secretary approached me a little later and asked if I was still looking for autographs. After my encounter with Sandy, I wasn't sure I wanted to be an autograph hound anymore, but when she said Hank Williams Jr. was in the building, I jumped at the chance. Hank was so gracious, and I still cherish his signature on that little scrap of paper.

The sessions got done and we had the tapes in hand, but Dad was furious with me about what he considered my unprofessionalism, and our next few hours were pure hell. He decided to give me an attitude adjustment. We left Exit Studios and pulled up in front of the Country Music Hall of Fame, where set in the concrete they had stars dedicated to the various entertainers. Dad sat there in the car looking like a storm cloud was brewing over his head.

"Tanya, take a good look at those names," he said. "Because your name is never going to be there the way you're acting."

For once I didn't have a comeback.

We went on to the Grand Ole Opry, and that experience, too, turned sour. Dad didn't say much to me, and when he did, he reminded me that it was obvious I'd made up my mind to sit in the audience, not stand on the stage. When my dad is mad, or disappointed in someone, it is like nothing you've ever seen. I huddled down in the seat at the Opry, dressed in a pair of green shorts and a little green and white shirt thinking about how Dad and Mother had sacrificed God knows what to make that trip, and I'd let them down. I spent those few hours watching the Opry stars and thinking about how I'd acted childish, pouting about a guitar player and running around asking for autographs. I felt about as lowdown as a person could be.

The next morning we were up and out early. We didn't know anything about the music business, so we'd see a record store and we wouldn't know if it was a place to buy records or make them. The first sign we saw that looked promising was K-Ark Records, so Dad pulled the car up to the curb in front and started to get out. All of a sudden he got a frown on his face and closed the car door.

"I wonder if we ought to have come up here in this Cadillac," he said. "Maybe they'll think we don't need 'em."

Now he says he'd rather walk to Nashville barefoot than to try to impress anyone with money he doesn't have. Dad backed the car up a few spaces and we headed in to K-Ark. It wasn't what we expected. The door to the president of the company's office was behind the receptionist's desk, and the entire bottom panel appeared to have been kicked in and semirepaired. We could hear people talking inside, so Dad stepped up to the receptionist's desk and asked if he could see the man in charge.

No way.

In what was the first of many such moves, Dad just walked on over and opened the door with the sign that read: John Capps, President. And I'm thinking, "Oh, man, you can't do that!" I guess Dad figured that kicked-in door meant people didn't get record deals by merely knocking.

John Capps was in his office talking to his secretary and a couple of guys who turned out to be songwriters and record producers, Ron Bellew and Peanut Montgomery. Peanut's wife was there, too. Peanut had written many of George Jones's great hits, and he would later write "What's Your Mama's Name" for me. Of course we didn't know any of that then. We just knew we'd arrived in the big time.

John Capps looked a little surprised and asked what we needed. Well, of course we needed all kinds of things, but Daddy said, "I've got these girls who can sing, and I was hoping you'd listen to the tapes."

John didn't say anything. He gave Ron and Peanut a look like they'd just had a visit from a mental patient. So Daddy went on, "I guess I want to know if I'm just being a daddy, or if somebody here in Nashville thinks they've got something. I think they do." He held out the tapes Costa and I'd made.

John probably just wanted to get rid of us, but he reached out and took them. He listened to Costa, and then he popped my tape in the player. Then he took it out, and handed both back to Daddy without saying a word.

"Well, sir, what'd you think?" Daddy asked.

John looked over at his secretary and said, "You just inherited some money from your mama, didn't you? How much was that?"

"Fifty thousand dollars," the woman said.

"And how much of that fifty thousand would you invest in either one of these girls?"

"Not a penny," she quickly answered.

It was an embarrassing moment. Costa and I couldn't even look at each other.

Peanut Montgomery seemed interested, though, and asked for our address and phone number.

Maybe that's why we weren't too discouraged. Or at least I wasn't. Embarrassed, but not discouraged. I don't know why, but I never lost faith that I'd get to make a real record. Maybe it's that wonderful thing that has to do with being a kid. It's why you can watch television cartoons where the coyote gets smashed up in every other scene and he keeps putting himself back together and chasing after the roadrunner one more time. As a kid you believe that's how things work. Scrape yourself off the road and head right on down it. I've done it many times in my life.

Next, we headed over to RCA, where Eddy Arnold was still riding high after over twenty years of hits. His "Then You Can Tell Me Goodbye" had been number one in *Billboard* for two straight weeks that year. RCA was then home to Connie Smith, Skeeter Davis, Jimmy Dean, Porter Wagoner, Dolly Parton, Jerry Reed, Charley Pride, Willie Nelson, and Waylon Jennings. The label was still having hits with Jim Reeves records, and he'd been dead since 1964! It was an obvious place to check out, and we did.

Chet Atkins had just taken charge of the label, and it was Chet who'd signed Willie, Waylon, Charley, and Dolly. Bandleader and producer Danny Davis was working for Chet, screening songs and singers, and his office was on the main floor of the building. Once again, Daddy ignored the receptionist, a Dolly lookalike, when she told him he'd have to just leave the tape with her.

"I drove all the way from Arizona and I aim to drive all the way back in a couple of days," Daddy told her. "This is the only tape I've got, and there ain't any way I'm leaving it anywhere."

Then he walked straight past her into Danny's office.

And once again, I was thinking, "Oh, man."

I later learned that Danny was a protégé of Chet Atkins. He'd met Chet several years earlier, after playing trumpet in bands with Gene Krupa and Sammy Kaye. Chet talked Danny into moving to Nashville, and he respected his taste in music so much that he hired him at RCA. The same year we met Danny, he'd started a band called the Nashville Brass and was starting to record instrumental music for the label.

Danny Davis was a gentleman, even if he wasn't interested in signing Costa or me. He told Daddy he did think Costa had some potential. And me? I was much too young for the label to even consider.

We made our way across Nashville, knocking on doors, walking into offices unannounced, always being told the same thing. No deal. Oddly enough, the one place we didn't go was CBS Records, where a producer and songwriter named Billy Sherrill was making hit records with Tammy Wynette and David Houston. We still don't know how we missed trying to get in at CBS, but it was the first of several near misses with Billy Sherrill, the man who finally took a chance and signed a much-too-young kid to a recording contract.

On our third day in town we heard that Roy Acuff was going to be signing autographs in his store on Second Avenue, so we headed over there. Roy didn't want to hear any tapes, and he sure didn't want a live performance in his store. As a matter of fact, he thought we were trying to get into a business that nice girls shouldn't be in at all.

"You take those girls on back to Arizona," he told Mom and Dad. "Take 'em home and put 'em in Sunday School. There's girls on the Opry doing things you wouldn't believe." Then he turned to Costa and me. "You girls ought to go home and plan on getting married someday and raising families. You'll be a lot happier."

Good advice, but in my case given to the wrong girl.

Having said that, I guess Roy's promoter mentality kicked in because he added, "And when you do get married and have kids, bring 'em on back to Nashville and see me on the Opry."

I never give people negative advice, and I think it's because of what happened right there in Roy Acuff's store. I know he meant well. The entertainment business is insecure, and it can chew you up and spit you out before you know it. But why rain on someone's parade? Years later I was in the lobby at Shutters on the Beach in Los Angeles, having a drink with Tom Berenger. Tom was talking about the difficulty in having a real life if you're in show business.

"Sometimes I just want to shake kids who are wanting to be actors and tell them to run," he said. "They have no idea what this life is really about."

I told him about Roy Acuff and said that I didn't think it was any entertainer's job to discourage someone wanting to get into the business.

Even if a person can't sing a lick, tell them to keep right on trying. First of all, who am I to decide what is going to happen to another person? It's like Billy Ray Cyrus once said, "Keep on swingin', you just might get a hit."

✻ ✻ ✻

We were big fans of Jim Reeves music, so maybe that's why Daddy got the idea of trying to find Jim's widow, Mary Reeves, the morning we were leaving town. I mean, can you believe us? I'm surprised somebody didn't call the law on the Tuckers that week. With the help of a Homes of the Stars map, Dad found out where Mary Reeves lived. We drove right up the driveway and knocked on her door.

Wonder of wonders, Mary opened the door, listened to our tales of being turned down everywhere, then invited us in for some iced tea. Mary Reeves is one of the most gracious women I've ever met. She listened to us sing and was very encouraging, especially to La Costa. She thought I was too young to be seriously pursuing a singing career, but she didn't try to discourage us in any way.

She even pitched us some songs! Once you get established in music, every publisher and songwriter in the world wants you to listen to their songs. But when you're a nobody, forget it. There we were, strangers who'd showed up on her step and asked for help because we couldn't find it anywhere else, and Mary Reeves not only asked us in, she offered us songs. It was amazing.

Before we left, Mary wrote down our names and address, and she promised to help us if there was ever any way she could. We did hear from her several times. She'd send us a song now and then, or write and ask how things were going. Those small acts of kindness coming from Nashville meant a lot and kept us feeling somehow connected to the business.

The one place we wanted to go before we left Music City was the Hermitage. Unfortunately we didn't know it cost money to get in, and when Daddy counted up what we had left, we had the choice of seeing Andrew Jackson's home or eating on the way back to Arizona. We were still driving a Cadillac but now were down to counting out change to pay for food.

On the other hand, we'd been to Nashville, the town that could make people country music stars. And even though we hadn't exactly been welcomed with open arms, we'd played our songs for some record companies and been invited for tea in Mary Reeves's home. And two very important things had happened to me. First, I had made up my mind that someday I'd be a star. Second, I'd made up my mind that I'd try to never again let my dad down.

SIX

*L*a Costa left home the following year for Cochise College in Douglas, Arizona, down on the Mexico border. It was the same school Don had attended to study aviation. All Costa's hard work during high school had paid off. She won an academic scholarship and that, together with a loan and a grant, allowed her the luxury of attending college and living in a school dorm. She packed up her clothes, record player, and records, plus an ironing board that stuck out of the back window of her old Metropolitan. I didn't realize how much I would miss her as I watched the car pull out of the drive.

Dad tried to make sure she kept that Metropolitan running. He used to send Costa letters with detailed drawings of how to make any repairs the car might need. Even years later I can picture him doing that late at night, sitting at the kitchen table, painstakingly drawing engine parts and writing out instructions. I wish the folks who call him a hard man could have seen that, too.

I went off to the sixth grade, and about halfway through the school year Daddy decided to pull up stakes and move to Phoenix where there were television and radio shows, and hundreds of clubs where somebody might notice me and help us.

I missed friends like Cindy Morris when I left Willcox, but I never had any regrets about moving. I knew we were headed to a place where I might get my career going, so I never looked back. The traveling around we did kept me from developing long-term friends, but I knew even then that it was a trade-off that had to be made.

We moved in with my Aunt Irene, who lived in back of the elementary school I would attend. But school had little meaning for me by then. I had a mission, and that mission was to find an outlet for my music. The minute we got settled, Daddy got right to it, making phone calls, trying to make connections with radio and television people. I met Waylon Jennings for the first time when I was living in Phoenix, and I got my first taste of what a funny man he is. He owned a club there called J.D.'s, and one night when Waylon was in town performing, Dad decided to try to get me on the show there. We went in, and the club was packed. Dad and I wound our way through the crowd and back to the office. We could hear a lot of laughing and horseplaying going on behind the door. Dad knocked on the door, and when Waylon opened it, he looked out at the packed house and turned back around to his band members standing behind him and joked, "We got their money, let's just go."

Dad introduced himself to Waylon, explained that I was a singer, and asked about the possibility of me doing a couple of numbers. Waylon turned us down. He didn't give us any real reason, but I think he didn't like the idea of an eleven-year-old girl in there around all those rowdy men.

One day when I was watching television, I saw a kids' program called *The Lew King Ranger Show*. I told my parents I wanted to audition. The show had been around since 1948, when Lew started taping a children's variety hour once a week from the Fox Theater in Phoenix. They had special guests each week, plus the show regulars, a group of kids who were to Phoenix a little like the Mouseketeers were to America. Wayne Newton had been on the show before he broke in 1963 with "Danke Schoen," and Marty Robbins performed an acoustic set once in a while. Part of the show consisted of a weekly talent contest, and the winner would get to go on the *Ted Mack Amateur Hour*. The folks took me down to the theater one Saturday morning for the talent contest. I didn't win the contest, but after I fired off a song Lew offered me a spot as a regular on the show.

He later said that several things caught his attention that day, in addition to my adult-sounding voice. First, he said, I acted older than my years, very mature. That led him to believe I'd be very professional and not throw any tantrums on the set. He was right about that. I wouldn't have acted any way but grateful, because he was giving me a shot. Another thing he later mentioned was that he thought I was a very pretty young lady, and that still stuns me. In the sixth grade I never thought about how I looked. I was very much a tomboy, so the thought that somebody was impressed by my looks was a mind blower. Lastly, and this is the big one, he said he realized I had a very strong family unit standing behind me. He'd seen plenty of stage moms and dads, and when he met my parents he knew they were different. They were there to help me do what I wanted to do, not to live out their own dreams through me.

The Lew King Ranger Show had singers and dancers and comics and mimes, and I felt closer to them than to my schoolmates. I felt temporary the whole time we lived in Phoenix, like I was biding my time and waiting for something to happen.

After eighteen weeks on the show, I felt like I'd progressed as much as I would in that setting. Even then, I knew I was a solo performer and not a part of the novelty kid acts that we did on the show. But I hated the thought of telling Lew, because he'd been wonderful to us. So I did what any entertainer does. I had my manager go explain things while I hid out in the dressing room. I said, "You go tell him, Daddy."

Dad liked Lew as much as I did, but he walked down the hall and broke the news that I was leaving the show. Lew said he hated to see me go, but he understood. After all, he'd seen hundreds of kids come and go.

La Costa came home that summer to find that I had already put together her vacation agenda. I'd been reading about the upcoming Miss Country Music Phoenix competition and decided that La Costa was a sure shot for the title. Somehow Mother and Dad got together the money to buy her a cowgirl outfit and a gown, and off we went. Now the weird thing about this contest was that you didn't have to sing. It was judged strictly on grace, beauty, and the ability to think on your feet, and La Costa won it hands down. She modestly says it was all due to spending several years in Rainbow Girls, an organization that, among other things, teaches its members to speak in front of groups and walk gracefully. I say it was because she was the best.

We had more good news about La Costa during the time we were living in Phoenix. Peanut Montgomery called and said he and Ron Bellew wanted to cut a record on her at the Widget Recording Studios in Muscle Shoals, Alabama. Actually, Peanut wanted to record me, too, but Ron convinced him, I was too young. Dad decided to take me anyway. Somebody might decide to let me cut a record, too. They needed Costa there right away, so instead of taking the car that Dad had just bought for her, a 1955 Chevy, we somehow put together the money for plane tickets and flew to Alabama. Just La Costa and Dad and I went. Mother said she wanted to save the price of an extra airplane ticket and would stay in Phoenix. What she didn't say was that she had been feeling somewhat sick for days: nothing she could put her finger on, just tired and out of sorts.

When we arrived in Muscle Shoals we found out that Peanut Montgomery and Ron Bellew couldn't agree on a direction for La Costa. Ron wanted to take her to more of a delta-blues sound while Peanut leaned toward straight country. They decided to go with the blues rather than country. What a shock to learn that industry veterans didn't agree about what was best for an artist. Up until then we'd just gone blindly along thinking that if someone—anyone—in the business took an interest, we were home free. They'd know exactly what to do and how to do it.

I didn't pay much attention to those discussions at the time, though. I was far more interested in my physical surroundings than in any talk of musical direction. I loved everything about the studio atmosphere, even the typewriters on the secretaries' desks. As the days went by I spent my time trying to teach myself to type. It helped distract me from the recording booth. I had the fever, and it killed me not to be behind a microphone. I'd sneak around and watch Costa sing, then kid her that night about how she'd closed her eyes and swung her hips to that swamp beat.

Back in Phoenix, Mother was in serious trouble. Soon after we left she'd started bleeding a little vaginally, and cramping. She wasn't pregnant and she wasn't having her period, and she was scared half to death. We had no medical insurance and no doctor there in Phoenix, so she packed up La Costa's '55 Chevy and headed back to Texas where she could get help from her family. Thinking about it now gives me chills. Mother piled towels under herself so she wouldn't bleed on Costa's car, and by the time she got home to Texas she'd damn near bled to death.

The Cunningham doctor checked her over and an additional problem was found. She had a lump in one of her breasts. Mother phoned us in Alabama. The doctors had decided they should go in and take care of the bleeding first, then do a biopsy when she got her strength back.

Dad went wild. He ran out and rented a car and headed straight for Texas, leaving La Costa and me with Peanut and his wife. He drove straight through with no sleep, and almost didn't make it himself. About halfway through the night he fell asleep in the car for a few minutes, awakening only as the car was leaving the highway going about a hundred miles an hour. He got back under control and took off again. When Dad arrived in Temple, Texas, they were just about to wheel her in for surgery.

This story has a happy ending. Mother just needed a D & C, and the lump turned out to be benign. Even though her recovery would take a long time, she was going to be all right. It makes you think. When people have very little, life is very fragile and your world can go straight to hell in a minute. Anyone's life can turn quickly, but the "haves" sure won't be the ones bleeding all across Arizona, praying they can make it home to a doctor who'll help them.

As soon as Mother could travel, she drove back to Alabama with Dad to pick up La Costa and me. Costa's sessions were finished, and Peanut even took me in and cut a few songs.

On the way back to Arizona, La Costa dropped a bomb and told us she'd made a decision to get married during the next school year. I couldn't believe it. She'd been dating this guy for quite a while. But now it looked like she was really on her way, and marriage seemed to me like the wrong move. When we got back and Costa left for her second year of college, I stewed around about it and finally wrote her a letter. In it, I detailed all the reasons getting married would put an end to the career that was just getting off the ground. "If you get married, you're gonna have kids," I wrote. "And if you have kids, you're gonna have to take care of 'em."

SEVEN

*W*e'd been in Phoenix about eight months when Dad heard from his brother-in-law about construction work in Page, Arizona. Dad's sister and her husband had moved to St. George, Utah, just across the border from Page, some months earlier. Now, my dad loves to rag me about spreading money around, but this is a case where he did it foolishly and paid dearly for it later. At the time his sister and her husband moved they were not only broke but having marriage problems. Dad had saved up a little money and felt like he was getting ahead for once, so he signed a note for a little trailer house to help them get started on what he hoped would be a new life.

When Dad learned that jobs in St. George were paying $9 an hour, he decided he'd better head up to Utah, too. By that time his sister and her husband were ready to move on, so we had a trailer and a truck waiting for us. Dad went ahead to get started on the job, so Mom and I packed up our belongings in the back of a pickup. The folks had just bought me some pigeons, and we strapped their crate on the top. We were towing our horse, Iveena, along in an old trailer Dad had bought for a few dollars, and we looked just like the Beverly Hillbillies. We didn't care, though, because Dad's job prospects looked so bright.

The trailer that awaited us in St. George was so tiny it could have fit into my kitchen now, but since we had so few possessions, we didn't ever feel cramped. What we didn't know was that back payments were owed. When Dad did learn about it, he pushed the problem to the back of his mind, thinking he could get caught up soon enough.

I had a great surprise in store when I started school. Suddenly, I was one of the popular kids. Sometimes just being new can make you the "kid of the day." Of course, it can also work the other way around. I don't believe I'd changed, so I credit the Mormon family structure for my newfound acceptance. The Mormons teach their children kindness and respect, and I was the beneficiary of that value system. As I mentioned early on, this was the first group of kids I'd ever been in where no one said a word about my discolored teeth. I soon noticed that the Mormon kids seldom, if ever, teased anybody. There was a girl in my class who wore a big, bulky brace to correct a spinal curvature, and I can't remember hearing one comment about it.

I thought then, as I still do, that Utah is one of the most beautiful, friendly states in America and one of the best in which to raise a family, too. It has a healthy environment and a healthy attitude about the importance of community. When you've lived all over the place like I have, you really come to appreciate places like that.

One of the icebreakers at school turned out to be Iveena. Like Willcox, St. George was horse country. It seemed like everybody had horses and everybody loved to ride. It wasn't long before I'd met several girls who shared my passion for taking long rides off into the hills. We'd pretend we were the James Gang or Calamity Jane and Doc Holliday or some other exotic bunch of outlaw types. While I'd had pals like Cindy Morris in Willcox, I'd never had the feeling of belonging that I felt riding through those Utah hills with not one friend but many.

I made my acting debut in St. George. My friend Terry Daugherty came to school one day, excited about the fact that a movie was being made in Zion National Park, forty miles east of St. George. She said the producers needed horses for the filming. I learned that the movie was called *Jeremiah Johnson.*

Sydney Pollack was the director and Robert Redford was the star, although none of those things meant very much to me at the time.

Terry explained that people were being asked to go to a hotel in town and talk to the associate producer, a man named Mike Moder. Dad had to work the next Saturday, so Mom drove me to the hotel and asked to see Mike. I'd planned my wardrobe carefully to help me get discovered: a turquoise gaucho outfit with a matching hat. Mike didn't seem to notice the clothes but inquired instead about our horse. I told him my horse was unavailable, but that I'd be interested in appearing in the movie myself. I was always trying to figure out a way to get a career going. I figured maybe if somebody saw me in a movie, they might think I should have a record deal. Years later I learned there are lots of people in movies who thought the same thing. He said he'd think about it, and we left. But we kept coming back, and Mike finally offered me $40 to play a bit part and wrote an extra kid role into a scene for me.

Jeremiah Johnson, the subject of the film, came to the West to be a mountain man. It's a "man against the elements" movie, and it doesn't gloss over the extreme hardships involved in pioneer life. At one point, Robert Redford comes up on a house where all but one child in the family has been slaughtered by Indians, and the mother has gone insane from grief. She later goes off in the mountains to die. Robert Redford comes looking for the woman and finds a settler creeping around the property, not knowing what has happened and fearful of an Indian attack. Redford figures out the man is hiding his family somewhere and he goes straight to the corncrib and throws open the door to find a mother and three kids, the oldest of which was me. My job was to look scared. I'm surprised I didn't look embarrassed, because my dad spent most of the day following Robert Redford around taking home movies of him. I knew the star didn't appreciate it.

Throughout my career I've tried as hard as possible to always accommodate fans, whether they want to talk or get an autograph or have their picture taken with me. Once in a while it's turned out badly, but those times have been the exception rather than the rule. I believe I have a good understanding of how fans feel about getting autographs and photos, and it stems from times like meeting Sandy Posey at Exit Studios and watching my dad dog Robert Redford with a home movie camera.

Our close-to-perfect life in St. George came to a grinding halt
several months after we moved there. Money had been in short
supply for quite a while, and to top it off, Mother had been sick.
I went off to school one morning without a care in the world,
and by the time school was out that afternoon we'd been
evicted and were living in a motel. Dad had helped Mother get
some breakfast down and was getting ready to go to Page to
work when there was a knock at the door. Dad opened the door
to find two men standing there. They were asking about the
back payments on the trailer.

"Are you Mr. Tucker?" one asked.

Dad said he was, and the man handed him an eviction notice.

"Oh, I'm gonna get caught up here," Dad started to explain.
"All it'll take'll be a couple of weeks of overtime."

"No, you're gonna have to get out today," the guy said.

"I can't move out of here right now," Dad said. "My wife has
been awful sick. You're gonna have to give us a little time." He
said later he couldn't believe anybody would actually kick a sick
woman out of her home.

"No chance," the other fellow chimed in. "You people pack
up your things, because we're locking up this place right now."

Dad was on the edge anyway, worried about Mother and
worried about money. He knew by then that La Costa's sessions
with Ron and Peanut had been turned down in Nashville, and
he still wasn't having any luck getting my career going. Dad
snapped. He jumped down out of the trailer, grabbed a lead
pipe, and chased the guys right back to their car.

"Get the hell outta here," he shouted. "I told you I could get
the money in a couple of weeks, and I damn sure will."

They jumped in the car and left, and Dad figured he'd convinced them to stay gone. He was wrong. Not more than an
hour after he left for Page to ask about overtime, they came
back and found Mother there alone. My mother might be a
fighter when it comes to her kids, but that day she was sick and
broke and about as down as she'd ever been. They told her to
get her things together, and she did. She didn't have the strength
to pack everything, so she just gathered up a few clothes and
put them in a sack.

There wasn't a phone where she could reach Dad, so Mother
somehow walked to a friend's house to wait.

When Dad finished working out his new overtime schedule he came back to St. George, and when he learned what had happened, he couldn't decide whether to go beat the living hell out of the men or to get Mother to a motel where she could rest. Fortunately for everyone concerned, he chose the motel option. All we needed was Dad in jail and us on the street.

When I learned what the realtors had done to Mother, I was screaming mad. I wanted to get a knife and chop them up. I wanted to blow them off the face of the earth. The idea of anyone kicking my sick mother out of her home was too much for me to comprehend. It's still too much for me to comprehend, and if I saw them today, I'd kick their butts. I've made an effort to let go of my own grudges, but I'll hold one to the ends of the earth for Mother.

I'm surprised I even found out what happened, since my folks always tried to hide our money problems from me. I'd ask about those big yellow government boxes filled with cheese and other food items, and Mother would make up some story about having to lug something home in a box from the grocery store. It took me years to figure out that we were getting government commodities.

The folks soon found another trailer, but it was much smaller, and the ugliest thing I'd ever seen. It didn't even have a bathtub. We had to go outside and use a makeshift shower. For the first time since moving to St. George, I was ashamed to ask friends over. I was afraid my newfound popularity would vanish as quickly and magically as it had appeared. But when kids did find out about our "new" circumstances, it turned into one of the most touching situations I've ever encountered.

Part of my self-consciousness came from my newfound interest in boys. I'd received my first kiss that year, from a boy named Kevin Burgess. Kevin was one of the school's "bad boys," a handsome blue-eyed blond who was popular with the girls but who was known to sneak out behind the school and smoke cigarettes. Kevin had tried to French kiss, and I thought it was without a doubt the grossest thing I'd ever imagined. Even though I hadn't cared for his attempt at kissing, I still had a crush on Kevin and prayed he wouldn't find out about our new living quarters.

My attempt to go underground was short-lived, because some of Kevin's friends discovered where we'd moved. Sure enough, one day there was a knock at the door, and when I pulled back the blind there was Kevin with a group of his pals perched on their bikes outside the trailer. A cold chill went all over me and I said, "Daddy, what am I gonna do? I can't ask him in here." Dad and Mother understood as well as I did just how bad this place was. They never invited anyone over anymore, either.

"Just say it's temporary, Tanya," Dad said. "Just temporary."

For the first time, I understood how La Costa must have felt when I exposed the jeans-stuffed rocking chair to her friend. That episode didn't seem half as funny when it was replaying in my life. But I sucked it up and walked outside. I asked Kevin to walk down the road with me, away from his friends.

"This place is horrible, isn't it?" I began, then went on before he even had a chance to answer. I knew the answer anyway. Of course it was horrible. "We don't really live like this all the time. It's just that we got behind—"

I kept on rambling and apologizing and explaining, until Kevin started laughing and stopped me from going on about it.

"Do you think I like you because of where you live?" he asked. "I couldn't care less where you live. I like you, not your house. You're very special, Tanya, don't you know that?"

I couldn't believe it. I was special. It didn't matter if we lived in a trashy trailer that we could barely afford. Kevin liked Tanya Tucker, the person. Seldom in my life since have men unconditionally accepted me for just what I am. So Kevin Burgess still holds a place in my heart.

❧ ❧ ❧

Between having boys start to show up at the trailer and riding horses with my girlfriends, I was beginning to cause Dad to worry that I was losing interest in singing. In St. George, school life was far more important to me than it had ever been. I really liked the kids, the classes, and the experience of being a real part of something instead of an outsider. Dad saw me getting more and more involved in school activities and less interested in talking about my future, and it worried him. One night as I was getting ready to go to bed, he asked me to sing him a song, and I balked. "Daddy, it's eleven o'clock, and I've got school in the morning," I protested. He kept after me, but I refused to sing.

"You've got the talent to make something of yourself," he said. "I'm gonna show you just what kind of a life you could have if you don't make it as a singer. You get yourself outside and weed that garden, because you could wind up doing it for the rest of your life."

The easy thing to do would have been to just sing him a damn song, but I never seem to do things the easy way. If there's a hard way, I'll find it. So I stomped out there in my nightgown and grabbed a hoe. I don't know how long I stayed out there. It seemed like an hour, but it might have been more like fifteen minutes. I hoed the hell out of that garden, too. Finally I'd had enough. I knocked on the door of the trailer and said, "All right, Daddy. I'm ready to sing."

That night was one of the few times I saw Mother get angry with Dad. She wore him out over sending me to hoe weeds on a school night. He told her he was teaching me a lesson, and in fact, he did. I was sure I didn't want to hoe weeds for a living.

EIGHT

*I*t wasn't long after the weed hoeing incident that Dad decided we needed more than the Nashville session to show to record labels. So he scraped together $400 and we drove to Las Vegas to make what he considered a decent pitch tape. After checking with the musicians' union, we located a bass player named Cotton Harp who said he would produce some demos. He booked time at United Recordings and we started going over material. I picked five songs: Hank Williams's "I'm So Lonesome I Could Cry"; "Proud Mary," which had been all over the air-waves in the past couple of years by both Creedence Clearwater and Ike and Tina Turner; Tommy Cash's "Rise and Shine"; Glen Campbell's "I Want to Live"; and "Put Your Hand in the Hand." When we got to the studio, Cotton decided he wanted me to sing "For the Good Times." I'd never done the song, and although Cotton didn't have a lyric sheet, he knew the words. So he stood in front of me and mouthed the words while I sang.

I don't think the Las Vegas sessions were as good as the one we'd done at Exit Studios in Nashville. Attitude and guitar picker aside, the Nashville tape had an honesty and simplicity that I still prefer. But no matter what I think, the Vegas tapes were the ones that got me my break.

After paying for the sessions and the tape duplication we had only a few dollars left for the trip home, but we were completely hyped up about what we were getting done. We drove back to St. George and mailed out the tapes, positive that something was getting ready to pop. Dad went back to work and I went back to school. Weeks went by and we heard nothing. Finally one tape got returned, from Bill Denny at Cedarwood Publishing. There wasn't an accompanying letter, so we weren't sure anyone had even listened.

Finally Dad got so frustrated he decided to try to make another trip to an entertainment center and talk to people in person. He never seemed to have much trouble getting in anywhere, and he sincerely believed that all it would take was for the right individual to listen. We packed a couple of bags and started out of town. Dad stopped at the crossroads on the edge of St. George and asked me if I was really serious. Was singing the one thing in this world that I wanted to do? He pointed back toward St. George, which stood for home and school and a normal life, and then pointed toward California, which stood for the unknown. "What's it gonna be, Tanya?" he asked. "We can keep on trying or go home and you can have this regular life you've started to love so much." I didn't say anything. I just pointed down the road to Los Angeles.

When we got to L.A., we checked into one of the cheapest places we could find, a little motel on Sunset Boulevard. It was also one of the seediest places in town. I could look out of the window and watch the hookers and street people out hustling. Everybody seemed to be trying to make a deal, which, of course, was just what we were trying to do. The first place we tried was MGM Records. Hank Williams Jr. was on MGM, and his record deal had been signed when he was underage, so Dad figured the label was at least open to signing kids. Bob Webb was the head of MGM at the time, and as usual, Dad talked his way in. Bob was a brisk-looking man, but that didn't intimidate Daddy. He handed Bob the tape and said, "If you don't listen to this, you'll be overlooking a gold mine." Bob listened, and he liked what he heard, but he was very doubtful about signing a country artist from the L.A. office. Yet he sat right there and made several calls to people in Nashville. Bob even tried to call his friend Billy Sherrill, but Sherrill was nowhere to be found.

Next we went to CBS, where we had yet another near miss with Billy Sherrill. Ted Glasser at Columbia listened, and he echoed Bob Webb's comments, saying, "Mr. Tucker, this little girl is a country singer, and I'd like to forward this tape on to Billy Sherrill in Nashville. I don't think Tanya belongs in Los Angeles."

Both Bob Webb and Ted Glasser were right about that. I didn't belong in Los Angeles, and I found it out the hard way several years later.

We went home thinking that finally something might happen. After all, an important executive in Los Angeles was pitching my tape to another important executive in Nashville. That ought to mean something. In the meantime, I was excited about playing the new sessions for some of my friends.

When I took them to school, the reaction from kids in my class was so positive I could have relived the moment forever and been happy. After school, one of the girls in my class, Darla Librand, approached me with an offer. She and her sisters, Diana and Dorothy, had an all-girl band, and they were in search of a singer.

I started rehearsing with the girls in their basement, and before long Darla's father decided we were ready for the big time. Mr. Librand owned a Cadillac, the ultimate success symbol, so when he wheeled down the road to our old trailer, he looked like the man who could make it all happen. He spoke with Dad and Mother and explained that he'd been in contact with Fuzzy Owens at Merle Haggard's Bakersfield, California, studios. If I was available, he'd drive us there and get us on tape. Was I available to record at Merle Haggard's studio? Is there a cow in Texas? You bet.

Mother and Dad warmed up to Mr. Librand right away. He was a gentleman, and he was a lot like my dad in many ways. He was a plainspoken, straight-ahead kind of individual who was determined to help his daughters with their dream. We left for Haggard country the next week with my parents' blessings.

On the drive to Bakersfield, I had what can only be an ESP experience. I announced that Merle Haggard was going to come to the studio, probably on his way to hunt rabbits. I don't know where the thought came from, but the Librand girls and their dad just laughed.

Fuzzy Owens was fantastic; he welcomed us in and treated us like we were a legitimate country music band instead of a bunch of school girls. I came out of the vocal booth after doing a couple of songs, just as the Man, Merle Haggard, was walking in the studio. I couldn't believe it. He was dressed all in black and was perhaps the most handsome, charismatic man I'd ever seen. I think I fell in love with Merle on the spot. Fuzzy was talking to him, and when Merle spoke to me it made my hair stand on end.

He must have got a kick out of seeing us girls there trying to be professionals, because he turned and asked if I wanted to sing with him. He hadn't even heard my voice.

I couldn't believe it. Merle Haggard wanted me to sing with him. Right then careers and big breaks were meaningless. The only thing that mattered was the fact that Merle Haggard had invited me to sing a duet with him. I'd met and performed with entertainers before, but it was because of my dad's insistence. This time a star had approached me.

He strummed his guitar. "What song would you like to do?"

"'Mule Skinner Blues,'" I said.

Merle grinned. "'Mule Skinner Blues' it is," he said.

After we sang together, Merle thanked me and left. When he told Fuzzy he was going rabbit hunting, the Librand girls almost dropped their teeth.

I realized years later that he's not one to sit around and make small talk with a bunch of kids, whether he liked one's voice or not. But I didn't feel let down by his sudden exit. Far from it, I was on a natural high and couldn't wait to get home and tell my parents what had happened. In fact, the rest of the trip was a letdown. We knocked on doors around town the next day, played the tapes for people, and nothing happened. Not only was the big break not happening as scheduled, I was sneezing and coughing and missing my parents. By the time I got back to my little trailer and my parents, I was almost at an anxiety attack stage.

About a month later the tape Ted Glasser had said he was going to send to Billy Sherrill came back to us in the mail. We didn't know whether it was a mistake made by someone in the mailroom or whether Glasser had listened again and reconsidered. Whatever happened, it was a blow to us all, and especially to Dad. He had it in his mind that I was going to be on Columbia Records.

NINE

$\mathcal{E}$ ven though I'd begged La Costa not to get married, she was determined to go through with it. She asked me to be her bridesmaid and promised that marriage would not dim her career goals. I was skeptical but too excited about being in the wedding to worry about it.

Costa had completed a two-year program at Cochise and was working in the medical records department at the hospital in Willcox. She set a date and we left for the wedding. I don't think any of the bride's magazines Costa had read ever addressed the wedding etiquette involved when the father of the bride arrives with a shiner.

It all started in Flagstaff, Arizona. We were driving through town when I spotted a sign that drew us like moths to a flame: Museum Records. We'd never heard of Museum Records, but then RCA, CBS, and MGM hadn't exactly been knocking on our door. Any record company in the world looked good about then. The company was both a record label and a bar, and the band-leader from the club invited me to "audition" that night. That meant I could get up and do a couple of numbers with the band at the club.

"What do you want me to sing?" I asked.

"You can sing whatever you want," the bandleader said. "This band can play anything." I borrowed a pair of white go-go boots from his wife and hoped they passed for costuming.

We went to get some food at a nearby diner and waited until showtime. When we got back to the club, it was almost deserted. Maybe it was the poor crowd that put the lead guitar player in a bad mood, or maybe the bandleader hadn't thought to inform him about me. Whatever it was, the guy seemed sullen and angry from the minute my name was announced. I took the mike and turned to the band.

"'There Goes My Everything,'" I said.

"What key?" the lead guitarist shot back like a bullet.

The tone of his voice took me by surprise, and the fact that I didn't know what key I sang the song in didn't help.

"I don't know," I gulped.

He shook his head and glared at both me and the bandleader. I didn't know what else to do but start the song and let them find a key, and that's just what I did. After I finished, I turned around to the band again. The guitarist's mood hadn't improved, so I decided to be helpful.

"I'll just start cold again," I said, not realizing he would take that as a slam of some sort. Maybe he was drunk, because what he said next was really shocking considering I was eleven years old.

"Yeah, you little bitch. Start 'em all off cold."

I'd never been called a name like that in my life; it sounded to me like the worst insult in the world. I could barely get through the song. By the time I got off the stage and across the room to my parents' table, I was shaking all over.

"What's the matter, Tanya? You sounded great." My dad immediately took my mood to mean I'd been unhappy with the performance. I couldn't say anything for a minute because I was starting to tear up. I blubbered out what the guitarist had said to me. At that point my mother knew we were in for it.

"Tanya, don't you start crying," she said. "You're going to get your dad in trouble."

It was too late. Dad's face was a deep shade of red and his jaw was set. "You two go in the bathroom," he ordered. "I'm gonna take care of this."

Mother rushed me into the bathroom, but then decided she couldn't just stand in there not knowing what was happening. When we got back to the bar, Dad was standing over the band's table shaking his fist at the guitarist. Then all of a sudden it seemed like the guy went flying off his chair. He was a little guy and he bounced right back up. Dad has always said it's the little guys you want to worry about in a fight. A big man will hit the ground and stay down, but a little, wiry guy'll come back at you, and that's exactly what this guy did.

All hell broke loose then. Some of the guitar player's friends jumped in on it, and Dad grabbed two chairs and was slamming them into first one and then another. I was screaming, and Mother was freaking. Dad broke loose from the pack and headed out the door for the car with Mother and me right behind him.

"Thank God, you're out of there," Mother said, her voice shaking.

"I ain't outta there," Dad said. "I'm gettin' my gun."

It took every ounce of persuasion my mother possessed, but she convinced Dad that we had to leave. As he was starting the car we could hear police sirens. We pulled behind a gas station on the corner and waited until the squad cars had squealed to a stop in front of the Museum Records bar, and then we blew town fast. My dad's face was already starting to balloon up. He told people in Willcox he'd walked into a door, but they knew Beau Tucker, and I doubt if one person believed that story. La Costa didn't have much to say about it all back then, but she thinks it's funny now.

The wedding was great, even if the father of the bride had a black eye. La Costa looked beautiful. She'd had a woman in Willcox make her dress from a pattern she found. It had an empire waist and was decorated with lace and tiny pearls. The three other bridesmaids and I wore pink flowered dresses. Costa had saved enough money to pay for everything, including my dress.

We stayed in Willcox about a week, then headed back for St. George, once again driving through Flagstaff. We figured things had blown over by then. I kept an eye out for the guitar player as we drove through town, and while we were stopped at a light, I saw a familiar face coming out of a Denny's restaurant. It wasn't the guitar player, but it was almost that bad. It was the bandleader and his wife, and they saw us. The two of them jumped in their car and headed after us. Dad shot down the highway, but he couldn't shake them. About ten miles out of town, Dad pulled off the road.

"What the hell am I doing, Juanita?" he said. "I ain't afraid of that guy."

The bandleader pulled up behind us, and Dad tensed up, ready to fight all over again if he had to do it. The guy came up to the car, but he stood back a little.

"We don't want any trouble, Beau," he said. "All we want are the damn go-go boots back."

TEN

*S*tories grow up around careers, and more often than not, the story gets bigger and better as the career does. Finally the stories take on lives of their own and become show business myths. The one about my dad gambling in Las Vegas to win the money for my first real demo tapes is a case in point. He did go to Vegas, and he did gamble. He gambled for days. But he didn't win. He lost every cent we had and came home desperate. But he already had the demo tapes. What Dad was trying to do was to win enough money to run with the big dogs in the record business.

We'd now been to both Nashville and Los Angeles, and nobody seemed interested in the tapes we'd made. Dad tried to figure out why. He sat up late one night going over in his mind every move we'd made, and what he believed he understood was that we had every element required for success except one. I had the voice, and he had the brass. What we lacked was financing. By the next morning, Dad decided that to get into the inner circle of the music business, he had to have cash. Somehow he got the idea $25,000 was the magic number, and the only way he could see getting that much money was to win it.

The first thing he did was to drive to the construction site in Page where he was working and auction off his tools to the highest bidder. Some of his friends on the job were worried about him, since a working man's tools are his life support. The last thing he said to them was, "I'm never gonna use 'em again. I'm sick to death of this life." Then he added, "I'm gonna get Tanya on Columbia Records with or without the help of those fellows in L.A."

Then he went to the bank and drew out all he had, which was about $600. He left Mother with the money he'd gotten for the tools and drove the three hours to Vegas. He had it in his mind that keno would be his game. After all, the stakes are high, and if you played the same number over and over, you'd have to win. Wouldn't you?

Dad gambled straight through for three days, drinking the casino's free coffee to stay awake. By the time he lost the $600 his nerves were jangled up on caffeine and he was badly in need of a shave and a shower. But he still believed he could win, so he did the unthinkable. He phoned Mother and said, "Bring everything we've got left to Vegas." She was mad as hell, but she came to Vegas with the money.

It was back to keno, and down $347. He had $3 left and bet it on a three spot. It hit, and he slowly worked his way back up to $100. Mother wasn't even in there watching him. She was so disgusted she'd gone out to the car and gone to sleep, something you wouldn't dare do these days. He sat there looking at the $100 and listening to them continue to call out the numbers, and he finally knew he'd lost. He'd been within $3 of having nothing. No grocery money. No paycheck coming in, and no tools to get a job with. He went back out and woke Mother up.

"Let's get the hell out of this town while we can still eat," he said.

Dad didn't sleep that night. They got home in the early hours of the morning, and Mother crawled into bed. Dad did, too, but the sound of the old air conditioner seemed to keep on calling out the keno numbers. Nine. Six. Ten. The next morning when Mother got up, he was already up having coffee.

"We're moving to Las Vegas, Juanita," he announced, still looking like he'd been on a three-day roll, and of course, he had. She just groaned.

He shook his head. "We're not going there to gamble. Las Vegas has show business people in and out of there all the time.

Somebody's gonna help us." Then he added, "We can't pay our rent here next month, anyway."

Moving from St. George was hard for me. I loved my life there, and I had many friends I was leaving behind. But I knew we had to go. Dad and I had already been at the crossroads, and I'd made my decision. If I was to get this career that could change our lives, I had to be in close proximity to people who could help. St. George, Utah, was not the place.

We packed up and headed for Vegas with less than $100. Dad drove around Henderson, which is the residential part of Las Vegas, and scouted out places we might rent. Then, on Navaho Drive, we saw a double-wide trailer with a covered porch and a neatly landscaped yard. It had a For Sale sign in the yard with a contact name: Mr. Day.

Mother took one look at the For Sale sign and asked, "Beau, how could we do this? We don't have any money!"

He shook his head and said, "I'll think of something." Then he went to a pay phone and called Mr. Day.

The trailer seemed like heaven to us once we got to see the inside. It was clean and bright. It was owned by a woman in Arkansas, whose husband had left her, signing over the trailer in the divorce.

Daddy sat down with Mr. Day and explained our situation in his usual blunt way.

"Sir, I don't have any money. We don't even have a hundred dollars to our name," he said, right up front. "But I've got this little girl who can sing, and I believe she's gonna be a star."

Mr. Day said he had a wife who was in a wheelchair, she'd had both legs amputated, and more than anything in the world she loved to play the piano and have people sing with her. So off we went to meet Dovie Day, who wheeled right over to the piano and began playing hymns. Some of them I knew and some I didn't. If I didn't know the words, I'd read them from her hymnals.

Finally Mr. Day said, "Well, Mr. Tucker, I believe you're right about your daughter's talent. How can I help?"

Daddy said, "You can put me in touch with people who lend money. I don't have any collateral except Tanya and a strong back. I'm a hard worker."

It seems unbelievable, but after Daddy and Mr. Day made the rounds of several savings and loan offices, they found someone who'd take a chance and give us a loan. Vegas was pretty free-wheeling in those days, though, and with Mr. Day's help, we had a trailer. Dad started lining up some part-time jobs that would bring in trailer payments and food money and still allow him time to pitch tapes. We were ready to take on Las Vegas.

Right after we got settled, Daddy met a guy who booked acts for several of the casinos. He listened to the tapes and said he could make me a star. No problem. Well, to us he seemed like a person who had the know-how, the experience, and the con-nections to get us rolling. What we didn't know was that he was on the take. He'd book an act into a lounge and demand a hefty piece of the artist's pay under the table. Otherwise he'd find another act. We found all that out after we'd signed a contract.

The day Dad learned what the guy's real game was, he went down and asked for the contract back. The guy just laughed in his face. My dad turned and stomped out of there and showed back up at the trailer.

"I'm gonna shoot that bastard," he said to Mother and me.

He hauled his pistol out of the drawer, loaded it, and left. Mother and I sat on the couch wide-eyed, not knowing what to expect. In Las Vegas, you never knew whom you might be deal-ing with. Thirty minutes later Dad was back with the contract, which he promptly tore into shreds. From then on, Dad tried to be more careful about what he signed.

Not long after that we set off for a talent show being held down on the Strip. It was sponsored by an independent record label. We'd never heard of the company, but they were sup-posed to have some money behind them. After we took off down the road, we realized the gas gauge was bumping empty. We didn't have a dime on us, so we pulled into the first station we came to, and Daddy got a jack out of the trunk. He walked over and told the man working there that he didn't have any money, but would he consider trading a few gallons of gasoline for a jack? The guy backed off and told us to get out. Well, that didn't stop us. Daddy pulled a U-turn, went to the station across the street, and offered them the same deal. This fellow was more receptive. He accepted the jack and told us we could have the gas, but he said we'd have to pump it ourselves.

Thanks to the jack, we made it to the talent show, I sang, and a few days later we got a call. The record company wanted to sign me to a recording contract. Daddy didn't waste any time getting down to the offices. He said when he walked in he thought he'd died and gone to heaven. The carpet seemed to be about four inches thick, and all the furniture was new. He was thinking about how he'd had to trade a jack to get enough gas to make it to the show, and that he was rolling his own cigarettes with Bull Durham to save a few dollars.

The man in charge didn't waste any time. He offered a singles deal, which means the label records and releases singles, hoping for a radio hit, then if the chart action warrants it, they record an album. He stressed that they believed they could make me into a hit act and that they had the resources to do it. "Now once you sign with us, you and your wife will need to back off from Tanya. I won't deal with any stage mamas or daddys. All decisions will be made by us, right here in this office. We'll own all recording rights, management, and booking. Everything." And he offered Dad a big check to confirm the deal.

Dad knew that the family needed money desperately. He knew this was a shot, and probably a good one, since these people had money. He knew he didn't know enough about record deals to know what was good and what wasn't, but the idea of somebody owning his daughter lock, stock, and barrel didn't set right. So with great reluctance, he got up and walked out empty-handed.

Mother like to have died when he told her he turned down cash money.

ELEVEN

*M*any elements played a part in my getting a recording contract. My dad's steadfast determination was probably the key factor. The fact that Billy Sherrill is an eccentric who does exactly what he wants and listens only to his own instincts is another. I'd factor in Billy's love of gambling in the music business as well as at the gaming tables. And it was necessary that publisher Al Gallico liked Las Vegas songwriter Delores Fuller enough to use his considerable influence to convince Billy to meet with her. I also think Billy and Al had to be in Vegas and in a crapshooting mind-set to finalize the deal. The odds against the most important producer in country music paying any attention to a kid from Henderson, Nevada, were astronomical.

The wheels were set in motion when Cotton Harp, who had produced my Las Vegas tapes, showed up again soon after Daddy turned down the independent deal. We'd let him know we'd moved to Henderson, and he came over one night. When Daddy told him about sending all the tapes to Nashville and the trip to Los Angeles, Cotton said he had an idea. He knew a songwriter named Delores Fuller who was promoting shows at the Flamingo Hotel. She'd once managed Johnny Rivers, and she'd written "Do the Clam," "Spinout," and "Rock-a-Hula-Baby" for some of Elvis's movies. Cotton thought Delores might be able to help us, and Dad didn't waste any time calling her up.

After they had a phone conversation, Delores invited Daddy to come to her house and play her the tape. She lived in a private community with a security gate, and her house was even more plush than the independent record company's office. Delores said she could get the tape to her friend Billy Sherrill in Nashville. Daddy thought she dressed too flashily and was too "Hollywood" for us, but he was grasping at straws by then.

Thank goodness he didn't know just how "Hollywood" she was. Delores had been the girlfriend of Ed Wood, the filmmaker who had directed what many think is the worst movie ever made, *Plan 9 from Outer Space*. That wouldn't have been a problem for Daddy, but Ed was also a notorious cross-dresser. The fact that Delores had a boyfriend who ran around Los Angeles in women's clothes would have been a big problem. Delores had starred in two of Ed's movies, *Glen or Glenda* and *Jailbait*, before heading to Las Vegas and a songwriting career. We didn't know about Ed Wood, or Delores's connection to him, until a movie about his life, starring Johnny Depp, was released in 1995.

Dad signed Delores up as my manager, and she sent tapes to both Billy Sherrill and Al Gallico, the two men who would play such pivotal roles in our lives. Billy was an Alabama preacher's kid who wound up in Nashville blowing sax in a rock-and-roll band, and Al had worked his way up through the publishing ranks pitching songs to every kind of act from big bands to rock stars. When Al heard Delores's story about my dad having knocked on half the doors in Nashville to get someone to listen, he must have felt a sense of sympathetic identification.

In 1961, just as Al was starting his own publishing company, a woman named Lillian Evans called him and said, "The next time you come to Nashville, you've got to meet my future son-in-law, Billy Sherrill. He's a genius." Al says he sluffed Lillian off, because he knew that everyone thinks they've got the next big talent, especially if it's a family member. She kept calling and finally wore him down. The next time he had a Nashville trip planned, he called Lillian. "All right," he said. "I'll meet this genius of yours." Lillian told him Billy was recording some songs he'd written at a little studio on Music Row, and Al stopped by unannounced. Billy was there all alone.

"I thought you were recording," Al said.

"I am," Billy answered, offering no explanation for the lack of session players. He fooled around with the control board and then went back in the studio and laid down piano tracks. Then he came out and fooled around with the dials again, and went back in and played the guitar tracks. He kept right on going. He played saxophone, he sang, he did everything, and when he was finished he came back in and listened. And during all this he didn't have one thing to say to Al Gallico. Al says he thought to himself, "Well, he's a little introverted, but I think that woman was right. The boy is a genius." Al offered Billy a songwriting contract with the newly formed Al Gallico Music, and he even helped him land his initial Artist and Repertoire job at Epic Records. Ultimately they went into a publishing business together.

Delores was pitching me to Billy Sherrill when he was without question the hottest producer in Nashville, working with stars like Tammy Wynette and Charlie Rich. He had no time to fool with some kid from Henderson, Nevada. I don't even know how he heard the talent in the first place. As I said, I never thought those tapes were very good. They were recorded in one take, since the cost factor made overdubs out of the question. In addition to the sound quality, my vibrato was not under control yet. I listen to it now and shudder. But Billy later said that the vibrato was one thing that interested him. He always said he was amazed to find a thirteen-year-old with a vibrato faster than Kitty Wells's.

Billy says he listened and liked what he heard, but since he was so busy, it took Al Gallico's prodding to make him meet with me. Billy Sherrill is one of those producers who may hear a voice he likes, but until he matches that voice with the right song, he doesn't get excited. And as it turned out, gambling played a big part. Daddy might not have been able to finance me by playing keno, but Billy and Al frequently came to Las Vegas to gamble. For all I know, those two might even have been in the casino when my dad was losing our rent money. But they're high rollers who play craps and twenty-one. They wouldn't have been playing keno.

Every time the two of them hit Vegas, Delores Fuller nagged them to meet her new "find," Tanya Tucker. Billy'd say, "Nah, I'm here to gamble, not to listen to acts." Finally, several months after she'd sent the tapes, the two were on another gambling junket, and Delores was bugging them about me again. Al says he turned to Billy and said, "Come on, Billy, Delores is a nice gal and a friend. Let's talk to her."

They went over to Delores's home, and after Billy listened to the tape again, he told Delores to bring me to the Riviera later that day. Delores called Dad and told him to get me dressed up, because at long last, Billy Sherrill had asked to meet me.

Billy remembers being stunned when he saw me walk up to the booth in the coffee shop of the Riviera. Even though Delores had mentioned my age in passing, he wasn't prepared for a kid to walk in. The face and the voice just didn't match up. It's probably lucky that Delores had downplayed my age, because Billy later told me he was a little like W. C. Fields when it came to kids and dogs. Of course, you ought to see him dote over his granddaughter now. And at his office he has a framed picture of his Himalayan cat on his desk.

Billy took one look at me, shook his head in disbelief, and asked, "Is that really your voice on those tapes?"

"You want me to sing something?" I asked, by way of an answer.

He smiled and shot a sly look at Al Gallico. "No. I guess the next time I'll be hearing you sing is in a studio in Nashville."

My first meeting with Billy Sherrill almost ended up as crazy as our trip to Costa's wedding. Bobby Vinton was playing the Riviera then, and he was sitting with Billy and Al. Bobby did something so outlandish that I still can't believe it. Billy introduced us to him, and of course I wanted his autograph. I pushed a napkin across the table, and he wrote: "To Tanya Tucker. No sex! Bobby Vinton." Maybe he thought that was a funny way to acknowledge that I was a kid, I don't know. My dad didn't think it was a bit funny, and when he started to turn red, I guessed we were in for another fight. Back then I never knew what to expect from my dad. I still don't, when you get right down to it. He says that the only thing that stopped him from decking Bobby Vinton was the knowledge that Billy Sherrill had the power to sign me to Columbia Records.

Finally Billy turned to Delores and said, "Okay, who's going to write a hit song for Tanya Tucker, you or me?" Delores said she'd go to Los Angeles and come back with a monster, and that was the last we heard from her for several months. What we couldn't know was that she was writing songs and sending them to Billy and he was turning them all down. He said they were all either too slick or too juvenile. Once again, we waited. But this time when we waited, we had a signed contract.

Dad and Delores negotiated it, and we didn't get any up-front money from Columbia. But Dad did insist on a three- instead of a five-year contract. I don't think Billy cared much one way or the other. He wanted to see if we had a radio hit. Otherwise, I was finished, anyway. But Dad believed I'd be successful, and he thought he could get some front money when he came to the table in three years.

TWELVE

I have Bette Midler to thank for the song that became my first hit record, because Billy happened to be watching Johnny Carson one night and heard her sing "Delta Dawn." Remember those show business myths? The tale told about "Delta Dawn" is that Billy immediately thought it was a hit for me. That's not the real story. Billy had never heard of Bette Midler before, but he loved her voice and wanted to sign her to a recording contract. He called Al Gallico in New York and asked him to track her down. Bette had just signed with Jerry Wexler at Atlantic Records, and when Al called Billy back and told him so, Billy said, "Well, let's find that song, 'Delta Dawn,' and I'll cut it on that little girl from Nevada."

It turned out that the song was close to home. Alex Harvey had written it with a former child singing star named Larry Collins. Alex was from Brownsville, Tennessee, and had written "Ruben James," a hit for Kenny Rogers a couple of years earlier. Billy called Delores and told her to bring me to Nashville, because we were in business.

The only trouble was that with no label advance up-front, we didn't have the money to get there. I believe if we'd spoken directly with Billy and explained that we didn't have the money to come, he'd have offered us travel expenses, but it never got that far.

Delores knew the extent of our poverty but didn't want the label to know. So she came to the trailer and talked with us. There were round-trip airline tickets to buy and hotel and food bills while we were in Nashville. No way was Delores going to truck across the country in a car and stay at the kind of seedy motels we were used to. And it was anybody's guess how long we'd stay. Delores's idea was that we borrow $2,500 from her boyfriend, and in return he'd get a percentage of my career.

"Well, Delores, it seems to me that you've already got a percentage," Daddy said. "If I keep on giving away percentages there won't be a dime left for Tanya when it's all over."

"I don't know what you're going to do then," she said. "Billy Sherrill's ready to record her. You're going to have to find the money to get her there."

Daddy sat there a few minutes and then offered a solution. "How about if your boyfriend loans me twenty-five hundred and I sign a note that I'll pay him back double? It looks to me like that would be a hell of a good deal."

Delores seemed doubtful, but she said she'd see. Her boyfriend must have thought it was a hell of a good deal, too, because he went for it. We booked the flights, then went down and signed the note for $5,000, exactly twice what we'd borrowed.

When we got to Nashville we checked into the King of the Road motel, and right away Dad saw how important it was that we had that extra money. We went to dinner and Delores ordered lobster. Not once in our lives had we sat at the table where anybody ordered lobster! She continued to dine in style, too. It was second nature for her. It got so bad that I'd order a hamburger and Dad would say he wasn't hungry. He'd sit there drinking coffee and smoking his hand-rolled Bull Durhams. Delores would sign the ticket charging the meals to our rooms, leaving a couple of dollars for a tip. Dad would say he needed to go to the bathroom or make up some other excuse to linger around the table until Delores was out of sight. Then he'd take the tip money and go off and get himself a hamburger. He lived in fear of running out of money and looking like a fool in front of people like Billy Sherrill.

Every day we'd go to Billy's office or to the Columbia studios and listen to songs. Even though Billy was banking on "Delta

Dawn," he wanted to find a strong B-side in the hopes we'd record a two-sided hit. Delores was pushing for a song she'd written called "Take Care of You for Me."

I quickly saw that Billy's personality wasn't going to mesh with Dad's. Billy isn't the sort who would glad-hand just to make an artist's family or manager or anyone else around them feel at ease. He believes his job is the music, not public relations and not record business politics. His strong aversion to playing politics accounted for the deal he'd cut with CBS. Billy had started out as a staff producer, thanks to his friend Al Gallico's pushing label executives in New York on his behalf. He went from a job as executive producer for Epic Records' Artist and Repertoire (A&R) to the vice president of both CBS labels, Columbia and Epic, and as he always put it, he had a "sweet deal." New York and Los Angeles left him alone as the unquestionable head of the creative side of the label. Still, even with that power, Billy wouldn't have been able to shove me down New York's throat if my first single didn't get some action at radio.

In fact, during the first sessions I'd asked him what would happen if the song bombed. He said, "I might have to drop you." He said it jokingly, but there was an underlying truth to the statement, and I knew it. I wasn't going to let anyone get the best of me, though, so I said, "Well, maybe I'll drop you instead." He cracked up. There's nothing Billy loved more than an artist who seemed to be full of confidence, and there's no one more confident than a kid who doesn't know what all can go wrong.

Billy decided to go with "Delta Dawn" and Delores Fuller's "Take Care of You for Me." Daddy had stayed at the hotel the day that decision was reached. Delores still says that Daddy's desire to protect me by controlling things was always a problem in the studio and at meetings and that Billy wanted him out of there. Billy doesn't remember it like that, but Dad was definitely uncomfortable around Billy Sherrill. Up to that point, my dad had been in charge. Now someone else was temporarily taking over. To ease the situation, and possibly to appease Delores, Dad stayed away from time to time. He phoned my mother and said he felt like he was being turned into a butt kisser.

"You don't have to do that, Beau," she said. "You're Tanya's daddy and you ought to be getting some respect out there."

"I don't give a damn, Juanita," he said. "We're just about to get this thing done. If it'll help Tanya get going, I'll kiss every rear end between here and New York."

Billy, Delores, and I listened to "Delta Dawn" and other songs all day, and by the time I got back to the King of the Road that night I was so tired I could barely hold my head up. It was late, and they'd decided to record at 10:00 the next morning. I asked Daddy to play "Delta Dawn" on our little tape recorder while I was going to sleep, so I could learn it even better. I wanted to knock everybody's socks off. Daddy says he sat up half the night playing the song by my ear, then rewinding the tape and playing it again.

I didn't really understand what the song was about. I knew that some lady had gone crazy and was wandering the streets wearing an old faded flower. I knew her daddy still called her baby. But the concept of losing a lover and going insane over it was beyond me. I liked the words and the musical feel of the song, though.

The next day, March 17, 1972, I arrived at Columbia's Sixteenth Avenue Studio at 10 A.M. sharp and for the first time met the musicians who were going to back me up. Billy brought in the best in town. Some musicians pay attention to the music tracks only, and the lyrics aren't particularly of interest to them. Billy tried to find those musicians who wanted to hear every line, every change of mood in a song, and back it up with their instrumentation.

The session leader was Pete Drake, a legendary steel player who Billy said loved making hits more than almost any musician in the world. Pete was a real "song man." Pig Robbins was on piano, Billy Sanford on guitar, and Charlie McCoy on harmonica and vibes, along with other members of the Nashville A-Team—Henry Strzelecki, Jerry Carrigan, Tommy Allsup, Ray Edenton.

I walked in and Billy introduced me to everyone. I loved everything about the studio, the seedy-looking carpets, overflowing ashtrays, and Coke cans strung throughout the place. I didn't feel nervous, although I figured the band thought Billy was headed for the nuthouse for signing a thirteen-year-old kid. I said, "Well, I know my part, boys. Do you know yours?" That loosened things right up. I belted out the two songs, and any reservations I had about the band's attitude were quelled by the smiles on their faces. Later many of them have said they never questioned my age. After all, Billy Sherrill believed.

Delores Fuller believed, too. She believed so strongly that we'd made a hit record that after we returned to Vegas, the first thing she did was to drive to L.A. and buy a brand new Lincoln and a house full of new sound equipment. She called us when she got back and said she had a present for me to celebrate the recording of my first hit song. Then she wheeled the new Lincoln in the drive and gave me her old taping equipment. Later she told the press that she'd taken me to L.A. and paid a lot of money to have work done on my teeth. That never happened.

"Delta Dawn" is the song I most often close my show with, and it is still one of the most requested. I'll go to my grave thanking whatever angel got Billy to tune to the Johnny Carson show that night. It made me a star back then, but it made me the proudest a few years ago. I was playing a show in Texas and received a note that there was a little girl with Down's syndrome in the audience who wanted to come backstage. When she and her parents got there, her dad told me that until she was eight years old she never spoke. They bought one of my tapes and were playing it around the house, and one day, the little girl stood in the middle of the room and began to sing "Delta Dawn." And she has spoken ever since. I teared up, it was such a miracle. It also reminded me that music can be a powerful thing.

THIRTEEN

"Delta Dawn" entered the charts on May 13, 1972, and we started getting some offers to play shows. We couldn't afford to get a bus or hire a band, so we'd take off in our old station wagon and I'd rely on house bands or the headliner's band. If we were using a house band at some venue, we'd send off to them a cassette tape of "Delta Dawn" and some of the songs I liked to sing. If we were lucky, they'd learn "Delta Dawn." More often than not, I just had to wing it and sing whatever standards we both knew.

I opened shows for artists like Tommy Cash, Nat Stuckey, and Marty Robbins. It was exciting to be around these stars, although since I was so young they usually didn't have much to say to me. Sometimes they'd talk to my dad about promoters or bus problems or getting stiffed on a show. I'd stand there listening and try to get some kind of a feel for what this business was all about. More often than not, I heard about the downside of it.

One person I was a little starstruck by from the beginning was Tom T. Hall. Maybe it's his manner—he has a very powerful presence—or the fact that he is a great songwriter, but you never forget that he's a star. I loved to sit and listen to him talk, because he's educated and so well spoken. I always figured that maybe I'd learn something just by being around him. If anything, I started to see how he dealt with all sorts of people. Entertainers have to be able to get along with fans, music people, political people, and sports people, and they have to be comfortable with that. I've become pretty good at it, and maybe my first training started all those years ago listening to Tom T. Hall.

I also got to talk with my hero, Merle Haggard, when I opened a show for him in Florida. I did my songs and then loitered around backstage while Merle was getting ready to go on. He was sitting in the wings, smoking a cigarette. It took every bit of nerve I could muster, but I finally went over to him and asked him if he remembered singing "Mule Skinner Blues" with me at his studio in Bakersfield. He looked at me for a while, then got a glint in his eye and, to my relief, said, "Yeah, I do, honey. I sure do."

We got to meet the headliners back then. These days you might open shows for an artist for months and never meet them. People stay on their buses and don't socialize as much now, although some headliners do make an effort to meet their opening acts and spend some time with them. Charlie Daniels is one, and George Strait is another.

It's easier for guys to socialize on the buses because you're always trying to get ready, and half the time you're in some state of undress. A couple of years ago I was playing a package show in Sidney, Ohio, with Ronnie Milsap and Confederate Railroad. Danny Shirley, who sings lead for Confederate Railroad, was on my bus. I had to start dressing, but I wanted to hear what he was saying, so he turned his back and I left my bedroom door open. I was standing there in almost nothing, when Ronnie Milsap came up the steps and through the door. My friend Sheila was with me, and she freaked out. "Oh, you can't come in here, Mr. Milsap," she said. "Tanya doesn't have any clothes on." Then she paused and added, "Well, I guess since you're blind it's okay."

My mouth dropped open, and Danny says his did, too. But Ronnie just cracked up. "I am and it is," he laughed.

I always wanted to get to know the other artists, and I still do. But everybody is on the road so much of the time you aren't in town enough to forge long-term friendships, even with neighbors. It feels awkward to pick up the phone and invite someone you haven't seen since the last awards show to come over to your house and hang out. Finally I did do that with Tammy Wynette. I am such a big fan of her music, and I respect her so much as a person. She is a woman who has been through so much pain and illness in her life, yet it never gets her down. So one day I was thinking I'd love to be able to spend some time with Tammy, and I called and asked her and her husband, George Richey, over for dinner. She said she'd love to. I flew right into action, getting the table set and the food ready. I can't remember whether it was chicken-fried steak or fried chicken that I made for them, but I do remember I was nervous about whether or not Tammy would like the dinner. But she polished off her plate and asked for seconds, and she was just as impressive and yet friendly in an informal setting as she is onstage.

In addition to having me open for as many artists as possible to help promote my record, Columbia decided I should hit the road that summer on a series of "meet and greets" at country radio stations. Delores came over to our trailer and told Mom and Dad they would not be assets on these trips. They didn't know anything about the record business, the radio industry, or politicking with movers and shakers. What she was really saying was that she thought they were a couple of interfering hicks.

I didn't see my parents as interfering. I knew what an interfering parent was. I'd seen it up close when I was on the *Lew King Ranger Show*. There was a boy on the show, and I believe his name was David, who did a lot of show tunes, songs like "Hello, Dolly!" and "Oklahoma!" He had quite an act, too, because in addition to singing in a Broadway style, he played trumpet.

David's mother literally defined the term "stage mother." She hovered around the theater when we were rehearsing, always making sure David was getting a fair share of on-air exposure. She went everywhere with us. One day Lew took us on an outing to the Phoenix Amusement Park. We'd been excited about the trip for weeks, and the first thing we all rode was one of the park's tamer rides, the ferris wheel. I should say, all of us except David rode the ferris wheel. His mother gave everyone a lecture about the dangers involved in the ride, then held David's hand the whole time we rode. In my mind, I can still see him standing there looking up at us, his mother looking fierce and clutching him close to her.

I don't know if David ever did anything in show business, but if he did, it was probably in spite of his mother. Risks are a part of anyone's life, and a parent who won't allow a child to take a few will repress needed development and experience. Now that I have children, I understand David's mother a little better. You do try to keep children away from anything that could hurt them. But I truly believe that by shielding them to an unnatural extent, you do them untold damage. If you're going to be an entertainer, that's even more important, because you've got to develop a very thick skin to keep going through rough times. And you can count on the rough times popping up frequently.

Delores convinced my parents to stay behind, and as soon as they were temporarily out of the immediate picture, Delores began talking about reshaping my image. As if a thirteen-year-old has an image. Suddenly I was being asked to tie my shirts up under breasts I didn't have, pull my jeans down to show my navel, and flirt a bit with the deejays. Country music's Lolita.

Delores's Hollywood and Las Vegas mind-set even caused a problem between her and Billy Sherrill. From the very beginning, Delores wanted me to put on a flashy stage show, and to that end she hired a choreographer. I was doing a straight-ahead country performance, not a Las Vegas review. But Delores wanted me to strut more, swing my hips more, move around on the stage more. I just wanted to sing, and I told her so. The strutting and hip swinging would come soon enough, and when it came it would be entirely my own doing. I didn't need anyone pushing me at the age of thirteen, when I was more tomboy than young woman.

Delores put me on report to Billy. Billy is an intensely artistic man and not inclined to sit in meetings involving anything that smacked of marketing issues, radio promoters' strategies, or managers' problems. Billy hated getting involved in anything except making records. When Delores busted in his office and told him I was a spoiled and uncooperative little kid who wouldn't work with her or the dance instructor she'd gone to great expense to hire, he told her to leave me alone. He said I was a little kid, and more important, I was a singer, not a dancer. Furthermore, Billy said, Tammy Wynette didn't tap dance around the stage while singing "Stand by Your Man," and she'd done just fine. Delores didn't like it, but Billy Sherrill had spoken.

Even if he hadn't taken my side, to choreograph a show you have to know what you will be singing, and since I was using house bands who played what they wanted, it would have been almost impossible to plan out any elaborate dance routines.

FOURTEEN

*P*eople often ask me what it was like to be a child star, and I have to say I don't know. I never felt like a star. I guess the best way to put it is that I felt like I was a part of a family business, and my role was to get up and sing. We didn't make much money, so the trappings of stardom eluded us for many years. I think that the first time I really understood that I even had a hit record was when I was invited to sing on the Grand Ole Opry during the summer of 1972. We didn't have a feel for what was going on while "Delta Dawn" was climbing the charts. If we'd been in Nashville, I think we'd have felt the building excitement that surrounds a hit a lot more than we did in the trailer on Navaho Drive.

I was on Ernest Tubb's portion of the show, and of course, my dad loved that. He said it was one of the biggest nights of his life, seeing me standing where all the stars stood. I loved the fact that I'd made it back to the Opry, the place where I had once sat in the audience feeling I'd failed my parents so badly.

For the record, the Grand Ole Opry was not a glamorous place in 1972. I love and respect the Ryman Theater, but back then it was hot in the summer and cold in the winter. The dressing rooms were about the size of an outhouse, and the stage slanted down, so you felt as if you might slide right down onto the people in the front row at any minute. The glamour was provided by the stars, and no star stands out more in my mind from that first appearance than Connie Smith. Connie is one of my favorite vocalists, and I used to tell people that I stole a lick from her every chance I got. She wore a light pink chiffon dress, tight at the waist, with cancans holding out the full skirt. Her hair was up, and she both looked and sang like an angel. Even now, when I think of the Opry, I can picture Connie standing there waiting to go on. As for me, I was wearing a little yellow flowered dress and white go-go boots, my own this time.

Ernest brought me out and told the audience about singing with me in Willcox. When he stepped back and said, "Ladies and gentlemen, Miss Tanya Tucker," I was so excited I could have peed my pants. I stepped up to the microphone and sang "Delta Dawn," then went offstage to see if I'd get an encore. Imagine my surprise to find that people didn't just automatically clap you back. The Opry announcers come out and keep the audience going, revving them up so you get an encore. And I did get one. I'd heard that Hank Williams held the record, receiving six encores one night. Well, shoot, I thought then, if the announcers are going to get the audience revved up for one encore, why don't they keep right on revving so I can break Hank's record!

⚜ ❦ ⚜ ❦

In July we were back in the recording studio to complete the album. We recorded nine songs over a three-day period, from July 12 to July 14, and from those sessions we got a double-sided hit, "Love's the Answer" and "Jamestown Ferry." Dad had one of those rare chances to say, "I told you so" during those sessions, and it was a sweet moment for him. We were walking down the alley toward Columbia's Studio B one morning, and who should we run into but John Capps from K-Ark Records. He immediately glad-handed Delores.

"Well, how're you doing, Delores?" he asked. "And what're you doing in town?"

"I'm managing Tanya Tucker," she said. "This is her daddy, Beau Tucker."

"How do you do, Mr. Tucker, glad to meet you. And you're the 'Delta Dawn' girl, aren't you, honey? I sure wish I'd signed

FIFTEEN

$\mathcal{S}$tarting my ninth grade at Henderson seemed strange after the summer of '72, when I'd been all over the country playing shows, performed on the Grand Ole Opry, and watched "Delta Dawn" become one of the biggest hits of the year. I'd always been an outsider, and my new celebrity status made me more of one. It was especially difficult to be treated like I believed I was special, a star, when what I felt like was someone who'd been working hard at a job.

I'd had a foreboding feeling about school in Henderson when I first came there the previous year. The building was big and gray and looked like a prison. The school grounds didn't seem that much different from the tension-filled prison yards I'd seen in movies and on television, either. The school was full of cliques, and I knew I wasn't going to fit in. There were black cliques, Mexican cliques, all kinds of white cliques, and mine, which was sort of a "nothing clique." We had nothing in common except that nobody else wanted us in their group.

After "Delta Dawn" hit, the Las Vegas newspaper sent a reporter out to our trailer on Navaho Drive to write a "local girl makes good" article. Nothing could have been worse for a junior high student, and I knew it the minute I walked in the school and a group of girls started chanting.

"Delta Dawn, what's that poo I smell on you? Could it be you need a bath and a shower, too?"

Like the Leroy Van Dyke song, I just walked on by. It was hard to know how to react. If I got mad or acted hurt, I knew it would get worse. Everyone knows how junior high is. It's not the best of times for most kids. If something has made you stand out from the crowd, it's very likely to be the worst of times.

I was standing in the girls' bathroom just before homeroom one day, when a group of girls slipped in and surrounded me.

"Come on, star," one said, shoving me a little. "Sing your hillbilly song."

I tried to shake her off, and another one closed in behind me.

"Let's hear you sing that old country song," she said, giving me a little push.

Then one of them opened one of the stalls.

"There's your stage, Delta Poo. Get on up there and sing for us."

There were so many of them, I had no choice. I couldn't have made it around them to the door, and even if I could, I knew I'd never make it home that night without getting beat up. So I did as I have done so many times in my life, I just shut down the hurt and anger and sang. But that time my stage was a toilet.

"She was forty-one and her daddy still called her baby, all the folks 'round Brownsville say she's crazy," I sang, my vibrato wobbling a little more than usual. As I wound up the song, the school bell rang and they ran out. I climbed down off the toilet and leaned against the stall, trying to make sure my emotions wouldn't show when I walked into the classroom. I didn't want any of them to know they'd got to me.

To this day I do not like to go to a public restroom alone. I always ask a girlfriend to accompany me.

❧❧❧

"They did what to you?" My dad's jaw dropped that night when I told him about having to sing on the toilet.

"Made me sing," I said.

"You're gonna have to fight 'em, Tanya," he said. "You've got to learn how to use your fists."

Dad did his best to turn me into a street fighter. He'd have little training sessions with me and offer bits of advice like, "Never agree to meet someone after school, Tanya. Always do your fighting in a very public place. Otherwise somebody'll have a friend sneak up on you with a beer bottle." A beer bottle in eighth grade? Well, you never knew. Now, of course, it would be an automatic weapon. But I never got very interested in being physically tough back then. I just wanted to get through school and get on with my career, with a minimum of trouble.

The girls didn't let up, and finally Rhonda Davis, one of the girls in my circle of pals, took it upon herself to be my bodyguard. She was a pretty wild redhead, and she already had her bluff in with most of the tough girls. She stuck close to me, and as long as she was around I didn't have much to worry about. The first day she was absent from school after taking over as my chief of security was another story. We sat in desks with two people in them, and without Rhonda there beside me the tension was thick.

One in particular, a girl named Terry, just couldn't stand me, and the minute the teacher left the room she made her move. In what seemed like a split second, she shot across the room and slapped me right in the face. I remember she was wearing a dress, and I thought, "How weird. She's wearing a dress and wanting to fight." It seemed like you'd be wearing jeans if you were looking for a fight. So I fought her back some but didn't get any good licks in before the teacher came back and we jumped back into our chairs.

The next day one of the black girls said she was going to kick my butt for not kicking Terry's butt any better than I did. I side-stepped that one, but I was thinking, "Damn, the only time I want to kick butt is when I walk out onstage."

I finished out that year and didn't go back to school the next. It was just too hard to go from a world where people were applauding you and cheering for you to a world where you were probably going to get beat up for just being what you are. But also, I was just flat tired. You can't play shows every week-end and have the energy to keep up your schoolwork. Especially if every school day involves a hassle in the halls and the school yard.

In retrospect, I wish I had finished high school. I've often thought about trying to get a GED like Waylon Jennings did. It would make me very proud. People are always asking me what advice I'd give young LeAnn Rimes, the thirteen-year-old

SIXTEEN

My last trip with Delores was to Los Angeles for meetings with promoters, deejays, and label people. We stayed one night at the home of a very wealthy friend of Delores's, an old man worth millions, or so Delores said. I don't know why, exactly, but I became so nervous around the two of them that the palms of my hands and the soles of my feet started itching horribly. I locked myself in my room and got out a hairbrush and used it to try to scratch my hands and feet to stop the itching. I sat on the bed alone, digging and digging until my hands and feet were bleeding. I finally fell asleep in the early hours of the morning. All I could think about was my parents and the safety of our trailer in Henderson.

The next morning we were to meet with some agents, and Delores told me in no uncertain terms to be on my best behavior. My feet and hands still felt like they were on fire, and I kept my hands clenched so she wouldn't see the scabs that were forming on my palms. I sat off to one side and watched her while she turned on the charm. I tried to pay attention and participate in what was being discussed, but all I could think about was the fact that my feet were burning. Finally I couldn't stand it anymore. I pulled my shoes off and started scratching my feet like crazy. Delores's mouth dropped open. She quickly wound up the meeting and pulled me out of there, furious. When we got back to Las Vegas she called a conference with Mom and Dad, telling them I was impossible on the road, and they needed to get me in line. All I could say in my defense was that something about being alone with Delores was making me so uncomfortable I'd started to itch. They took one look at my hands and feet and fired her.

I don't think Delores understood just how uneasy all her image-creating made me. To her it was entirely natural. Delores had started her career running around with a cross-dressing film director and had later moved on to the glitz of Vegas; she couldn't possibly relate to the Tuckers, whose idea of heaven was a trailer with a picket fence and an indoor shower.

Delores wasn't the only one wanting me to grow up fast. At CBS in New York there was an entire group of promotion and marketing people who wanted me to be a rock-and-roll singer dressed in skintight black leather. At the same time Billy Sherrill in Nashville wanted me to sing country songs and grow up whenever the spirit moved me. The flashiest image Nashville came up with was an airbrushed poster of me looking something like a 1940s starlet. A very innocent looking starlet, I might add.

When it's all said and done, I sometimes wonder if Delores's Hollywood flash didn't cover up a good heart. It sure happens in this business, and sometimes I'm afraid it happens with me.

SEVENTEEN

*S*oon after Delores Fuller was out of the picture, John Kelly came back into it. He initially approached Dad about me opening some shows for Judy Lynn, but what he really wanted to talk about was handling my career. It seemed perfect to Dad, since John had managed Judy Lynn's career very successfully. John knew people, and no one had a bad word to say about him. Besides, he'd allowed me to sing on Judy's show long before I had anything going. Our immediate finances also played a role in the decision to sign with John. I'd had a hit record, but we were still having a hard time making ends meet, and Dad believed John Kelly's booking expertise could help. The first thing John did was release Buddy Lee as my booking agent and sign me with his own company, Artist Talent, in Las Vegas.

When I first went on the road, it was in our Chrysler station wagon with one or both parents along. We didn't have any idea how to run a tour, and more than once that lack of knowledge cost us money.

On one run during the summer of 1973, we were driving from

Louisiana to Atlanta to play a show with Dave Dudley. Columbia had lined me up to do several radio interviews along the way, but Daddy kept checking his watch and estimating how long we still had to drive, so we thought we were fine. I always tried to get some sleep in the car. We'd folded down the backseat and put a mattress there, so I'd curl up under a blanket while Dad drove the long roads between shows. I was sound asleep when I heard Daddy calling to me.

"Tanya, you better get up and get dressed, because we're coming up on Atlanta," he said.

I did what I usually did and held the blanket like a tent over me while I slipped out of my jeans and into my stage outfit. All of a sudden it seemed like the world got brighter even through the blanket, so I stuck my head out and looked around to see what was going on. The only thing I could see was a continuous stream of car lights, all going the opposite way we were going.

I freaked. "Daddy, everybody's going home! The show must be over."

He checked his watch again and said, "Nah, there's probably just so many people coming to see your show that they're havin' to turn 'em away."

When we pulled up backstage, Dave was already on his bus eating his dinner. They'd figured me for a no-show and Dave had gone on without an opening act. Daddy kept shaking his head and saying how he'd checked his watch dozens of times all the way from Louisiana. Dave asked, "Did ya change your watch for Atlanta time?"

I'd like to say that success changed all that, but every so often I'm reminded of those days in the station wagon. Once during the summer of 1991, when I was very pregnant with my son, Beau Grayson, my assistant and I flew to Denver, Colorado, then rented a car to drive to a show in Greeley. We had directions from the road manager, who had gone ahead on the bus. My assistant had been driving an hour or so, and I was rereading the directions, when all of a sudden I realized we'd taken a wrong turn. "Oh, Lord, we're headed the wrong way," I said. "Turn the car around and hit it." We had given ourselves plenty of time for me to change clothes in Greeley, but with the time we lost, we rolled into town just in time to get to the venue. Just like all those years ago, there I was, changing in the car again. I was pulling on a pair of stage pants and had to half stand up in the front seat. We were slowing down at a four-way light when the man in the next car turned. All he saw was half of a face and a big pregnant belly. He came within two inches of pulling into a light pole. We took off and made it to the show. And I always wondered if he saw who it was and told his friends that Tanya Tucker had mooned him with her stomach coming into Greeley.

Since we made it to the show in Greeley, we got paid. That night at Dave Dudley's show, we didn't. Daddy sat down on the bunk and looked like he was going to cry. He's been very conscious of time changes ever since, because we'd counted on the $600 I was going to earn to get us home. When we got back to Vegas, John Kelly was hopping mad.

"You tell me the truth, Beau, why'd you miss that show?"

"Because I didn't set my watch, John," Dad explained.

"Well, I'm gonna tell you—" John started, but Daddy'd had it by then.

"No, you ain't gonna tell me anything," Daddy shot back. "You lost twenty-five percent of six hundred dollars. We lost seventy-five percent. We're the ones who are sick to our hearts and broke to boot. I'll promise you this one thing. I won't miss another show." He didn't, either.

John started out treating Daddy like he didn't know anything about the music business, and, of course, he didn't at the time. But he was willing to learn if people would just treat him with some respect. John Kelly never learned that. He continually reminded us that we were supposed to mail him the payments for shows the minute we got them. He even went so far as to write his address on a stack of envelopes and place stamps on each one, so we wouldn't have any excuse not to send in the money.

After all the years he'd been on the road with his wife, Judy Lynn, John should have known what a big problem it was when we were getting started to get the payments from some of the show promoters who might not be professionals.

In one place where we played we drove up to the fairgrounds to find that the stage was a flatbed truck, and it wasn't equipped with any sound and light equipment. The promoter tried to tell us we were responsible for bringing our own, but Daddy pulled the contract out and showed him where it said the fair association would provide it. The guy wouldn't budge, and he said if I didn't do a show the crowd could hear I wouldn't get paid. We stood there and Daddy looked around and saw that the announcer had a bullhorn. He handed it to me and said, "Hell, Tanya, sing through that. They'll hear you then." So I just got up and started singing. We got paid that night, thanks to Dad's ingenuity and my loud voice.

We returned to Nashville in January of 1973 to start recording my second album for Columbia, and the very first song we laid down was the number-one hit, "What's Your Mama's Name." Our old friend Peanut Montgomery wrote the song with Dallas Frazier, and Billy Sherrill had already recorded it with George Jones when I first heard it. I knew the song was for me the minute Peanut played it, and it came out so strong Billy made it the title cut of the album.

We recorded Curly Putnam's "Blood Red and Goin' Down" in March of '73, and it became another number one. Once again, the minute I heard that song I wanted to record it. In both cases there is a strong story with a dark twist, and a powerful, surprise ending.

Al Gallico once again entered the picture during the time we were in Nashville recording and, once again, profoundly changed our lives. My whole family came to those sessions, including La Costa. She and her husband, Darryl, had been living in Toltec, Arizona, where he was working as a pilot. Dad was never one to give up on anything, and he'd been thinking about La Costa's derailed career. He knew the Muscle Shoals sessions had been mishandled, and he still believed, as we all did, that La Costa's talent deserved a better shot than she'd been given so far.

One night he got on the phone to her and said, "I think you ought to pull up stakes and move to Henderson with us. We've got Tanya going now, and I believe we can get you going, too." So La Costa came to Vegas in a renewed search of a career, and I got my sister back.

We were in Billy Sherrill's office one afternoon, and Al was there, in Nashville pitching songs. He approached La Costa and asked if she had any interest in recording. In what was a great understatement, she said she did.

"Can you sing something for me right here?" Al asked.

She went back to her old favorite, Dean Martin's "I Will," and Al was sold.

"I think we need to record you," he said. "You go on back home and let me work out something. I'll call you."

In the music business, "I'll call you" means about as much as "the check's in the mail," but when Al said it, we believed it. He was one person who didn't make idle promises. I went back to Henderson on a natural high. I knew two things: that we'd made some hit records and that Al Gallico was going to help La Costa.

He kept his word, as we knew he would. Within a couple of months Al called and said he had sessions lined up, a producer, and a bite from Capitol Records. He just needed the songs down. We didn't understand it at the time, but Al had done more than pitch her to a record label. He'd offered to pay for the demo tapes they'd need to make a final decision. La Costa and Darryl piled in their old VW bus and headed for Nashville. She says they slept at every roadside park between Nevada and Tennessee. Her first sessions were recorded in November of 1973 by one of Al's staff producers, Norro Wilson. By the following July, Al and Norro had her signed to Capitol.

EIGHTEEN

I remember only once feeling resentful that my career inter-
fered with my life as a teenager. Even though school was a very
tense place, I was excited about some of the activities. And even
though my parents wouldn't let me go on dates, I was hoping
they'd let me attend the Sophomore Reverse, a yearly event
where the girls in ninth and tenth grades got to ask out the boys.
I'd been thinking about Sophomore Reverse in connection with
a boy I'd had a crush on since we'd moved to Henderson.

Del Ford sacked groceries at the local Albertson's. For two
years I'd found all sorts of excuses to head down to that grocery
store every chance I got. Del probably thought I was a total
harebrain, since on some days I conveniently forgot first one
thing and then another and had to return several times. I knew
I'd never have the nerve to ask him out, so I asked one of my
girlfriends to find out if he'd go.

When Del told my friend he'd love to go with me, I made a
date. My plan was to take him to the Top of the Landmark for a
$4.99 prime rib dinner. Mother and Dad didn't say much about
the "date," but then again, they didn't tell me I couldn't go.

The days went by and all I could think of was getting to go
to Top of the Landmark and have prime rib with Del. A few days

before the big event, I got home from school and Dad was waiting for me.

"You're booked at Bobby McGee's this Saturday," he said.

"That's the night of Sophomore Reverse!" I wasn't believing it.

He shrugged. "It's also six hundred dollars, and we're not turning it down."

I was just sick, it was such a letdown. I went back in my room and had a talk with myself about the responsibility of a career and paying the bills and all the sacrifices people had made for me. Then I called Del and canceled our date for Sophomore Reverse.

Bobby McGee's was not one of my favorite places to play, anyway. It was in Gilroy, California, and it was one of the roughest clubs I've ever been in. It was the kind of place where if you said something a guy didn't like, he might just pull a gun on you. At one show, I was changing into my stage clothes in the dressing room, and a guy got knocked right through the wall and landed at my feet. So that was what I was trading my first date for.

We pulled up to the club that Saturday night and there wasn't a soul in sight. Not only that, but the doors had been boarded up. Dad drove into town and a fellow at a gas station said it had been closed down by the law because of prostitution and drugs. We didn't have much to say to each other on the way home. I didn't really blame my dad. He was sick, too, that we'd spent money for the drive to Gilroy and come home empty-handed.

I might have missed out on the Sophomore Reverse, but later that year I discovered two important new loves: my first real boyfriend and cutting horses.

When I was playing the Flamingo Hotel in Vegas, the World Cutting Finals were being held at the Stardust, and I'd been asked to participate as a celebrity contestant. Cutting as an event grew out of the cattle drives, when a cow was sick or had to be removed, or cut, from the herd. Cowboys took a great deal of pride in how they maneuvered the cow, and it eventually turned into a formal competition. Pat Patterson, who later became my cutting trainer, won that year, but the big moment for me came when a young cutter named Mike Mowrey rode out into the arena. He was blond, gorgeous, and at sixteen, the youngest guy out there. In those days cutting was primarily an older man's event. The younger cowboys rode broncs and bulls. But Mike loved cutting, and he was good at it. I watched him ride and thought to myself, "There is the boy for me."

We met at a lunch with a group of the rodeo people at the Stardust. I didn't say much to him that day, but I already had a class-A crush. We stayed in touch, and the next time I played a show close to the California ranch where he worked, he invited me to come along the morning after my show to a cutting in Turlock, California. I worked late and jumped out of bed early. A lack of sleep was the last thing I was concerned with. We loaded up Mike's horse, a champion cutter named Rancho Dick, and drove through the foggy wee hours of the morning to the grounds. I got to ride, too, and came in third.

It was probably a combination of having what I now considered a "boyfriend" and actually placing in my first cutting, but I felt like I owned the world. What I didn't know was that the love for cutting events would last much longer than my feelings for Mike.

Participating in the cutting events during that time made me realize that there are some real benefits to being an entertainer, perks that you don't anticipate in the beginning. You have the opportunity to do all kinds of things you might not be able to afford to do on your own, like ride in limos, sail on yachts— and, yes, cut horses. Cutting is a rich man's sport, and if you're going to go after it full-time, you'd better have a pile of cash ready. I found out just how expensive a sport it was soon after meeting Mike. Thinking I wanted to get serious about the event, I phoned a special cutting school in Los Angeles and asked about signing up. "Sure," the guy said. "We'll just need a check for twenty-five thousand dollars." I said I'd think about it and hung up, figuring I'd have to settle for the celebrity events and whatever training I could get there. I still have a serious desire to train, really train, as a cutter.

I continued to see Mike over the next couple of years at celebrity events and rodeos where I was hired to perform. But he had rodeo and I had country music, and those two careers don't make getting to know another person easy. In the long run, Mike didn't like the idea of a girlfriend who was up onstage performing. He wanted a very traditional relationship, and traditional is hard to come by for an entertainer.

NINETEEN

I soon found that I couldn't rely on house bands as my backup, and it was while we were in Nashville trying to put together a band that Dad heard Sonny James had a bus for sale for $32,000. Of course we didn't have the money, and of course we didn't let that stop us. Luckily, the bank decided it was a sound investment, and finally we had real wheels. The difference in driving along cramped up in a station wagon and in a bus where we could sleep comfortably, kick up our feet, and actually move around when we wanted to was unbelievable. Now we could take the whole family along on tour. It was the beginning of what has become a family business involving every member of the Tucker clan.

Things were starting to happen for La Costa, too. Her first single, "I Wanta Get to You," was released in April, and while it didn't burn up the charts, it moved ahead steadily, ultimately becoming a top-twenty record. Her second release, "Get on My Love Train," which became her career record, was far more successful, rocketing to number three in *Billboard* and establishing her as far more than just Tanya Tucker's sister.

In August of '73 we were back in Nashville to record a third album. Billy had found a song he believed was perfect for me.

It was to be a number-one country single, a top-forty pop hit, and my first taste of career controversy. I didn't know it at the time, but the third album would also be my last with Columbia and Billy Sherrill.

"Would You Lay with Me (In a Field of Stone)" was a song David Allan Coe wrote to perform at his brother's wedding. When he brought it to Billy Sherrill, the title was "Tell Me Lady, Can You Pray," and Billy told David he had no idea what that had to do with the lyrics. In fact, Billy said he wasn't even sure what the song was about. David explained that the song was about eternal love, love that doesn't stop at the grave. The line, "Would you lay with me in a field of stone," referred to a couple who would ultimately be buried together. At the time, I thought of it as "The Wedding Song."

Mother and Dad didn't like it a bit. They both felt it had a sexual connotation and would be entirely inappropriate for me to sing at such a young age. The day we recorded it we also recorded "The Man That Turned My Mama On," which was a top-five hit. Hits or not, those kinds of songs were not Mother's style, even if the messages in the lyrics were less suggestive than the titles.

One month before I started recording "Would You Lay with Me," Helen Reddy released "Delta Dawn" to the pop radio stations. I wasn't thrilled about it, but I wasn't anywhere near as burned up about the release as Billy Sherrill. Billy went nuts. I remember going to a CBS convention in San Francisco with Billy just after Helen hit the charts with what we considered "our" song. Billy was dressed in a black suit, and to me he looked just like a gangster in an old movie. All the record executives did, as a matter of fact. He stormed in and immediately started bending people's ears about it. What really griped him was that Helen's record was so similar to Billy's arrangements. The problem as far as Billy was concerned was that his country recording would sell about 200,000 copies, and Helen's pop release, using his arrangements, would top 2 million. That amounted to a lot of money out of Billy's pocket. When the song hit number one, Helen's producer sent Billy a telegraph. It said: "Thanks for the arrangement." Billy didn't know if he was being gracious or sticking the knife in deeper.

That was probably the first time I really started to understand the difference between a pop record and a country record. Since Billy's arrangement had been used, pop and country couldn't be all that different. The lyrics had certainly appealed to all audiences. The difference was in the money earned.

"Would You Lay with Me" was released in January of 1974 and was immediately met with opposition from several radio stations. Some went so far as to ban the song, and the record label learned that some preachers in the country were even using the song as an example of how country music was getting as evil as rock and roll.

My parents were quick to tell the press that they'd been against their fifteen-year-old daughter cutting the song in the first place. I felt I had to defend both the song and the fact I'd recorded it. On interview after interview I said the same thing: "It's not a bad song. It was written as a wedding vow."

Articles started appearing with titles like, "Did Tanya Have to Grow Up Too Fast?" All of a sudden people were asking me if I was "crossing over" to pop music. Again, I kept giving the same answer: "I'm a singer. I love all kinds of music. But this is a country record, not a pop record." The controversy didn't bother me like it did Mother and Dad. In fact, sometimes when people have criticized me, both as a child and as an adult, for better or worse, that's when I stand most firm. Also, I thought the controversy might sell some records.

TWENTY

*T*anya, you got some good news just then," Dad said, hanging up the phone. "You're not gonna believe it, but you've been nominated for the Country Music Association's Female Vocalist of the Year. Loretta Lynn's up for it, too."

"Me and Loretta Lynn!" That was my main reaction. I couldn't believe that Loretta Lynn and I were in the same category of anything, let alone an award. I didn't quite grasp what an honor it is to receive a CMA nomination. Just being mentioned in the same breath with Loretta was enough for me.

The whole Tucker family went to the awards show that was held on October 15, 1973, at the Grand Ole Opry. We were all involved in the business now, since my brother Don had joined the organization as my bus driver. We were thrilled to see so many stars in one place. I kind of split into two people that night. I was a nominee and accorded star status, but I was also a starstruck kid in awe of people that I didn't really understand were my peers. I wore a little blue chiffon dress to the awards, probably because I'd been so impressed with Connie Smith and her pink chiffon at the Opry. Loretta wore a blue-and-white flowered dress with a huge, antebellum-style skirt, and she looked just like a fairy princess. It was the first time I'd seen her in person. It seemed like every singer I'd ever listened to on the radio was there. Tammy Wynette and George Jones looked like the definition of country stars. Tammy had on a sweeping blue beaded gown, and George had a light blue studded suit. Loretta and Conway Twitty presented the Male Vocalist Award to Charlie Rich. Maybelle Carter was there, as well as my favorite intellectual, Tom T. Hall.

I was part of a segment toward the beginning of the show called "New Girls in Town," with Barbara Mandrell, Barbara Fairchild, and Jeanne Pruett. Johnny Cash hosted the show, and he introduced me when it was time for our part.

"Ladies and gentlemen, this young lady just recently celebrated her fifteenth birthday, Miss Tanya Tucker." I walked out and sang "Delta Dawn," and then Barbara Mandrell came out and sang "Midnight Oil." Barbara Fairchild sang "Teddy Bear," and then Jeanne Pruett sang her classic, "Satin Sheets."

The Female Vocalist Award was announced by Glen Campbell and Merle Haggard. Glen was wearing a flashy orange suit decorated with studs, and a Hawaiian shirt, and he looked every inch the huge star that he was. But it wasn't Glen who impressed me the most that night, it was Merle Haggard, who was dressed in a tuxedo and a blue ruffled shirt, the man who had actually remembered me singing "Mule Skinner Blues" with him in Bakersfield. When they called Loretta's name out as the winner, I never had even a quiver of jealousy. In fact, if I'd won over an artist of Loretta's stature, I'd have thought something was screwy.

Loretta was great when she did her acceptance speech, and we could all learn from her. She walked out and said, "I ain't gonna take up all a' your time, since I know we're runnin' late. I'm just gonna thank Owen Bradley, my A&R man, and all them deejays and other folks who voted for me."

I sat in the audience and watched with big eyes as three legends walked offstage: Loretta Lynn, Glen Campbell, and Merle Haggard. That girl in the blue dress seems a far cry from the one who, just a few years later, was raising hell with Glen and running off with Merle right in the middle of it all.

TWENTY-ONE

I toured off and on with Johnny Rodriguez throughout 1974, and the experience allowed me to see up close what celebrity can do to a person. Johnny had his first hit with "Pass Me By" in 1972, and within a year he was one of country music's biggest heartthrobs. Since we were both identified as Texans, a tour of that state was put together that included every fair, festival, and honky-tonk the promoters could dig up. Some of those clubs were dives I wouldn't go in even now, but we hit every one of them back then.

Wherever we played, Johnny Rodriguez might as well have been Elvis. I had never seen anything like it, especially in Johnny's home state of Texas. On our tours, girls brought Johnny dozens of roses, cooked up trays of tacos and tried to bring them backstage, and tried to grab his pants while he was performing. Extra security guards had to be hired to keep the girls from tearing off Johnny's clothes. He almost never had any privacy. I could go out back of the motel and play Frisbee with the band, but if Johnny tried to do it, some of those girls would have broken past the guards. It was unbelievable.

The only time he could be himself was when Joaquin Jackson stepped in. Joaquin was a Texas Ranger who years earlier had arrested Johnny for stealing a goat, as the legend goes, then taken him under his wing and helped him get his career going. Joaquin had a ranch, and if we were playing nearby, between shows he'd take us there. We'd shoot guns, ride horses, and kick back. Those were some of the best times of the tour as far as I was concerned. Riding horses and playing practical jokes was still my idea of the fast lane. My concept of boy/girl relationships was daydreaming about Mike Mowrey and the rodeo. For me, running wild was to sneak down the hall at the motel, knock on doors, and run. Actually, that's still my idea of a good time. Once in a while when my friends and I check into a hotel, I'll stick them with the luggage and then race down the hall knocking on doors, leaving them to face the music and hotel guests.

Not that I didn't understand what the excitement was about. Johnny had a tremendous amount of charisma and sex appeal, and an amazing talent to boot. I had a little crush on him at first, and it even gave his promoters the bright idea to marry us off and grab as much publicity as we could from the tour. My dad flipped out and vetoed that idea before it got past the "what if" stage. Besides, after weeks of seeing half the girls in Texas throwing themselves at Johnny, I think my interest turned to something close to pity. The girls even started coming around to cry on my shoulder when Johnny dumped them!

I think Johnny was emotionally torn by all the adulation. On the one hand, he was a guy who loved the attention and having girls swooning over him. But he was also a shy, private individual whose eyes sometimes reminded me of those of a deer caught in the headlights. As the tour progressed, I saw Johnny change a great deal. It got so he'd be doing one of two things, running wild with girls on both arms or trying to hide. Either way, the fans believed he could do no wrong.

To be given carte blanche when you're young is a heady experience. That's when you start to make mistakes and don't even count them as such. You think there are no consequences. There were times Johnny missed our show dates. I asked the guy who was driving us around on our tour why he thought Johnny could get away with it. I knew I wouldn't have been able to. The driver said, "He can't do it, Tanya. It'll catch up with him." Johnny had personal and career ups and downs over the years, and I think many of his problems stem from being considered the Little God of Texas back then.

We've stayed friends through the years. You can't help but love him. Johnny came out and performed on a benefit I threw a couple of years ago for a friend of mine who had cancer, and he's still got that old stage magic. He recorded a new album this year, and from what I hear, he's still got the studio magic, too. I think he's happy. He's married to Willie Nelson's daughter Lana, which means his father-in-law is the Big God of Texas. It should keep things in perspective.

❦ ❦

In a strange turn of fate during the fair season of 1974, I met a man who would years later become very important in my life. I was scheduled to play a Labor Day show at the Mahonig Valley Fair in Canfield, Ohio, with a regional act called the Sound Generation opening. It had been raining for days in Canfield, so by the time Don pulled the bus into the fairgrounds, the infield was soaked, and the bus sank clear to the axles. I looked out the window toward the stage and could see the Sound Generation onstage. It was a group of what appeared to be twenty or so musicians.

Don tried to drive us off the infield, but the wheels just whined and spun. We were creating a huge distraction, and little by little, most of the crowd of seven or eight thousand people turned and were watching our lack of progress. I was already dressed in one of my favorite stage costumes, an Elvis-type gold jumpsuit, and was ready to perform, should I ever make it to the stage. Don opened the door to the bus and got down to see if there was any hope at all, and I could hear the lead singer and keyboard player of the act onstage making an announcement over the PA.

"Ladies and gentlemen, with all due respect, the show is here on the stage, not out in the infield. I promise you we'll get Miss Tucker up here in time to perform."

I cracked up. That lead singer was Paul Moore, who became my Nashville-based agent in 1979, a job that has often involved hauling me out of the mud.

❦ ❦

About the same time in 1974, CBS introduced us to a man from Little Rock, Arkansas, who would profoundly affect our financial status. On the surface, Bill Carter was an unlikely person for the music business. He had spent years in the U.S. Secret Service, working in both the Kennedy and Johnson administrations, and for a time he was assigned to the Warren Commission. During his tenure with the government, Bill worked both in Arkansas and in Washington, D.C., and he made some powerful contacts, as well as learning the ins and outs of the political workings in the nation's capital. After he left the Secret Service, he went back to school and got a law degree.

When the State Department banned the Rolling Stones from returning to America after their 1972 tour had caused riots in several cities, Bill was hired to help get the ban lifted. With the help of his friend, Arkansas Congressman Wilbur Mills, who was chairman of the House Ways and Means Committee, Bill ultimately did get the the Rolling Stones reinstated, and in the process he became close friends with the Stones' manager, Peter Rudge. Through Peter, Bill met several CBS Records executives, including Don DeVito and Jonathon Caffino. Those two were worried about my career, since as near as they could tell, my father didn't have a clue about developing an artist for the big time. Bill says a nice way to put it is that Jonathon Caffino told him the Tuckers were naive, and that maybe he could give them advice from time to time.

Bill Carter hit it off right away with Dad. Bill didn't have a flashy show business personality. He was a low-key, but direct, Arkansas lawyer who was genuinely interested in seeing us succeed. He not only liked my dad, he treated him with respect, which was all Dad asked for and seldom received in those days. When Dad first met Bill, we were ready to try to sever ties with John Kelly. I had been ready since the opening night of the Pikes Peak or Bust Rodeo in Colorado Springs that year.

The incident that turned me sour on John started as I stood by the bull pens and watched Judy Lynn ride out into the arena. She was astride her big white horse, waving her white cowgirl hat while the fringe on her jacket was flying in the wind. I was wearing my little handmade miniskirted dress and go-go boots waiting for my part of the show. She looked like the Queen, and I felt that I looked like Cinderella. My face might even have been dirty, because I'd been hanging out at the cow pens listening to the rodeo hands talk "bull" all day. I saw John Kelly was standing over by the backstage area, and I walked over to talk to him.

"John, I want to ride in the arena, too," I said. "Like Judy."

"Go on, Tanya," he said. "I don't have time to talk right now."

"I want to ride," I repeated.

"You don't have a horse," he said, absentmindedly, as though I were an afterthought in his daily world.

"Well, I could get one."

He mopped his forehead and pointed to an old horse grazing beside a trailer.

"I'll see if you can ride that one," he said.

I didn't think so. I'd already seen the horse I wanted, and it was a big, beautiful black flag horse that was used to the spotlight and would have been a dream to ride. So I brought it up.

"Listen, John, that black horse over there is one of Mike Serby's, and I know he'd let me ride him. We know Mike," I explained.

John barely paid attention to what I was saying. He just blew it off and pointed to the nag he'd picked out. "If you want to ride, that's the only horse I can get for you, Tanya," he said. "Beggars can't be choosers."

Beggars can't be choosers?

I don't know of an artist in the business who wouldn't be furious if their manager referred to them as a "beggar." I was just dumbstruck. My dad had been pissed as hell that John kept booking me as the opening act, when I was the one with a recording contract and hit records. But up until that moment, I couldn't have cared less. I didn't feel like a headliner, and to tell you the truth, I still don't. In my mind, headliners are people like Garth and Reba with the fireworks and sixteen-wheelers following the buses to all those mammoth venues. I'm just a singer out on the road. Was then and am now. It was Dad who was grinding his teeth over the Tanya Tucker/Judy Lynn opening act or headliner question; my teeth were grinding over a horse.

I walked straight over to Mike Serby and asked if I could ride his horse in one of the preshow processions. He said, "Sure, Tanya." And the next night, when the band struck up the parade music, I was riding in the front of the line.

John Kelly never tried to cheat us or purposefully lead us astray. He was an honest man. The problem was that his first and most important act was Judy Lynn, and I was always going to play second string to her in his eyes. Dad didn't get mad enough to fire John until they started renegotiating my CBS contract, but in my mind he was gone from that day on. John didn't trust my dad to be involved in the negotiation process, which was stupid, because Dad was the one who insisted my contract be for three years instead of five. He always believed I could become a valuable property for Columbia and wanted to be able to renegotiate as early as he could.

But John kept him in the dark and flew to New York to handle the negotiations without even telling Dad he was going. The first Dad knew about it was when John called and told him to come to New York and sign the contract. He was stunned, but he flew in and met with John and CBS. John took Daddy out in the hall and showed him the agreement. It was a long-term contract and offered us $50,000 to re-sign. Daddy was humiliated at the way John put it to him.

"Beau, that's more money than you've ever seen," he said. "Why, you could get it in cash and take it home and take a bath in it!" Those words went all over my father, because he felt that John was treating him like white trash, as if he'd really get fifty grand in $1 bills and pour the money over himself in a bathtub. Daddy told CBS he'd fly back to Nevada and think about it. John tried to get him to sign on the spot.

"Do what you want, Beau," he said. "But I promise you this is the most money you can get for Tanya." Nevertheless, Dad flew home with the unsigned contract and asked Bill Carter what he thought.

CBS must have been surprised when their handpicked Arkansas lawyer didn't advise us to re-sign right away. Bill Carter wasn't a manager back then, and he wasn't sure what financial arrangements might be appropriate. So he asked the opinion of his Rolling Stones friend Peter Rudge. Peter read the contract in disbelief.

"Bill, I don't know anything about the country music business," he said. "But this isn't any money at all! The girl's got hit records. She ought to be worth a lot more."

"Well, what should we do?" Bill asked. "Try to talk them up?"

"First, I'd go to some other labels and see what kind of offers you get," Peter said. "You might want to start with MCA in Los Angeles, because the pop labels are throwing money around everywhere right now." Peter Rudge had inside knowledge about MCA because he was working with MCA's Lynyrd Skynyrd at the time, who were fresh off their big hit, "Sweet Home Alabama." Peter said he'd try to arrange something with an A&R guy in L.A., and Bill thanked him and hung up, wondering exactly how much money the pop labels were willing to throw around.

At that point in my career, Billy Sherrill's sweet deal with CBS presented a problem for us. Billy's desire to stay out of the politics and the business decisions left my contracts in the hands of the New York office.

I was determined to stay with Billy Sherrill, and I said so. Billy represented complete studio security to me. We didn't have any kind of a relationship with him outside of the studio, so it's not like we were pals around town or anything. My parents and I didn't go over to his house for dinner, that sort of thing. But in the studio there was something special between us. He not only let me be a part of the process, he actually listened to what I had to say about songs and music.

Plus, and I realized this much later, Billy's Baptist upbringing played a major role in the success of my early songs. Many of his arrangements have an underlying religious urgency, that old Southern Baptist feel. I can still hear Billy telling the vocal groups, "Don't move around so much. Lock onto that C-minor and stay there a few bars." That sound was an important part of some of my early records.

Out of respect for my wishes, Dad and Bill promised me that if CBS would even come close to what another label offered, we'd stay with Billy. But with the New York office doing all the talking, things got quickly out of hand, and by the time Billy got involved, negotiations with MCA were all but finalized.

TWENTY-TWO

ohn Kelly's negotiating with CBS pushed his relationship with my dad to the edge, and his saying Dad could take a bath in fifty thousand $1 bills pushed it right over. Dad's only question about getting rid of John was how to get out of the management contract without going broke. Bill and Dad came up with a two-part solution. Bill was afraid if I signed with MCA, John would get wind of the potential for big money, and he told my dad he didn't see how we could get out of the management contract without a very big payoff. Dad said he believed he could buy John out for $50,000, the amount CBS had offered. Bill just laughed. "You'll never be able to do it," he said, adding, "but you might as well try."

The first thing we did was pull up stakes in Nevada and move to Little Rock, where Bill and his family lived. Even after all the hit records, we still didn't have much in the way of material possessions, so most of what we brought could be transported in our station wagon.

As soon as we got settled, Dad got on the phone and informed John that he wanted to buy him out of the contract. He also said we were close to broke. They talked awhile, and Dad convinced John that he couldn't come up with a dime to buy a cup of coffee. Finally he said, "I'll tell you what. Give me a week to come up with fifty thousand dollars, and we'll call it quits."

John didn't believe Dad would be able to get his hands on that kind of money, so he agreed. Bill Carter was sitting there listening and he wrote Dad a note: "Get him to send a telegram and confirm it." John sent the telegram, and the minute they had it in hand, Dad and Bill went to Bill's banker and borrowed fifty grand.

"Now you just watch," Dad said. "We'll get this cashier's check to John and he'll try to double the price."

So Dad and Bill worked out a plan. They'd fly to Las Vegas, where John had his offices, and Bill would deliver the check and ask for the release. Dad would show up a little late. He had to go pick up a car he'd left there when we moved, anyway. When Dad got there, if the release was signed, they'd leave. If John was screwing around with the deal, Dad would blow his stack, threaten to sue, and storm out, leaving Bill, as the voice of reason, to close the deal. Well, that's exactly what happened. John wanted more money, Dad showed up, blew up, and walked out. John saw $50,000 slipping through his hands and signed the release.

∗⧸⧹∗⧸⧹

In the middle of the John Kelly and CBS upheavals, I had a press coup that I neither understood nor fully appreciated. *Rolling Stone* magazine sent writer Chet Flippo to do a series of interviews with me out on the road. *Rolling Stone* was rock's bible, and although I was getting interested in some rock music, I was still country to the core and far more interested in country music fan magazines like *Music City News* and *Country Song Roundup*. But Bill Carter was ecstatic, because not only did the magazine want a story, I was to be on the cover. Throughout *Rolling Stone's* history, very few country artists have ever made the cover—Dolly did, and a few years ago Garth did. But it's a very unusual situation.

It seemed like Chet Flippo was on the road off and on with us for months, and he and I hit it off right away. He asked quite a few questions about rock-and-roll music, and I told him about acts I loved—Redbone, The Allman Brothers, Elvis—and acts I didn't like—Black Oak Arkansas, David Bowie. Most of the acts

I loved were acts that had country or southern roots. What I especially liked about rock concerts was the audiences. They were young and energetic, and the entertainers were able to elicit a huge response. I was beginning to wonder how I could expand my live show and get that same response from a country crowd.

I don't know what the *Rolling Stone* readers thought of Tanya Tucker when they read that I sometimes might break up a poker game among the band members by turning a hose on them, or that one of my goals was to be able to get $20,000 for a show so I could lie back and just go fishing and ride horses for a month or so. Chet also wrote about us going to a freak show at one of the fairs, where I was fascinated by a hunchback who stuck nails up his nose.

About the biggest revelation I offered was the fact that Larry Collins, who co-wrote "Delta Dawn" with Alex Harvey, tried to pick me up at the King of the Road motel in Nashville right after we recorded "Delta Dawn." Larry damn near died when I told him who I was, how old I was, and that I'd cut his song. I also told Chet that I'd heard of a deejay who announced Tanya Tucker singing "Would You Lay with Me," and he tagged the announcement with, "I'd slide down a razor into alcohol if I could, darlin'."

Chet listened to all this and he reminded me that some people were saying I was the sex symbol of my generation. I said, "Well, I guess that's cool." I'd still never had a real date, and on my off-time—when I was just hanging around the house—I still felt like a tomboy. But I was starting to like the feeling of looking a little sexy, and I was working on making my show more flashy. Everything, in fact, that Delores Fuller had wanted me to do.

Bill Carter's old friend, Arkansas Congressman Wilbur Mills, turned up again and helped Dad and Bill begin serious negotiations with MCA. Around the same time we'd been trying to get loose from John Kelly, Bill had mentioned the possible MCA deal to Mills, who casually said, "Oh, why don't you call my friend Lew Wasserman?" Lew Wasserman was chairman of the MCA Corporation, which included Universal Pictures. Dad and Bill knew that to a man like Lew, the $50,000 offered by

CBS would be pocket change. Dropping Wilbur Mills's name paid off, and Lew Wasserman took Bill's call immediately.

"I've got a country singer named Tanya Tucker I want to talk to you about," Bill began, thinking he'd have to give Lew a rundown of my hits and a pep talk about my potential.

"I'm familiar with Tanya," Lew said quickly. "As a matter of fact, I've thought she could cross over into the rock and pop charts."

That was the beginning of the courtship from MCA. Mike Maitland, who ran the record division, came out on the road to see my show, and even as loyal as I was to Billy, I began to like and respect Mike a great deal. He not only loved my music, he believed I could sell millions, just like the pop stars.

Dad and Bill finally decided we should sign with MCA and flew to L.A., where with surprising speed MCA offered me $1.5 million. It was an unbelievable offer, since this was after three very difficult years of the Tuckers trying to make it out there on the road with no up-front record label money. So Dad shook hands with Mike Maitland on it. By the time Bill and Dad were back in Little Rock, CBS had heard the news and decided if Lew Wasserman wanted me bad enough to pay a million and a half, maybe they'd blown it. Also, Billy Sherrill was raising hell with the New York office about their handling of my contract negotiations.

I was completely torn up over it. I loved working with Billy, and I didn't want to leave him or the label. But Mike Maitland was a wonderful person, too, and he was offering $1.5 million. We couldn't even imagine that much money. It's hard to imagine it even now, let alone in 1974. When CBS finally flew in with their counter offer, Dad turned them down. He and I had shaken hands with Mike Maitland. Even if the contract wasn't signed, the deal was done.

MCA orchestrated a big event in Little Rock on my sixteenth birthday to officially announce the signing, and they flew in people from all over the country—their own staff members and press and radio people. They rented an entire amusement park there in Little Rock and turned it over to the guests for the celebration. In between interviews and photo opportunities, I was running around everywhere riding the bumper cars, tilt-a-whirls, and ferris wheels.

Part of the reason for the big hoopla was to distract from what the doomsdayers in Nashville were saying. They were shaking their heads and predicting the end of Tanya Tucker's career. After all, it was Billy Sherrill who had brought me to the dance, and without Billy everything could, and most likely would, fall apart. It was the first of many times that doomsdayers would predict my career demise.

TWENTY-THREE

*E*ver since we started making any money out on the road, we'd dreamed of one day owning a ranch, and when we moved to Little Rock we saw firsthand what living that dream could be like. The Carters had a 365-acre farm about an hour out of Little Rock, and we spent every available minute out there. It was a wonderful place, and just the sort of place we'd always dreamed about. They bred horses and kept around fifty on the farm, so we rode and worked with the animals nonstop when we were out there. In some ways it was like camping out, because the farmhouse had only one bedroom—a long room with a double bed and a lot of twin beds for the kids.

Little Rock was a very curious time for me. I became close to the Carters, especially Bill's wife, Jan. I loved her fried chicken, which she prepared by frying it until it was crisp, then baking it until the meat fell right off the bones. I also spent an enormous amount of time with the Carters' daughters, Joanna and Julia. When I first met them, Julia was nine and Joanna was seven, and the two girls quickly became almost like younger sisters to me. I'd spend hours fixing our hair, putting makeup on all of us, and dressing up. One of our favorite pastimes was playing model, where we'd all dress up in stage clothes and parade around the

Carters' living room pretending we were on a fashion show ramp. I even took them trick-or-treating one year in their model getups. Having never experienced anything close to it, I loved playing big sister.

Then I'd get a gig and take off to a county fair to sing. Bill says he used to feel like he ought to apologize when I'd have to turn back into a performer, but it never seemed weird to me at all. It was the only world I knew.

The downside to living in Little Rock was that when we had business to take care of in Nashville, we had to drive or fly in, get motel rooms, and live out of suitcases. And even with hits, during the years we were on Columbia, we weren't flush with cash. I was successful musically but still out there paying those hard road dues for money in the three-digit range, certainly not like an artist today, who can be raking in thousands of dollars a night after just a hit single or two. Our overhead—travel expenses, paying the house band, the occasional new stage outfit—ate up a lot of the cash.

The MCA money gave us financial breathing room for the first time, although to tell the truth, I've never really felt like I had breathing room. I've made and spent a lot of money. But since I don't write many songs, the lucrative BMI and ASCAP royalties, the ones entertainers can retire on, go somewhere else. I have to stay out on the road to stay alive, and overhead expenses still eat up a lot of the profits.

When Dad got our advance check, he decided to buy a 220-acre ranch about twenty-five miles southwest of Nashville. Bill Carter advised against it. He put a pencil to the deal, figured in taxes and upkeep against our newfound wealth, and told us in no uncertain terms we couldn't afford it. The ranch was not a working one by any stretch. We bought it anyway. Strangely enough, it was already named Tuckahoe and carried the double-T brand. The man Dad bought it from had purchased it long after it was named, so he didn't even know why it had the name, either. As far as he was concerned, Tuckahoe was just the name on the gate; as far as we were concerned, it was destiny. We bought horses and cattle, geese and ducks. Even if we didn't have a working ranch, we wanted the feeling of one.

Tuckahoe had three houses on the property when we bought it. My brother Don and his wife moved into one; Mother, Dad, and I took another; and we used the third house as an office. There was a big swimming pool, and Dad had painters come in and paint a Tanya Tucker logo on the floor of the pool. La Costa and her husband were living in Los Angeles, and the ranch gave them a home base when she came to town.

I got a great idea one day while I was sitting in my room at Tuckahoe listening to a James Taylor album, and it resulted in Mother meeting one of her musical heroes and George Jones having a hit record. I heard James sing the song "Bartender's Blues," and I thought it was perfect for George. He'd had a little dry spell in 1977. He released two songs that year, "Old King Kong" and "If I Could Put Them All Together (I'd Have You)," and neither one did much on the charts. Then Don and I saw him out on Old Hickory Lake, and I told him I had a hit song for him.

A few days later the doorbell rang, and when Mother answered the door she about freaked. There stood her hero, George Jones, looking pretty sharp in a pair of patchwork Bermuda shorts, a tank top, and sunglasses. She asked him in and came to find me, stunned that Mr. Country Music was standing in her living room. I got the James Taylor record and played it for George, and he loved the idea of doing it. He even brought James in to help sing on it, and it ended up being a big hit.

I watched "Bartender's Blues" climb the charts as closely and with as much anticipation as I watched my own songs. It was kind of like my baby, since I'd been the one who brought it to him. Songpluggers—the people at publishing companies who pitch songs to artists and producers—must feel that same pride when they've called it right and brought an artist a hit. I sure did. It was kind of like winning an award.

Being able to help my family move to a ranch and start this new life was better than winning an award. I was so very proud, although I didn't really feel like I was giving my mother and dad anything. The Tuckers were a team, and I figured we'd all earned it. Right about then I started telling the press that my plan was to work hard out on the road and make enough money so that in a few more years I could retire, get married, have a bunch of babies, and raise them on the ranch. That was my little fairy tale future, and one I'm still waiting for.

I thought about my old dreams and plans again this year, when I recorded "Some Day My Prince Will Come" for an album titled *The Best of Country Sing the Best of Disney.* After all these years, it's still such an appropriate song for me to sing.

TWENTY-FOUR

*M*CA decided to team me up with one of L.A.'s top producers, Snuff Garrett. Snuff had done well with Cher, and the label thought he would be the perfect man to bring out a blockbuster on me. I sincerely hoped they were right. I also prayed that Snuff Garrett would be the Billy Sherrill of this second stage of my career. My first clue that this was not to be was when Snuff told me I didn't need to come to the studio while they were cutting tracks.

The difference in production style was unbelievable. Snuff Garrett talked to his musicians about technology. Billy Sherrill talked to his about feeling. Whereas Billy asked my opinion and made me feel like an integral part of the entire process, Snuff couldn't have cared less if I even met the musicians. I wanted to be included in each step of the process, and I showed up anyway. I was used to cutting live and by the hair of my chin, and I liked it that way. These sessions were like an assembly line. The musicians acted very formal; they read music and played it note for note as written. In Nashville, the guys use the number system: They listen to the demo and write down a series of numbers, which stand for chords. They also improvise a lot, and for that reason, I think the final recordings are fresher than when musicians play note for note. I'm not saying all the music coming out of L.A. is stale, but what we did during those sessions felt stale to me. I knew I wanted to come back to Nashville to make my next record.

I wasn't a control freak, by any means. I have never insisted that my way is the only way in or out of the studio. But I had always felt very much a part of the whole creative team: the producer, engineer, musicians, and background singers. However, the system didn't work that way while we were recording that first MCA album, which was titled, simply, *Tanya Tucker.*

The sessions taught me to be careful when someone starts to talk about a producer's "track record." Lots of creative people have track records a mile long, Kentucky Derby–winning track records. It doesn't necessarily mean they'll be the right person for the next job or the next artist.

⚜ ⚜

Despite my feelings about the Snuff Garrett sessions, we had two number-one hits from the album, "Lizzie and the Rainman" and "San Antonio Stroll." I was actually competing with myself on the charts during that time. Columbia had a great amount of material in the can, and two months after MCA released "Lizzie and the Rainman," Columbia released "Spring" as a single, from an album they later released titled *You Are So Beautiful.* It followed "Lizzie" up the charts for fifteen months, peaking at number eighteen. As "San Antonio Stroll" headed to number one, Columbia released a second single, "Greener Than the Grass (We Laid On)," and it topped out at number twenty-three. While I understand the reasons record labels do this, I also know it can hurt both chart action and sales figures. Luckily, my two MCA singles held their own.

⚜ ⚜

Elvis Presley came to see me perform once during this time. I'd already seen his show in Las Vegas. La Costa and I went when I was around fifteen, and evidently someone told him ahead of time that I was in the audience. Elvis came down off the stage, leaned over me, sexy as all get out, swinging his body around and smiling at me. "This is how you do it, girl." I knew he was right, too. He had the moves and I wanted me to have them, too. We were introduced after the show, but we didn't get to talk much.

I didn't get to talk to him at all the night he came to hear my show. It happened while I was playing a show in Denver, Colorado, and Elvis was visiting some of his police pals in the Mile-High City. Mae Axton, who wrote "Heartbreak Hotel," was also in Denver that week, and she told Elvis he ought to come hear me. I don't know how Mae managed it, but she got the club owner to section off a small area close to a side door, where Elvis and she could slip in and watch in private. She didn't let me know he was coming, because she believed, rightfully, that I'd be a nervous wreck. This was a time when I was working hard to liven up my stage show, moving around on stage more and singing edgier songs. I was definitely moving from the kid singer to the adult entertainer. He liked the show and paid me an unbelievable compliment. I only learned about this later, when Mae called to tell me about Elvis's reaction to my performance, because as I was closing my show, they slipped back out. Elvis didn't want to take any chances of being spotted and mobbed. According to Mae, she asked his opinion as they got into the waiting Cadillac, and he said only one short sentence: "She's a female Elvis Presley." I'd stack any awards in the world up against that one comment.

What I loved most about Elvis was that incredible charisma he had onstage. I started watching Elvis's stage moves when I'd see him on television. He could hold an audience right in his palm, and they were mesmerized. I wanted to be able to do that, too. I mentioned this in several interviews, and very quickly other journalists picked up on it and Elvis was popping up in every article anyone read about me. I did emulate him and I did idolize him. But I also loved other performers, like George Jones and Merle Haggard and Loretta Lynn and Tammy Wynette. I love all kinds of music. But before long there was the feeling that I was more into the rockers than into country artists, and that perception would later bite me on the butt. God help me if Mae Axton had released his quote about my show to the press.

※ ※ ※

My life in show business was confusing to me when I was a teenager. But it would have been almost as confusing as an adult, I think. One day I was in the Los Angeles fast lane with people who were trying to keep me out of the making of my own music. I could be talking to Mae Axton and learn from her that Elvis thought I was his female counterpart. And then, I could head out on the road with people like Miss Minnie Pearl. During this time, I played a show with Minnie in Pierre, South Dakota, and got to observe firsthand this wonderful woman's wit.

I was backstage at this big out-of-doors package show, listening to Minnie do her show, when I heard her coughing. I looked out on the stage and it appeared she had experienced one of those events that can be a nightmare at an outside show—a bug flew into her mouth just as she was taking a breath. She stopped and coughed, trying to get the bug up or down, and someone ran out with a glass of water.

"No, I don't need any water," Minnie said, waving them away. "He got in there by himself. Let him just walk down."

Now maybe that was a part of her act, I don't know for sure. I certainly hadn't ever heard her pull it as a gag before. But I'll bet she did after that.

Minnie Pearl was one of those rare, completely uplifting people you are blessed to know in your life. She was a truly fine woman, not only a great entertainer but a smart business-woman, too. She was also very lucky—if you can call it luck—to have a loving husband and manager by her side every step of the way. Minnie and Henry Cannon were one of the industry's golden couples. There's no doubt in my mind that nobody can make it in this business without someone they can trust standing by them. In my case it was because I was born into the family I was.

One of the things that working on a memoir has done is make me realize how special some folks have been to me. And it's also made me see how easily we let people drift away. Minnie died in March of this year. Several years earlier she had a stroke, and when she died she was in a convalescent home. I should have gone to see her more often. Every entertainer who was touched by this woman should have been stopping by to see her, and I'm putting myself at the top of the list. I hate the way your career sometimes just overwhelms you and you don't get the things done that are really important.

Waylon Jennings once told me one of the biggest lessons he ever learned was to cull the riffraff out of his life and take the time to be with his real friends. "None of us has as much of real friendship today as we did yesterday," he said. My answer was, "Well, Hoss, I think there's a song in there somewhere." I do believe this, you're better off in life when you learn to spot the angels, and Minnie Pearl was definitely one of the angels in mine.

TWENTY-FIVE

I had just turned eighteen when I came within inches of being killed in a car crash. I was working almost all the time, and I had some freedom and some money to spend. And yes, sports fans, this is when I first started to run a little wild. I was sneaking drinks when I could get clear of my folks, and I'd take a drag from a cigarette every chance I got. I bought a new Jensen automobile, and I figured I was hot. I probably wasn't behaving any worse than most teenagers. I was still a virgin and I wasn't doing any drugs. But I'd take a drink with the boys.

We'd hired a young piano player named Tony Brown for the band, and he and I immediately struck up a close friendship. We weren't exactly dating, since I still wasn't officially allowed, but we liked to go to clubs in Nashville. As I said, I was starting to like to party, and of course I had to sneak around to either hang out or drink. Tony and I hung out and drank together.

On November 5, 1976, we were in TGI Friday's after a band rehearsal, and I'd had some wine. A musician friend, Bobby Seamore, had wanted to trade cars earlier that day, so I was in his black 1973 Mercedes-Benz, and he was driving my Jensen. I'd been thinking about buying a Mercedes anyway, and I saw it as a good opportunity to try one out. After hanging with Tony at Friday's for a couple of hours, we parted company and I started home. I wasn't really that drunk, but I shouldn't have been driving. When I went over the bridge about twenty yards from the entrance to the ranch, I skidded on gravel and lost control of the car.

I think the pigskin jacket I was wearing saved my life. It was thick, and when I flew through the front window it helped protect me from the glass shards. My face was a mess, though. I don't really remember anything about this, but they say a nearby farmer found me talking to a tree and he went to get help. When I woke up in the hospital my parents were there, and Dad had already fired Tony Brown. I know he blamed Tony for my drinking that night, but as I have always said, I never followed anyone down that path. I was already starting to consider myself to be a trailblazer when it came to nightlife.

I wouldn't have admitted who I was with, and Dad probably wouldn't have known, except that Tony came to the hospital as soon as he heard. Dad put it all together and gave him his walking papers. Tony got a job playing piano for Elvis after that, and he never once acted like he resented taking the heat for me. He also came to visit on the day I was released, and I know it must have been hard for him to face my family after all that had happened. But he did, and to this day I have the highest respect for him. Ironically, Tony is now president of MCA Records, the label that almost lost their million-dollar property that cold November night. If he has even half the nerve and honesty he displayed over that car wreck in his life as an executive, then he's standing head and shoulders above many in the music business.

Because Tony and I remained close friends after he went to work for Elvis, I could keep tabs on what one of my music idols was doing. And through Tony, I know that working with Elvis could be a tough gig for a musician. If you went to work for him, he might hand you four hundred songs on Tuesday and say, "Learn 'em by the weekend." I remember Tony telling me about one of his first shows with Elvis, and all of a sudden Elvis calls out, "Big Boss Man." They'd never practiced it, and Tony started the song in the wrong key. When Tony left the stage, Elvis's producer, Felton Jarvis, who was standing in the wings, shot him a look and said, "Don't ever let that happen again." When Tony was telling me about it, my eyes got wide, and I said, "Man, what did you say?"

"I didn't say anything," Tony laughed. "I ran right back to my dressing room and started practicing 'Big Boss Man'!"

Not long after Tony started playing in his band, I came to one of Elvis's shows in Vegas, and he introduced me to the audience and said I was dating one of the guys in the band. That really got under my skin. No woman likes to be introduced as simply somebody's girlfriend, especially if it isn't true.

I guess because Elvis thought Tony had a girlfriend in the audience, he started needling him. "Let's do 'Bridge over Troubled Waters,'" Elvis said. "And Tony, don't mess it up." After the show I told Charlie Hodge to tell the King he'd better get his facts straight. Tony Brown and I were friends, but we were not an item.

On one of the last times Tony Brown invited me to a show, I couldn't believe the change in Elvis Presley. He was completely zoned. I got to go backstage, but nobody took me over to say hello. And even though that pissed me off, I knew Elvis wouldn't have known who I was anyway. There was the most fear-inspiring blank look on his face, and a complete lack of understanding of what was going on around him. World War III could have broken out and Elvis Presley wouldn't have known it. One of the band members told me that Elvis had instituted a ban on marijuana smoking for all those in his band and crew that same week. I guess he didn't consider his prescriptions as harmful as marijuana.

※ ❦ ※ ❦

We came back to Nashville to record the second MCA album, and the label teamed me with another man who has had a tremendous effect on my life and career, Jerry Crutchfield. Bill Carter suggested him to Dad and me after hearing Jerry's production on Dave Loggins's "Please Come to Boston." Jerry had come to Nashville following a short stint as an artist in pop music, and he had quickly established himself as a songwriter, musician, session singer, and record producer.

As soon as Snuff Garrett found out that I was changing producers he called up Crutch and went off on a tirade. He said, "Jerry, I cut two number-one records on that girl! It's her daddy that's the problem. Nobody can get along with him in the studio!"

It certainly wasn't my dad that wanted the change; it was me all the way. And I was surprised Snuff even mentioned the studio, since he didn't want any of us there most of the time. I can imagine Jerry, with his quiet, businesslike manner listening with that nice, noncommittal attitude, saying very little or trying to be diplomatic.

Jerry Crutchfield is one of the most unflappable, kind, and patient people I've ever met. Maybe someone could get under his skin, but I can't imagine how. I've tried his patience several times over the years, and I've yet to see him lose his temper. On the surface, Jerry and I appear to be opposites. I have so much going on every minute that I get scattered and unfocused. Jerry is focused at all times. But in the studio we mesh, because when I'm singing, it's the one time in my life that I stay completely centered.

Jerry is very different from Billy Sherrill in his production style. Whereas Billy wants to get in, put it down, and get out, Jerry is meticulous and willing to redo something over and over until it's right where he wants it. I tend to be more like Billy in that I like to get in, get it done, and get out. But Jerry and I worked well together from the beginning. He understood that I needed to have a more mature musical image, and he set about finding songs to complete my transition from child star to adult entertainer. *Lovin' and Learnin'* had two big hits, "Don't Believe My Heart Can Stand Another You" and "You've Got Me to Hold On To." The title cut on the next album, *Here's Some Love*, topped the country charts. Jerry and I worked on *Ridin' Rainbows* during the latter part of 1976, and it was released in February of '77.

Even though we were having success with most of my releases, I began to grow very discontented with my music during the late 1970s. I'd been working to energize my show for several years, and I felt I was close to where I wanted to be. Just not close enough. Crutchfield wanted me to move cautiously, knowing that audiences sometimes balk at sudden and drastic change on an artist's part. It had nothing to do with success or a lack of it. I was doing fine careerwise. I was making hit records, I'd been nominated for a CMA Award, a Grammy, won *Billboard* and *Record World* awards, been on the cover of

Rolling Stone, signed a million-dollar contract, and bought my parents a ranch. Most important, my fans seemed content with what I was doing. But "content" has never been a part of my vocabulary, and to my way of thinking, things didn't seem to be happening fast enough. It was that dissatisfaction that started me down the road to new managers and new producers, and it almost destroyed my country career.

TWENTY-SIX

On August 16, 1977, the world lost a hero. I couldn't believe it when I heard Elvis Presley was dead. I had to call one of his former girlfriends, Linda Thompson, and talk to her for the thing to sink in. Linda is one of the women who I believe really loved and cared for Elvis. The papers said he died of a heart attack, but people who knew him were telling stories of prescription drug abuse.

I'd had very little experience with drugs in 1977, and the idea of hard drugs scared me. I'd had my first experience with smoking pot a couple of years earlier, and it happened when I was in Hawaii performing at a Dr Pepper Convention, of all things. My girlfriend and I were talking one night and I mentioned that I'd never tried marijuana. Her eyes lit up. "Let's get some, then," she said. "Why the hell not," was my response. I flagged down a bellman and asked him if he could oblige us. He could, and did.

We sat there in our room and smoked dope that night, and I laughed more than I ever had in my life. The next morning I didn't have a hangover and I thought to myself, "Man, that stuff was pretty good. I'd better take the rest of it home." I stuffed it in my luggage and we headed back home.

Well, I don't know why he did it, but within an hour of my

dragging the luggage into my bedroom, Dad had gone in there and searched it. All hell broke loose when he found that little bag of dope. It just figured that the very first time I tried dope, my dad busted me. He said he had a feeling I'd been up to no good, and he wanted to check. That was the beginning of my parents' fearing I was on the road to drug addiction. He also says he could tell you the first time I had sex. That's how close tabs they were trying to keep on my doings. I don't think he ever quite trusted me again after finding the pot, and Dad tells me that even today, even a thousand miles away, he knows if I go in somewhere and order a drink.

But when Elvis died, I was still more of a drinker than a drugger. With the exception of my ill-fated pot experiment, I just wasn't into drugs. But I could understand how a person as isolated as Elvis might turn to them, and I knew from firsthand experience that Elvis had been in very bad shape. Even knowing what I did about his condition, his death hit me hard, because he was the King, and the King doesn't die. I felt a little the same way when I watched O.J. Simpson's Bronco chase. Like the sky was falling. American heroes don't die from drugs or run from the cops.

When I heard the news about Elvis, I booked a flight to Memphis. I didn't go as a star, but as a fan. Nobody invited me. I felt like I had to go see Elvis's body. It didn't even look like him. He seemed so small, and his face and hands looked like plastic. You could see what looked to be a makeshift dye job on the white roots in his hair. The Elvis I'd met was a big, robust guy. People like to trash him saying he was fat and bloated during his last years, but I prefer to remember him as big and robust. I looked around and listened to all those hangers-on talking about how much they loved him and how he was so wonderful, and it made me sick. I knew that half of them had done things like sell special gifts he bought them to the highest bidder.

I have often felt lonely and alone on this planet, but never like the day of Elvis's funeral. The most lasting memory I have of that day is the fact that Elvis was dressed in a tacky-looking suit. I thought it was a crime that Elvis Presley, the King of Rock and Roll, who was famous for his fabulous stage clothes, was being buried in a cheap polyester suit.

I don't know if anyone was there for Elvis, really there for him. I wonder if he ever reached out at the times he felt like he was falling apart. I know that I've reached out at times when I felt like I was drowning. Sometimes I've been down, had a few drinks, and called friends in the middle of the night to talk. What generally happened was that they phoned the next day to remind me that I got drunk the previous night. Maybe he felt like he had to always be "Elvis" in the same way I always think I have to be "Tucker tough."

Elvis died in August of 1977. In October of the same year, on my nineteenth birthday, I lost my virginity, although I know lots of people thought I'd been burning up the sheets since I was about fifteen. Maybe younger for all I know. Until I started working on this book, I hadn't really thought that much about why I never had sexual intercourse before I was nineteen. Part of the reason is that I couldn't get clear of my folks a lot of the time. But maybe the biggest reason is that I was "acting out" when I was doing my stage show. I could parade around and act like I was a very sexual young girl without actually having to produce. But whatever the reasons, I didn't "do it" until the night I turned nineteen.

I loved going to a Fort Worth country music club called Speakeasy's, where Monday night was Cowboy Night. I've always loved cowboys, and so any time I had a free Monday I could be found in Fort Worth, at a corner table at Speakeasy's. My parents just hated it, but by now I had my own money and the freedom to buy a plane ticket or gas up the car and come and go as I wanted.

One night at Speakeasy's my friend Cindy Crow and I ran into a friend who asked us to lunch the next day. We went, and at the restaurant was a saddle bronc rider I thought was very cute. We didn't really go out at first, but he started joining us at Speakeasy's on Cowboy Night whenever I was in town, and I thought he was one of the hottest guys I'd ever met.

One night I got to the club and my bronc rider wasn't there. When I asked where he was, I was told he'd gone skiing with some other rodeo guys at Steamboat Springs. I jumped right on the phone to say hi, and he insisted that Cindy and I fly to Steamboat on the next plane. We went straight to the Dallas airport and caught the next plane out. We didn't have any extra clothes with us. But I had a credit card, which is just one more of the reasons my parents hated it every time I got out of their sight. We caught a commuter plane from Denver and flew into Hayden, Colorado, where the guys picked us up. He and I still slept in separate beds, but that trip made me think we were a couple.

On October 10, 1977, my friends in Fort Worth threw me a big party, and that night my boyfriend and I finally had sex. I have to say I didn't like it as much as I had figured I would. I'd had all those thoughts about bells ringing like most girls do, and when it was over I wondered what all the fuss was about.

He and I stayed friends for years, long after we broke up, and that was very important to me. Like with my first boyfriend, the rodeo circuit and the concert trail are two paths that sometimes cross, but they don't make for a long haul as far as relationships go. Neither one of those men had any desire to be Mr. Tanya Tucker, and I don't blame them.

TWENTY-SEVEN

$\mathcal{T}$desperately needed career management. Dad knew it and Bill Carter knew it. Most important, MCA knew it. Dad and Bill had their hands full with the business and legal aspects of my career. What I needed now was good, solid career guidance. Bill recommended we talk to a company called Far Out Management in Los Angeles. It was the firm who had guided the blues/rock group War to stardom, and they had expressed some interest in helping a country act cross over.

The first time we met with Far Out they kept us waiting for about two hours in the reception area of their Los Angeles office. I was impressed with the gold records that lined the walls and thought War had sold billions of albums. It appeared that Billy Sherrill and all of Nashville were runners-up as far as record selling went.

Dad walked around the room, staring at each framed record, shaking his head.

"Most a' these are the same damn album, Tanya," he said with disgust. That was the beginning of his mistrust of Far Out. Dad never trusted nor liked them, but he still believed my career should be handled by professionals. Once again he was being introduced to people he considered too "Hollywood."

Finally a big, booming voice came over the intercom. "Bring the Tuckers back here."

The receptionist motioned us on back. We went through three or four doors and had to be beeped through at each point.

"Man," I said. "This looks like a fort."

"No, this looks like people with something to hide," Dad said.

When we finally reached the inner sanctum, I thought I'd die. The walls of the office Steve Gold and Jerry Goldstein shared were lined with animal heads. Bear, deer, elk, and moose heads looked down on you with glassy eyes, like so many gold records. I'm not a vegetarian, and I know that if we eat meat, animals have to be killed. I've grown up around the cattle business, after all. But killing something just to cut off a head and hang it on a wall grosses me out. Especially when the walls start to look like the San Diego Zoo. I think that's how they saw me, another trophy to hang on the wall and forget about.

Steve Gold was balding and had one big gold tooth right in the front of his mouth. Jerry Goldstein seemed more like a hippie, with long hair parted in the middle and a more casual style.

"Tanya Tucker," he said, ignoring my dad. "Are you ready to be a superstar?"

"You bet," I said, forgetting the animal heads, the duplicated gold records, and the locked doors.

"What do you want from a career, Tanya?" Steve asked.

"I want the biggest audience I can get," I answered, thrilled to have someone even ask. Usually I got told what I wanted. By record company executives, by managers, and by my dad.

"Country is holding you back," he said. "Rock and roll is where the money is. You, my dear, are a rock star."

My dad sat back in his chair and folded his arms over his chest, a sure sign he was sizing up what he thought was a bad situation.

"The first thing you've got to do is move to Los Angeles," Steve explained. "You've got to be where the action is, and it sure isn't in Nashville. Those hicks can't sell records. You should be selling platinum with every release."

"In fact," he went on, "if your first album with us doesn't sell platinum in a year, you can walk away from your contract and not owe Far Out one cent."

As much as Dad didn't like the setup and the slam at Nashville, he did believe I should be selling platinum. And he liked the idea of built-in platinum insurance. And so did I. We listened as Steve outlined his plans to expand my music, my audience, and—most important—my ability to generate income. He was a very boisterous big talker and capable of making you believe anything. As full as my head was with dreams, Steve made them bigger with every word. It was an "anything's possible" period in my life.

"The thing is, Tanya, you haven't had a chance to show the world your capabilities," Steve said. "You haven't been allowed any input. That's going to change right now. We're going to be a team, and we're going to make Tanya Tucker a household word."

I sucked right into it. The idea of me being in charge of my life and career was just what I needed to hear to sell me on Far Out. Like a good little client, I rented an apartment in the same building as Far Out. At $2,700 a month, the rent was too stiff, though, and I soon moved into a little stucco house on Linnington Avenue. Mother and Dad took a house in Los Angeles, but they kept Tuckahoe and divided their time between the two homes. This was my first real freedom from my folks, my first time living completely on my own.

We even brought my sister La Costa to them. All they did for her was put her out on the road playing shows in some of the worst dives on the West Coast. There was no thought given to building her as a star or to finding the big, substantial hit songs she needed to sustain a lengthy career. She also moved to Los Angeles because Far Out thought it would be a good career move. All it did was take both of us away from Nashville, the town that had the songs and support we needed.

Soon after I moved to Los Angeles, we started recording *TNT*, and Steve Gold's prediction that I'd go platinum proved right. *TNT* was my first million-selling album, and the one that almost killed my career. When I hear *TNT* now, I know it wasn't a great record. And I know now that I didn't have any more control over that record than I ever had. I had far more input with Crutchfield.

There are great records, and there is great hype. Any artist knows when they've done good work and when it's just the record company machine that's working. That's when you have the marketing dollars, the hottest publicist, in short: the Big Push. *TNT* had the push. You can sell records and book concert dates on hype, but you can't sustain a career on it.

Want to know what I did the most of during those sessions?

I learned to play Ping-Pong while we waited hours upon hours until Jerry Goldstein felt moved to arrive at the studio. Meanwhile, MCA was paying for musicians and studio time for all those hours he held us up. The people we held up were a formidable bunch, too. Phil Everly and La Costa sang backup on "Lover Goodbye." Mickey Raphael played harmonica on "Not Fade Away." John Prine sang on "Angel from Montgomery," and Jim Seals and Dash Crofts accompanied me on "The River and the Wind." They pulled in great musicians: Billy Joe Walker Jr., John Hobbs, Paul Leim, Jerry Scheff, and Jerry Swallow. There was all that talent playing Ping-Pong for hours with the singer, waiting on the producer.

While I was cooling my heels waiting on Jerry in the studio, Steve was working with MCA to market *TNT* with a sex-driven sales machine. The clothing selected for my photo shoots was all leather and spandex. On the album cover I appeared in black leather pants with the microphone cord pulled up between my legs, and on the inside foldout was the infamous red-hot spandex backless bodystocking shot. The cover was outrageous to many, and all the more so because people were used to my album covers portraying me with a puppy, or at least looking fairly demure. To add fuel to the fire, Far Out took an ad in *Hustler* that said, "*TNT*—this album will make your ears hard."

My parents hit the fan. Dad was beside himself trying to find out how the *Hustler* ad came about, who was responsible and who okayed it. I don't know if anybody actually okayed that ad, but I admit that I liked it at the time. I thought it was kind of cool, and back then if somebody had wanted ad copy approval, I'd have given it. I think I was like a lot of girls in their late teens. On the one hand, I was still a tomboy who wanted to ride horses and goof off. But at the same time I was also starting to want to look cool and sexy. I had my parents trying to hold me back, but I also had a management team pushing the sex bit right out in front.

Far Out canceled over a million dollars' worth of country concerts and set up a tour of rock clubs across America. It was a terrible decision, since even though those clubs might have been hip, they didn't pay like a fair or a festival show. But by that time Far Out was so much in control, we were doing anything they told us to do. And we did get good response at the rock clubs, so it appeared we were on the right track. The album sales were strong, as Far Out had predicted, and our live show was good. The concert reviews were great, and they paid tribute to both my performance and the band's underlying Leon Russell–type hot rock and soul feel. I thought things were going great until the revisionist articles began appearing. One article had a headline that said, "Tanya Tucker Forsakes Nashville."

I tried to counter that impression every time I gave an interview. I explained that I was a singer who loved rock, but I certainly hadn't given up on country music. After all, one song on *TNT*, "Texas (When I Die)," was one of the most country songs I'd ever cut. I tried to explain that for me it was more a case of show production, that I no longer wanted the little speakers, the small stages, the clubs. I wanted to put on a show that would rock the house. I wanted arena shows. The problem became, in part, one of language. What I meant by "rock the house" was that I wanted to put so much energy into a performance that nobody could stay in their seats. But the word "rock" translated to "anti-country" for many people.

Categories and boxes are so damaging in an artistic field. If Jerry Garcia hadn't been heavily influenced by Bill Monroe, would his music have had as many dimensions? The Beatles admired Elvis as much for his country roots as his early rock releases. Johnny Cash was and is the idol of almost every rock musician in the world. Bob Dylan loved Nashville so much he made one of his finest albums with our musicians. And Mark Knopfler's work with Chet Atkins is brilliant.

Garth Brooks has done a great deal to knock down the walls between country and pop and rock. In a lot of ways, what I wanted was what Garth has pulled off—a big show that draws in people who never thought they liked country before. It's rare that an artist can come along like Garth did and just take charge on his own terms. Country music owes artists like Garth, who break down barriers, a big debt. Not everyone can break down the barriers without breaking themselves. He seems to have done just that, and God love him for it.

I learned just what a mistake all that hype about *TNT* had been at the 1978 Deejay Convention in Nashville, where once a year deejays from across the nation gather in Nashville for a week of parties, meetings, showcases, and schmoozing. The Deejay Convention is one of the most important events in the country music industry, because we depend so desperately on radio airplay. Rockers like the Grateful Dead might be able to keep on keepin' on without hit radio records, but country artists have to have airplay to book good venues and to sell albums.

Careers can be made at this event. Labels fight to get their new acts on the New Faces Showcase, where radio can feel the excitement of a career launch right up close. Current hitmakers show up to remind radio that they're hot right then, and artists who haven't had a hit in a while show up to remind radio that they could easily get hot once again. But careers can also be damaged if something goes wrong, and for me the convention took a nasty turn.

I was very excited to premier my *TNT* album at a show for the deejays, and I flew into Nashville feeling like I owned the world. For one thing, I was coming off a big radio hit with "Texas (When I Die)," the album's first single. We—the band and I— were proud of our hot new sound and my Elvis-inspired stage moves. I was nineteen years old and ready to knock 'em dead, so that night I walked out onstage with all the confidence in the world. The band was "on" and so was I. But we didn't start with "Texas (When I Die)." We came out of the chute with the rockin' side of *TNT.* I'd planned on saving my new hit until later in the show.

When we went into "Brown-Eyed Handsome Man" and "Heartbreak Hotel," I figured people would go nuts. They did, but not in the way I'd hoped. At first there was just a lack of response, but then came some scattered booing. I didn't even understand booing a Chuck Berry song, but the fact that a country crowd would boo "Heartbreak Hotel," a song written by Mama Mae Axton, one of the industry's greatest ladies, stunned me. Later, I decided that they weren't reacting so much to the music as to the sexpot hype that had preceded it.

Up onstage I was sweating rocks. These were the guys who either let you on the airwaves or kicked your butt off them. There was an amazing amount of power out there. Lord, when that power and energy is negative and directed toward you up onstage, it's a fearful thing. I knew I had to do something quick or I was dead in the water, so I changed the song lineup and we did "Texas (When I Die)." That brought 'em home. I somehow finished the show and when I left the stage I was shaking, but at least I felt like I hadn't blown my whole career right there on that Nashville stage.

"Texas (When I Die)" was a top-five country hit, and the flip side, my version of Buddy Holly's "Not Fade Away," got onto the pop charts. You'd have thought Far Out had taken me to the top of the rock charts to hear them talk about that little bit of pop success. The follow-up, "I'm the Singer, You're the Song," barely cracked country's top-twenty, and the flip side of that release, "Lover Goodbye," couldn't even make it into pop's top-100. Maybe the Deejay Convention hadn't destroyed my career, but I could tell that something was going sour, because after "Texas (When I Die)," the singles weren't working.

When I tried to communicate my concerns to Steve Gold and Jerry Goldstein, it was as if I didn't exist. There were still the two- or three-hour waits in the outer office and the wild behavior from Steve—screaming at secretaries, storming around the office. At the same time, they were telling me that the album was going platinum and things were right on target. Platinum or not, things were obviously not even on the rifle range. For one thing, I knew that some of those sales were because of the controversial nature of *TNT*'s marketing, from the red bodysuit to the microphone cord through my legs to the *Hustler* ads. I'd understood ever since "Would You Lay with Me (In a Field of Stone)" that conflict and controversy isn't always bad—it can be great publicity. But even at the time I knew that *TNT* was a hype, and it wasn't working to my benefit.

As the weeks went by, I started to feel like a sword was sticking through me. I could feel what little control I had slipping away. In fact, I realized that Far Out had hyped me into believing I had any control at all, the very same way they were hyping album sales.

Then, a couple of days before the platinum-in-a-year deal was up, they showed up at a concert and presented me with a platinum record. I was stunned. They'd pulled it off. I hurried offstage and looked down at the album and saw that it wasn't even an authorized platinum award. They'd had a fake platinum record made for the presentation. We asked Mike Maitland about sales, and he assured us that even though we weren't certified, we were very close to platinum. So we stayed with Far Out. We didn't know what else to do.

It seems like all my life I have been fighting to get some sort of control over what was going on around me. I know that I should have grabbed control myself or trusted my dad to do it for me, but I didn't. One thing was becoming clear to the Tuckers, though. Even if Dad didn't want to be a manager, he could probably do a better job than the ones we'd been through.

TWENTY-EIGHT

I may not have been in charge of my career, but I could sure take charge of my daily—and nightly—life. I was ready to hit the fast lane, and that's exactly what I did. L.A. was a wild town in 1978, and it wasn't long before I was the leader of the pack. I loved to party, to drink, to tell jokes—I loved to raise hell. There was no shortage of people who wanted to raise hell with me, either. There was a whole crowd of actors and actresses, as well as some second- and third-generation rich Hollywood kids who could and would do just about anything, and I got in with them.

There was a party somewhere in L.A. every night, and I figured I ought to hit every one of them. I was invited to a lot, and those I wasn't invited to, I'd crash. I partied with people like Cher, Candy Clarke, Don Johnson, Jan Michael Vincent, Katy Seagall, and Linda Hart; I don't know who all I partied with back then. Remember "I Got Stoned and I Missed It," the old Dr. Hook song? Sometimes that's how I feel about certain periods of my life.

Candy Clarke was a bubbly little blonde who never seemed to have a bad day. I'd met Candy and Don Johnson when I made *Amateur Night at the Dixie Bar and Grill*, a "Nashvillesque" movie about the clientele of a bar that sponsors a talent contest, starring Candy, Don, Dennis Quaid, Henry Gibson, Joan Goodfellow, Jamie Farr, Victor French—and a lot of others. I was playing Dennis Quaid's girlfriend, and my character had two qualities no one else did—talent and sanity. But that was my character. I don't think any of us back then qualified as completely sane.

I ran around with Jan Michael Vincent for a while, and he was a perfect match for me, because he's a good old boy at heart. He drove around Hollywood in a pickup, the kind of guy who seemed more natural talking to a mechanic than a casting director. I'm kind of a good old boy at heart, too, so we ended up pals rather than passionate lovers.

I never got to know Cher very well, even though I went to several roller skating parties that she organized in Los Angeles. It was the start of the 1980s' health craze in L.A., and roller skating became the trendy thing to do. What little I knew of Cher, I liked. Cher is a romantic kind of person, and she is definitely crazy about the boys. But she's also one of those women who seems to have a core of inner strength that pulls her through anything. I was around during her Gene Simmons days as well as the Gregg Allman ones, and although I guessed a lot of bad stuff was going on all around her and her relationships, she seemed to sail through it all relatively unscathed. But now that I think about it, she did, later on, win an Academy Award for her acting. I don't know if anyone is ever unscathed. But I have a lot of respect for what Cher has done in her life. Whatever she's tried, she's done well. And I don't see anyone but Cher making her decisions.

Katy Seagall and Linda Hart were working as two of the Harlettes, Bette Midler's backup singers at the time. I loved to party with them, but I also loved their harmonies and what they added to Bette's concerts. Their work impressed me so much that I hired three women to sing in my band, too. Audiences loved it, so that was one positive outcome of this fast lane I was in. I always thought Katy was a crack-up, so I loved it when I was channel surfing one night and discovered *Married, with Children*. Katy and Linda introduced me to a girl named Beverly Hills (oh yeah, it was really her name). Beverly was both real L.A. and real southern—wild, yet with this drawl that killed me. She smoked like a chimney and was always looking for a good time. A perfect pal for me. When I first met Beverly she worked at Tree, a music publishing company, so in addition to liking to party with me, she liked to talk music. That was a big factor in our friendship, because in L.A., most people talked about the movie business.

Beverly sort of took over my life. First, she hauled my luggage around when we traveled, then she started making the travel arrangements herself. If I needed something done, she usually did it before I even thought about it. I did enjoy the luxury of having someone in charge of details I didn't want to have to deal with, and since I was uncomfortable with my management, and my parents were dividing their time between Nashville and Los Angeles, Beverly stepped in.

So there I was, twenty years old, running wild in L.A. with Beverly Hills. Only in Hollywood would you find that kind of casting. I'd be lying if I said I wasn't loving every minute of it, too. The fast lane is a fun place until you start to skid out of control.

At first I thought Desi Arnaz Jr. must have heard some wild stories about me, because I had to pass a small inquisition to have even one date with him. Later I discovered it wasn't just me who had to pass the test, it was everybody who went out with him. I saw Desi Jr. and Dean Paul Martin one night at Roy's, a Chinese place across from the Comedy Store. They were musicians, too, and, with their schoolmate Billy Hinsche, as Dino, Desi, and Billy, had done those teenybopper records that kids loved back in 1965. We talked quite a while about the music business. Desi was by far the more serious one. Dean Paul had a joke a minute. He was a very "up" type of guy. When I heard that Dean Martin never really got over Dean Paul's 1987 death in an airplane crash, I could understand it. Everyone says the loss of a child is the hardest thing in the world, and Dean Paul would leave a big hole in anybody's world. I liked both of the guys, and the three of us had a great time that night. When I got ready to leave, Desi said he'd like to see me again and we exchanged phone numbers. A few days later he called me.

"I'd really like to go out," he said. "But I've been under a doctor's care and you'll need to talk to him first." I had no idea what he was talking about, and he didn't go into it on the telephone. A day or so later I got a call from a guy who introduced himself as Desi's shrink. The doctor explained that Desi had been going through some rough times, and that if I wanted to date him, I'd have to follow some very strict guidelines. There were to be no drugs. No alcohol, not even a beer. I don't know why I wasn't insulted. Instead, it aroused my curiosity. I've always been drawn to wounded pups. Then the shrink told me another requirement that intrigued me. We had to meet at his mother's home. I was going to meet Lucille Ball? Man. Like everybody else in the world, I loved Lucy.

I arrived at the appointed day and was disappointed to find that Lucy was not there. But Desi took me on a tour of every room in the mansion, even the bathrooms. It was very posh. He played some of his music for me, and then sat down and told me he was still torn up about his relationship with Patty Duke, and he thought that was contributing to his mental state. She'd evidently had a son by Desi and refused to tell the child who his father was. He said that someday she'd regret it, and I wonder if she did. Desi might have kissed me a couple of times, but it was a very innocent date. I followed the guidelines to the letter. But nothing really clicked between us. I ran into Desi and Dean Paul around town later, but Desi and I never got to be an item.

The fact is, many of my so-called hot celebrity love affairs were not all that hot. Throughout my career I've seen some of the same names pop up everywhere, and it always appears that they were momentous in my life. I didn't really discourage the myth. With one notable exception, the men who have been significant loves in my life are not public figures. But if a tabloid wants to link me to someone, a public figure makes a better read. Don Johnson is a case in point. When I met Don he didn't have much going careerwise. He was driving an old beat-up orange Volkswagen and often didn't even have gas money. Don was in *Amateur Night at the Dixie Bar and Grill*, but I didn't really get to know him then. I was dating a rodeo guy, Bobby Brown, when I made that movie, and he'd drive me to the set in his Jeep in the morning, then pick me back up every night. It wasn't exactly limo service, like some of the people in the film had, but it worked for me. And because I didn't hang around after the filming stopped each evening, with the exception of Candy Clarke, I didn't really get to know most of the cast well at the time.

I ran into Don months later at Robert's on the Beach, and we had a few drinks and really hit it off. Don was as wild as me, and he loved to hang out. We started seeing each other, hitting the clubs and the party scene every chance we got. Don was a frustrated singer and songwriter and was fascinated with music business professionals. I think the night he probably enjoyed the most while we dated was when we attended an Allman Brothers concert at the Forum, and afterward we jumped in the Allmans' limo and went to Don's house in Santa Monica. We stayed up all night while Dickie Betts tried to help Don write a song. I don't know for sure, but I never heard that the song saw the light of day, like Dickie and Don and I did with bleary eyes.

It didn't last too long, though, because Don was a very cocky guy with an enormous ego and a strong will. Things pretty much needed to go his way, and I was always thinking that things ought to be going my way. I can be a little cocky myself, especially around a guy who thinks he's a gift. The big issue between us was that I didn't want to sleep with him. I'm very funny about sex. If a guy seems like he expects it, or that I somehow ought to feel grateful to him for propositioning me, that's when I am most likely to say "no way." I doubt Don usually had problems along those lines with the women he dated. So we ended up quarreling a lot and the relationship cooled.

I saw Don later at the Le Dome club in L.A., when he was living with Patti D'Arbanville. He must have said some nice things about me—or at least admitted we'd never had sex—because Patti, who was about eight months pregnant, jumped out of her chair and dragged me clear back to a broom closet in the kitchen to tell me how wonderful I was and what a good friend I was to her and to Don.

Too bad that friendly feeling didn't last. Several years ago I wanted Don to appear with me in a video. My staff placed phone call after phone call to his manager, his agent, to his home in Aspen, where he and his then-wife, Melanie Griffith, were staying. No one ever responded. Even at the house, the only answer we could get was, "We'll give him the message." Right. And the check's in the mail.

Friends have always been very important to me, and one individual I met during the wild L.A. years remained a true and steadfast friend until the day he died in May of 1993. Michael Tovar is a man who will be in my heart forever, and one I've missed every day since his death. He is far more important to me than most of my lovers, real or fictionalized. I met Tovar in 1979 at Jon Peters's salon in Beverly Hills. I dropped by the salon, even though I had no appointment, hoping someone could cut my hair. The manager explained that no one was available except Michael Tovar, who was not a full-fledged stylist. His job was to shampoo customers and sweep the floor. Well, I've always been a gambler, and I really needed a cut and style, so I said, "What the hell? Give me Tovar."

When I sat down and we started to talk, I felt like I'd met a soulmate. Haven't you had that happen? You meet someone, and it's not a romantic or a sexual thing, but you feel like they'll be a part of your life for a very long time and that you're gonna love them. Tovar was just about my age, and he had big dreams of a big career as a Hollywood stylist, the same sort of big dreams I'd had about my music. The next time I made an appointment at the Peters salon, I requested Tovar. It was the beginning of a beautiful friendship, and he was a man who taught me a lot.

Of all the people from back in my L.A. days, I got closest to Tovar, and it's probably because he wasn't an entertainer. The so-called friendships you forge with other entertainers are often surface ones. As I mentioned earlier, that's why I finally got the courage to call Tammy Wynette and ask her to dinner at my house that night. Even when you wish you could really get to know someone, there often isn't a chance for you to spend enough time together. I just wanted to get to know Tammy better as a person and not simply as someone I quickly hugged at an awards dinner. Or worse yet, someone I posed for a photo with, leaving the impression that we're soul sisters who go grocery shopping together. I wish that was the way it is, but it's not.

Even when you tour with people, you don't often spend any time with them. There have been some exceptions in my career, most notably Travis Tritt. After a season of opening shows for me, he became a good and lasting friend, but only because I made a conscious effort.

I'll have to be honest, when I met Tovar, I was one of those people who thought gay was the wrong way and straight was the right way. I thought homosexuality was some kind of environmental thing that people could "get over." Man, I had so many wrong ideas. I'd had gay guys tell me, "Oh, if I'd met you . . ." At the time, I believed that maybe if they'd met the right woman, they might be straight.

But Michael Tovar was so honest and so pure about his sexuality, I had to start changing my thinking. For Tovar, gay was a natural state. I changed partly because of knowing him, and partly because as I've become older I've become smarter, not a lot, but a little. At least I've learned to question stereotypes.

Tovar and I shared many personality traits. Both of us took our profession more seriously than we did ourselves, and we laughed at ourselves easily. We both denied that we were looking for Mr. Perfect, but we both were, and we both knew it. I've learned that people are people and life is too short to take offense if someone is seemingly different from me.

Another important thing that happened to me in 1979 was that my brother Don saved my life, and because of it, he may very well have saved two additional lives. We were playing a show in Minnesota, and Don was driving the bus. I had one of the worst headaches I'd ever had and was taking aspirin to try to get rid of it before show time. In my usual desire to get on with things, I threw all three aspirin in my mouth at once and took a big swig of water. The water didn't cut it, and the aspirin lodged in my throat.

Choking is a panic situation. You just stand there trying to dislodge whatever's in your throat, but without help, it's nearly impossible. Everyone on the bus just froze: the tour manager, the wardrobe woman, the makeup artist. Everyone that is, except for Don. He grabbed me from behind, lifted me up, and applied the Heimlich maneuver. After three hard jerks all three aspirin flew out onto the floor of the bus. I literally couldn't move. I just stood there and stared at those three little white pills that had stopped me from breathing.

But even with my throat clear, I still couldn't seem to get started breathing right. Don ran back to the bathroom and got a wet washrag and put it across my neck. "Come on, kid," he said. "You're a singer. You've got muscle control, so use it. Start breathing." Slowly I began to relax and get some air into my windpipe. I just sat down and shook from the experience. When I finally got my wind and my nerve back, I asked him to show me exactly what he'd done. I'd never seen anyone choke, but I knew that if I ever did, I didn't want to just stand there staring, like everyone but Don had done that day. Twice since that time I've had occasion to apply the technique. The first time was when my friend Roe Farone got a piece of steak caught in her throat at one of my baby showers, and the second was when my press agent choked in Atlanta at the 1994 Super Bowl. Both times I've silently thanked Don for my knowledge of the Heimlich maneuver.

TWENTY-NINE

*F*ar Out almost succeeded in removing Dad from the management loop. I truly think those guys had no idea who or what they were dealing with. I guess they just thought of Beau Tucker as an old Okie with no sense whatsoever. So it seemed odd when Steve Gold called Dad one day and said he guessed he could use some help in negotiating marketing and promotion budgets. Dad came in to see him and waited the usual three hours in the lobby, before finally being ushered in through all those locked doors.

Dad asked Steve how he could be of help. Steve was pacing around in his usual state of agitation.

"I need some things okayed, and I need you to make MCA okay them."

Dad nodded. He was willing to help any way he could.

Steve got wild-eyed and started waving his arms around. "You've got to go in and tell Mike Maitland if he doesn't give us what we need, you're going to tear hell out of his office."

"What?" My dad thought he was hearing things.

"You smash up those damn records on his wall, and he'll know we're serious about what we need," Steve said.

Of course, Dad refused to do anything of the kind. He

guessed right then that drugs had completely taken over the company. He didn't know for sure, but he certainly suspected it. Then he fired them, and one more management deal was history. For the time being, my dad was back in charge. I have few regrets in this life. I don't believe in looking back and saying, "If only I hadn't done that." If cows could run they could catch rabbits. Those "ifs" will get you every time. My philosophy is this: You stumble, you fall, you get up and get over it. But if I do have a regret, it's that when we were waiting to meet with Far Out that first day in 1977, I didn't walk out of the office and run like hell back to Nashville.

They sued us when Dad fired them, and it ended up costing us a lot of money to leave, but it was worth every penny. I used to tell people that because I signed the contract right after Elvis died, it ought to have been invalid by reason of Tanya's insanity.

THIRTY

*T*n the fall of 1980 I was in Las Vegas, staying at the Desert Inn and taping a television show with Wayne Newton and Tony Bennett. I'd been doing my usual hell-raising around town—partying, drinking. My girlfriend Rhonda, my old pal and bodyguard from Henderson High, was with me and we were having a blast. But we weren't causing any real trouble. About the biggest mess I got into was when I spilled a bottle of bubble bath into the Jacuzzi in my suite at the Desert Inn and bubbles ran out all over the carpet.

After we bubbled up the carpet at the Desert Inn, Rhonda and I thought we should get out for a while, so we slid over to see the Glen Campbell show at the Riviera. We showed up, and Glen did what many entertainers do for a visiting singer, he called me up on the stage and had me sing a couple of songs. After the show, Rhonda and I went backstage and hung out for a while. Glen introduced me to his wife, Sarah, Mac Davis's ex. I had never seen such a tiny woman. I'm not particularly big, but I felt like an Amazon next to her. Her hands were the size of a child's hands, and she was also thin, thin, thin. I don't see how she could have weighed seventy-five or eighty pounds. People talked about our relationship like he was dating a child, but they should have seen his wife. Sarah was a lot more childlike than me, age be damned.

After Rhonda and I hung out backstage at Glen's show that night, we went back to the Desert Inn with a songwriter named Michael Smotherman. Luckily we hadn't been kicked out over the bubble escapade, and the three of us sat around drinking and listening to songs half the night. Before Michael left, he made us promise to come back for Glen's show the next night so we could party some more. Hell, we didn't have anything better to do.

That next night Glen was really coked up. I was drunk, of course, so you'll have to take a drunken woman's word for it, but there's a big difference between someone who's drinking and someone who's doing blow. Sometimes he was just bouncing off the walls. This is the truth: I had never done cocaine in my life at that time. Frankly, it scared the crap out of me. I was one of those people who justified getting drunk by saying, "Well, it's legal and it isn't dope." We can find lots of ways to justify shit. There is one other thing I want to set straight. Glen wrote in his book that I took him to some mysterious house where people were freebasing cocaine. I did no such thing, and Glen and I never freebased. He's got me confused with some other girlfriend in that story.

After the show Rhonda was about half sick and wanted to go back to the Desert Inn, but when Michael Smotherman suggested going over to Glen's place to listen to songs, I said I was in. I was way too drunk to be going anywhere, and the minute we got there, I curled up on the couch. Michael—who is an unbelievably talented songwriter—played a lot of his stuff and then switched to other writers he admired. Glen left the room for a while, and I remember wondering why. I didn't have to wonder for long, because when he walked back out in the living room he had nothing on but tennis shoes and socks. Not one stitch of clothes.

There I was on his couch, drunk as I could be, thinking, "Man, I ain't believing this. There's the Rhinestone Cowboy naked as a jaybird and walking around in his tennis shoes."

Then I crashed. That's one difference between being drunk and being high. If you're drinking, you're bound to pass out sooner or later. If you're on cocaine, you can get into trouble for days. I found that out firsthand later.

Glen took me back to my hotel the next day and I didn't see

him again for several months. But I couldn't quite get him out of my mind after that night. He was interested, too, and we stayed in touch by telephone. Our conversations turned more and more personal, until I was positive we'd be together one day. I even started making veiled references about him to my friends.

One of those friends was Paul Moore, who had been the lead singer for the Sound Generation that time my brother Don got our bus sunk in the mud at the Mahonig County Fair. Paul was now my booking agent. In 1979 he was working for William Morris in Nashville. He got a call from Los Angeles and the agency told him that he had a new client, Tanya Tucker, the former child star who had tried her hand at rock and roll and just might be on her way down the tubes. Did he want to book her, anyway? He just said, "Oh, my God! I would love to work with her again," and didn't mention his only other experience was when I was mired down in the mud.

One night in Knoxville, where I was sharing the bill with Charlie Rich, Paul took Beverly Hills and me to dinner, and I started in about this new guy I thought was cool. It was "Glen, this," and "Glen, that," and Paul sat there with a frown on his face. Then all of a sudden he said, "Are you talking about Glen Campbell?" I grinned and said I sure was. He told me later that he could barely finish the meal. All he could think of was, "Oh, my God, what a scandal this could turn out to be." As it turned out, it could and did.

⁂

A month or so later Glen phoned to ask me to come to a show he was playing in Tahoe, and I jumped at the chance. I was in Colorado Springs with Reba McEntire and Larry Mahan for the opening of the Cowboy Hall of Fame. The show went great, even though Reba kept having to remind Mahan and me to tone it down. "Now keep it country," she'd say during rehearsals. "Ya'll are getting kind of rock and roll." It's funny how times and tastes change. Now Reba does everything from R&B to pop to a Broadway-style show.

Glen didn't want the press to find out I was in Tahoe. He had me picked up at the airport and taken straight to a suite at the hotel, instead of the house where he was staying. I think we both knew this was the big night. He came to the room after his show, and we slept together for the first time. Afterward, I was lying there thinking that this was the man for me, that this was what love was all about. I thought we'd be together forever. I didn't even think about Sarah, since he'd told me it was over between them.

I was lying there in my little fantasy when he spoke.

"Tanya," he said. "Sarah's pregnant."

I froze up.

"She had her IUD removed and didn't tell me."

I still didn't say anything. He'd gotten her pregnant, no matter who stopped using birth control. I really couldn't react to this, because it took a while to sink in. I don't like people knowing when I'm hurting, either. I'd rather throw a fit or something. Anything to cover up pain. After I had my act back together I started sympathizing with him. Glen had a way about him that made you want to try to make everything right for him, and I played right into it. I agreed that Sarah was a terrible woman to have done that awful thing to Glen. And yes, she was just trying to hang on to him, since she knew he couldn't throw out the mother of his child. In some ways, it made him even more attractive that he seemed to be hurting and needing me. Many women will relate to that dangerous syndrome.

I knew I loved this man, as crazy as he seemed to be. But I also knew there was no chance he was going to abandon his pregnant wife for me. When I finally left Tahoe, I was one confused woman. So I showed it by running off with Merle Haggard.

THIRTY-ONE

*T*here had always been something between Merle and me, going back to my childhood crush when the Librand girls and I recorded in his Bakersfield studio. As I said, the night of my first CMA Awards show, even with all the star power there, it was Merle that I thought was the main man. I'd opened shows for Merle, and I even talked with him about the possibility of doing an album called *Tanya Sings the Hag*, adding in the tape of "Mule Skinner Blues," from that long ago day in Bakersfield. Unfortunately, Merle's studio had burned, and the tape was lost along with it. But I still thought the album was a good idea, and so did Merle. I'd still like to make that record. Once, when I was sixteen, I went to his show at the Bottom Line in New York, and he called me up to sing. And after I moved to Los Angeles, I'd see him at parties that Tree Publishing threw at an apartment they kept in town for special occasions. I flirted like the devil with him every time I saw him.

I'd just returned to L.A. after playing a show at the 1980 Lake Placid Winter Olympics when Merle called me from out on the road. He wanted me to hop on a plane and come to his show in Beaumont, Texas. I thought it over for about two seconds and said, "Hold the bus, I'm on my way."

I was in a very strange state of mind. I'd made a career change that I thought was going to be the best thing I'd ever done musically, and it hadn't worked. Nashville seemed angry I'd even tried. I'd slept with Glen Campbell, who I thought was going to be the big love of my life, and then he'd turned over in bed and told me his wife was pregnant. Rocking around Texas on a bus with Merle seemed like great therapy, and I felt I needed it. At least it would take my mind off Glen and his pregnant wife.

I flew to Houston and caught another plane to Beaumont, where Merle was waiting to pick me up. I realized right away that Merle was wanting a party between the sheets, not a traveling companion. If I hadn't been so confused about my life, I would have known when he called that he was looking for more than I was prepared to offer. When we got to the club in Beaumont he introduced me to the band with a "guy attitude," saying, "Well, boys, look what I've got." Then, during the show, Merle was nervous and kept forgetting the words to his songs. He wasn't drugged up, either. I got a charge out of thinking it was because of me that he was sweating bullets up there.

After the show, we left the club and got on Merle's bus, heading for the next stop on down the line. Merle had a big, expensive-looking bus. There was a living area up front that opened onto a big bedroom. Beyond that there was a nice, fully equipped kitchen. I probably would have wanted to buy it myself, except that I couldn't imagine having people truck on through the bedroom every time they wanted a cup of coffee. But that night I was mainly interested in my hero, not his bus. I'd started drinking at the club and I had a million questions for Merle Haggard once we were alone on the bus. I thought I'd start out clever.

"So, Merle," I joked. "Did you really turn twenty-one in prison or was it thirty-two and the number didn't flow with the song?"

He just looked at me.

"Have you ever heard of Nostradamus?" he finally asked.

I'd heard of him, but Nostradamus wasn't who I wanted to talk about. I wanted to talk about the living legend sitting across from me on the bus. Merle wasn't having it.

"Did you know that Nostradamus knew that the planet Pluto existed centuries before it was discovered by scientists?" he went on.

I'm going, "Yeah, yeah, but how about the time you wrote 'Sing Me Back Home.' What inspired you to write that song?"

I must have sounded like a refugee from Music Journalism 101 to Merle Haggard.

We spent the next four or five days on the road, playing guitars, drinking, singing, and raising hell in general. It only took a day or so before Merle knew I was there for the music and the party, and not for sex. We fooled around some, but for some reason, I just couldn't bring myself to actually have sex with him. Maybe it was because he was Merle Haggard, or maybe I was still smarting over Glen. Whatever the cause, I couldn't quite do it.

Merle was scheduled to stop in Meridian, Mississippi, Jimmie Rodgers's hometown, for a meeting with Peavey Amps, with whom he had a product endorsement. So we stopped and went into Linebaugh's for a beer before his meeting. My father loves Jimmie Rodgers music like it's sacred, but it was Merle Haggard singing it that got me hooked on the Trainman. I felt like I was directly linked to country music's past that afternoon. I sat there in that historic bar with this connection to music history and thought, "Man, this must be like sitting at Tootsies, talking to Hank Jr. about his dad."

Then Merle decided he didn't want to go visit Peavey after all.

"Man, you can't blow them off," I said. "They're paying you money." I sounded just like Beau Tucker talking to Tanya. Merle grumbled a little, but he went to his meeting, anyway.

Rolling around the country on a bus can be great, and when I had the chance to do it with Merle Haggard, it was out of sight. I still love bus trips on many levels. Falling asleep in the back of the bus when it's raining is the most peaceful thing in the world. Or maybe it's nostalgia for my childhood spent in trailers. There is such a wonderful feeling of self-containment when you step into a tour bus, and the doors close behind you. Whatever problems you have often seem to fade with the sound of the wheels roaring down the highway and the sight of the towns looming ahead that then just get lost in the distance. That feeling of safety can turn on you, of course. There are some problems that will always be waiting for you when the ride is over.

On the trip with Merle, what I most enjoyed was the music. The party aspects were overshadowed by the experience of spending that many days listening to one of country music's greatest legends sing his songs. I love so many of them. "If

We Make It through December" is one of my favorites, because it reminds me so much of our family while I was growing up. That song nails it, that feeling of wanting to be able to give your family a Christmas and knowing you'll be lucky to keep the heat turned on in the house. Merle told me later that he wrote his 1983 hit, "What Am I Gonna Do (For the Rest of My Life)," about me, and I hope that's true. I did tell him that I bet he'd never again sing the line, ". . . the last thing I needed was somebody messing with my mind" without thinking about me. There's nothing that messes with a man's mind more than a woman who's just along for the good times. They all figure you're going to fall all over yourself for them. Especially stars.

But I do love Merle, and underneath my coming off like a party girl, I think I did fall all over myself for him. Sometimes I think I love Merle Haggard better than any of his wives except Bonnie Owens, and I think she's the one who's loved him best. I never was his wife, of course, but I do love him. I have a tape of one of Merle's television specials, and sometimes my kids and I watch it together. I'm continually telling them—and anybody else who happens to be around—that the man they are watching is one of the greatest artists in any form of music. My daughter, Presley, and I love dancing together when Merle sings "Working Man Blues." My son, Beau Grayson, plays along with his drumsticks.

I had a blast, and I wasn't even worried what my folks would think, because I figured they thought I was still at the Winter Olympics. I thought wrong. My dad was on my trail, thanks to George Jones. George was playing a show at the Palomino in Los Angeles, and Merle suggested we call him.

"Hell, yes," I said. "Let's call Possum!" Now, you may think this is a lie, but I'd rather have a few drinks and start calling friends than almost anything, and that includes sex.

Once upon a time I thought it was great that there were no other Tanyas in country music. That was before Merle and I called up George Jones at the Palomino. Dad took Mother to see that show, since George Jones is her number-one hero. After George finished his performance, my folks went backstage to say hello. While they were talking, a stagehand came up and said George had a call from Merle Haggard, and that he could take it down the hall. After a few minutes, Mother and Dad decided they ought to say good-bye. Dad walked down the hall to tell George they were leaving, and as soon as he was within earshot, he heard my name.

"And Tanya's there on the bus with you? Where'd you say you are?"

George hung up on us when he turned to find my dad standing there with his mouth open. Good ol' Possum. Rather than admitting he knew anything, he shot out the back door and onto his bus. He called us from the bus and explained about the hang-up. I might have figured I couldn't run anything past my dad. At least in twenty years I hadn't been able to.

Dad went straight home and phoned a booking agent and asked him to try to find out Merle Haggard's tour schedule by the next morning. Fortunately, it took the guy a couple of days to track us down, and by that time I was on a plane to L.A. By the time I left, Merle wasn't putting any rush on me. I don't think I wore very well on him. He's far too introverted and intense, and I'm too loud and rowdy for us to really go the distance.

This is a hard thing for me to admit, but I know I put my parents through hell back then, and for more years to come. All they ever wanted was for me to be happy, and as I got more out of line, they knew that even though I had a great time while I was out partying, I wasn't satisfied with my life.

They had other worries at the time. Dad was having problems in his relationship with La Costa, and that about killed him. She hadn't been able to stand being around Steve and Jerry at Far Out Management, and in the winter of 1979 Dad was managing her. Dad was being torn apart between worrying about me and my personal and career problems and my sister's career problems.

Although she'd had five albums on Capitol, only one single had cracked top-five. "Get on My Love Train" was a big song, and she had two other top-ten singles, "Western Man" and "He Took Me for a Ride." The albums were all well received by the critics, but she couldn't very well sustain a career on three hit singles. It was obvious something had to give. La Costa had heard Dad say that you can't really have more than one horse in the stable, and she figured that the Tucker horse was always going to be Tanya. So she fired Beau Tucker.

He was almost physically ill from it all, but he asked Bill Carter to take an offer to La Costa. He wanted 10 percent of her earnings, which he would put into a savings account as a trust fund for any children she might have. La Costa doesn't remember hearing about that proposition, so maybe Bill didn't fully explain it to her, or maybe she was just so frantic out there on the road with nobody to help give her direction that she didn't understand it. At any rate, she didn't respond. Those were very dark days for our dad.

Luckily for me, something came along that temporarily distracted Dad from me and the Hag. He had a call from a guy named Mike Chapman who wanted to produce me, and he didn't want any up-front money to do it.

THIRTY-TWO

$\mathcal{M}$ike Chapman and his songwriting partner, Nicky Chinn, had sold well over 150 million albums with worldwide acts like Sweet, Mud, Smokie and Suzi Quatro by the time they relocated from the United Kingdom to the United States. As soon as Mike got here, he jumped right on the charts as the producer of Exile's "Kiss You All Over" and also found success with Debbie Harry and the Knack. Mike's license plate read: MC HITS.

If I'd learned one thing it was not to pay much attention to so-called track records, but Mike had one credential that interested me. He was the kind of a producer who wanted to be intensely involved in every step of the recording process, up to and including writing a lot of the songs his artists recorded. He also wanted his artists involved. That's all I needed to hear to decide he was the man to do my next record.

When my dad asked him what kind of up-front money he wanted, Mike won him over right away.

"Nothing," he said. "If I can't produce a hit record on this girl I don't deserve a cent."

He was speaking my dad's language.

Because he could be absolutely outrageous, he spoke mine,

too. He liked to sing and dance around the control room. He liked to work fast, much like Billy Sherrill had done, only with a more maniacal attitude. He'd say things to me like, "What are those horrible slacks you're wearing? Did your seamstress steal a set of drapes from the Beverly Hills Hotel?" Or, "I don't want respect. I want disbelief," or, "Giorgio Moroder is the *only* disco producer. I steal everything from him."

Well, I had to love a guy like that. Especially when I found out that underneath the mania was a sweet-tempered marshmallow of a man who really believed in me, wanted input, and wanted success for me above all else.

Life around Mike was an extension of the wild L.A. lifestyle, but without the destructiveness. I'm not saying we didn't party, because we certainly did. But we weren't into drugs and we didn't fight. We just ran around having fun when we weren't working in the studio. He had no temper to speak of, and there was a childish sexiness about him. Mike loved to hop on a jet and head to New York to party at Studio 54 with Debbie Harry, The Knack, and Blondie. He was a part owner of Le Dome in Los Angeles, and we went there a lot. Le Dome remained one of my favorite hangouts long after Mike and I finished the record.

I guess the only real argument we ever had, if you could call it an argument, was about my signing up to drive in an off-the-road Jeep race in Riverside, California. I was the only woman entered, along with guys like Gary Busey, John Schneider, Larry Wilcox, and Jan Michael Vincent. Mike could not believe I was going to drive in that event, and he was very vocal about it. Driving fast came natural to me, though. I mean, I once picked up a couple of hitchhikers in Nashville, and by the next interstate exit they were begging me to let them out. (These days I sponsor a NASCAR racing car, and I love watching it fly around the track.) So I piled myself into a Jeep and waved good-bye to Gary and Jan Michael and the rest of the boys. Even though I outran them all and drove off in my prize-winning Jeep, Mike was angry about it.

The recording sessions were refreshing, and not just because Mike and I were such close friends. I had a great deal of input on *Tear Me Apart*, from putting the band together to choosing the material to helping with the production technique. I was more involved that I had ever been, and I was convinced we were making a good record. I do think *Tear Me Apart* was a good recording, but country radio thought otherwise.

In the meantime, Glen Campbell kept calling to say how much he loved me and how one day we'd be together. I decided that day should come sooner than later, and on New Year's Eve of 1980 I foolishly took matters into my own hands.

THIRTY-THREE

I played a show at the Palomino in L.A. that New Year's Eve, and a bunch of my girlfriends showed up. Around midnight, when the show was over, we all piled into a limousine and decided to party all night. Someone had sent a huge horseshoe bouquet to my dressing room, so we hauled that into the limo. I sat in the sunroof and rode down Sunset Boulevard throwing roses to everyone walking, or in some cases dancing, down the street. It seemed like all of Los Angeles was out rocking around in honor of 1980.

Glen had told me he was throwing a party at his house, but early in the evening I was still smart—and sober—enough to avoid it. We partied everywhere else in Los Angeles. Now, the interesting thing is that no matter where we went and what guys wanted to pick us up, we were having none of it. I can be one of the boys and I can be one of the girls. That night we were just a bunch of good ol' girls out on the town. We weren't out trolling for guys, just for a big New Year's Eve.

Finally we decided to hit the Playboy Mansion. My friend Audrey was along, and since I hadn't been able to start drinking until after I finished my show at the Palomino, she was even drunker than I was. We pulled up in front of the Playboy

Mansion, and the doorman asked for a name. I stuck my head up through the sunroof with my horseshoe full of roses around my neck and smiled brightly. "Tanya Tucker," I said.

Just then Audrey stuck her head out of the limo door and puked right at the doorman's feet. Needless to say, Tanya Tucker and party were denied access.

I decided we should get Audrey to my house immediately, so we headed back home where I cleaned her up, forced some coffee down her, and put her to bed. Then I called Glen's house to see what was happening. My pal, singer and songwriter Billy Burnette, answered the phone and told me to get my rear end right over. That was all the invitation I needed. "Perfect," I said. "We're on our way."

It was around 2:00 A.M. when I decided I should make my big entrance. Before I left my house I stuck an M-80 firecracker in my pocket. I walked in the house, and when I saw that Glen was holding court in the library, I lit that M-80, rolled it into the middle of the room, and shouted, "Happy New Year, everybody!" Just as Glen whispered, "Oh, my God," the firecracker blasted off. Do I dare say it went over with a big bang?

Of course, all my buddies like Billy Burnette and Michael Smotherman thought it was hysterical. Glen didn't think it was all that funny.

My girlfriends and I waltzed into the kitchen and made ourselves at home. It's weird, but even with all that bizarre stuff going on, I remember thinking that this was the kitchen of my dreams, beautiful flowered tile, everything looking perfect. I was still sitting there admiring Glen's kitchen when a very pregnant Sarah came in and ordered me out of the house. Glen had told me he and Sarah were waiting to separate until after the baby was born.

"Aw, come on, Sarah," I said innocently. "I got all my girlfriends with me. We're just having a good time." She cussed me up one side and down the other. Obviously, Glen had been running his mouth about our little fling. Either that or she'd had all his phone calls traced. Then Glen came into the kitchen and cussed Sarah for cussing me. She stormed out, and I pulled myself down off the counter where I'd been sitting admiring Glen's taste in kitchen tile.

"You've got two months, son," I said. "In two months you better make or break your mind up about me." Then we all piled

THIRTY-FOUR

I called Glen immediately. He was sick with double pneumonia, and in a bad depression. Mother and I practically moved in with him while he regained his strength. Mother made him soup, and I tried to keep him off cocaine while he was recovering. I'm not trying to sound like a saint, here. I'd been running wild for several years. In fact, when I first started going out with Glen, Jerry Lee Lewis cornered me at a show and said, "Now Tanya, this ain't going to work. You're a fast horse, and I don't believe old Glen can hang on." My reputation preceded me into the relationship. But that February I just wanted Glen to get well.

I thought that I was starting off on a love affair that would end in a marriage that would last a lifetime, just like my parents' marriage had. But you can't build a marriage like that of my parents when the man gets up off his sick bed and says, "Want to do a line with me, honey?" And the woman says, "Sure, why not." Why did I do cocaine that first time? I wish I knew.

I've tried to say very little in print or on television about my time with Glen. But when I decided to do an autobiography, I knew that was going to have to change. It would be silly—to say nothing of dishonest—to try to act like it never happened or that it didn't affect me. The continuing interest in our relationship has always been a mystery to me, though. It seems like it's one of the first questions anyone asks in about half my interviews. "You won Female Vocalist of the Year in 1991? Great, now what about Glen in 1980?" When Glen's autobiography came out it stirred it all up again.

Anytime two people tell stories about their affair and subsequent breakup, you're going to get each one's personal spin—just ask any divorced couple what happened to their marriage. And before I give you my spin, I want to explain two things. First, I don't think either one of us remembers this saga perfectly. We weren't videotaping these fights. And second, while I was with Glen, I was very much in love with him. He was the first great love of my life, and there's still a part of me that loves him, even though I haven't been "in love" with him for years.

In Glen's book, he likened going out with me to wading through a swamp filled with poisonous snakes, and while one of my friends said she'd take that as a compliment, it hurt my feelings. Glen and I had fun for a long time. We had some horrible times, but we had some great times, too. When I first got together with him he was so unhappy he'd even stopped golfing, which next to music was probably the biggest passion of his life. I handed him his clubs and told him to hit the course again. I may not always do the right thing, but at least I do *something*. He did start playing golf again, and I believe he started coming back into the world right then. Maybe not the real world, because according to him we were both on cocaine almost every moment of every day we were together. Here's what I wonder. If he was that out of it, how did he remember all that stuff he wrote about me?

At first it looked like Glen Campbell and Tanya Tucker might make it. We had some great times. We spent hours and hours just talking—about life, families, music, everything. We traveled to each other's concerts and to vacation spots. We flew to Paris and did the whole tourist bit. We saw the sights, sat in little outdoor cafes and drank wine, and shopped. Lord, did we shop. We'd set up private showings at big design houses, and Glen would have me try on every gown in the place. Sometimes we bought things, and even if we didn't, I'd have Glen take my picture in the outfit. I bet the designers loved that.

Looking back on it, we seemed to spend 80 percent of our time in airplanes. For example, when Glen was playing a long-term gig at the Las Vegas Hilton, and I was out on the road doing my shows, he'd send the Hilton's private plane to pick me up after my show and fly me back to Vegas to walk onstage during his second show. Then the plane would turn around and take me back to whatever town I was playing next. It was definitely a "Lifestyles of the Rich and Famous" kind of time, and that in itself made the whole thing unrealistic. That you aren't going to get grounded if you're always up in the air goes without saying.

Glen was always trying to spend money on me, and it frequently made me uneasy. He'd give me his credit cards and tell me to go buy clothes or jewelry or something—anything. It makes me nervous when people spend money on me, so lots of times I'd buy something myself, bring it home, thank him, and give him back the credit cards. He never paid any attention to credit card bills or money, so he wouldn't know who paid what. Don't get me wrong, I love to spend money, but I'd rather it be money I earned.

He did buy me lots of things. He bought me clothes and jewelry. He hired Learjets to fly me to his shows, and he chartered them to come see mine. He flew both our families to Hawaii for a show. He spent almost $60,000 throwing me a party at Bistro on my twenty-second birthday. I can't even imagine how much money he spent when all was said and done. Of course, I laid out some cash myself. I bought him a Rolex that cost about ten grand, and it was $10,000 I probably didn't have to spend.

I learned a lot about performing from Glen. I don't think he's ever blown a show in his life. He is an amazing musical talent, and he gives 200 percent every time he walks on stage. I don't care how drugged up he was, or what mood he was in, he gave the show everything he had. I always told him, "You never seem too high to hit the high notes," and it was the truth. And Glen will go ahead and do a show no matter what else is going on. Once, a few days after we'd gone roller skating and he broke his arm, he not only made it to opening night at the Vegas Frontier Hotel, he played his guitar. He connects with his audience, and I always admired his commanding stage presence.

Glen's broad-based audience was the one I'd always wanted, too. All I'd ever asked for in this business was to make good music, to be able to just get out there and perform the songs I loved and entertain people. I loved the way he was able to sing anything, and the people loved it. Yet there was never the feeling he turned away from his roots in country music.

This book would run into two volumes if I were to detail all the problems we had in that relationship. I'll tell you about the ones that stand out in my mind, and I think the reason they stand out is because they were incredibly stupid. We fought over the silliest things, things that didn't amount to anything.

For one thing, Glen didn't think I acted ladylike enough around the celebrities such as Milton Berle, Jack Lemmon, and Joe Namath and other rich people he liked. I never tried to put on a front for any of them, and I don't think many of them expected me to do so. The problem, I think, was in Glen's mind.

One night when we were at a party in Dallas at some oilman's house, we were talking to James Garner. Somebody must have looked at me the wrong way, because I made some little comment about it. Jim laughed and said, "You're so paranoid you think that when the football team goes into the huddle, they're talking about you." Jim Garner is a funny guy and a nice guy and he meant nothing by it. It was just a little joke, and I thought it was funny. Glen was so pissed he barely spoke to me the rest of the night. Talk about paranoid. He said James Garner would never have said that to a real lady. I said I never promised I was a real lady.

Another thing I did that always got me in trouble was hanging out with my friends at Le Dome. When Glen was out of town he ordered me to stay away from the place, and of course, being me, I went anyway. The people at the limo service we used were always ratting on me, even though I wasn't charging the car to Glen. He was a big customer, and therefore they had loyalty to him and not me.

Glen never understood that I went to clubs to party and have a couple of laughs, not to pick up men. He couldn't understand that because he always had to have a woman around. Some men are like that. They always need to have a new girlfriend standing in the wings before they drop the old one. I guess they can't stand to be alone. I'm the opposite. I can go without a man in my life for long stretches of time. It's not because I don't want one, but if I can't find one that's right, then I'd rather hang with my buddies.

My family liked Glen at first. We'd all watched his television show and listened to his records. Glen's public image made him seem like a great guy. For all my folks knew, he was Mr. Perfect. And he might have been for some woman. What he turned out to be was the man who could bring out all the bad in me, and I turned out to be the woman who could bring out all the bad in him. We dragged our families right along into our soap opera, too.

Glen was playing the 1981 New Year's Show at the Sheraton Waikiki. This was the show he flew everyone to when I came up with the big idea that everyone should be together in Hawaii for New Year's. I got along well with Glen's family. When we first started dating, he took me to Arkansas to visit them. Right at first they seemed a little nervous around me, and I don't know if it was because I was a singer, or because I was one of a trail of women he'd brought home. It didn't take long for them to warm up, though, and within a day we were fishing together and singing around the house. I even cleaned out the ice box and made fried okra and polk salad for them. So when we talked about this trip to Hawaii, I really wanted to include both families.

Off we went, our parents, his brother and sister, and his nephew. Beverly Hills went with us. By that time she'd left Tree Publishing and was working for Glen's publishing company, Glentan. Even though it had my name in it, I wasn't a partner. A pal of Glen's was promoting the show, a guy I didn't like at all. He was Mr. Hollywood Hawaiian-style, and very oily. He was the one who started the trouble.

Beverly Hills was trying to seat some people down front at the show, close to where the two families were sitting, and this promoter came up and jumped all over her. He said she shouldn't be seating people and that she should just go sit the hell down. Well, Beverly protested, because part of her job with Glen was to see to it that his friends had good seats. So right there in front of people she knew, including my family, the guy called her a bitch. I was backstage with Glen at the time and didn't hear about it until after the show.

When we got back to the hotel suite, Beverly wasn't there, so I called her room to see what was going on. She was upset, to say the least. I said, "Well, we'll just tell Glen and he'll tell that guy to go to hell. Glen will be furious about this!"

Wrong. When I told Glen he was so ripped he couldn't have cared less. I was ripped, too, so I didn't let it pass. I told him Beverly was embarrassed and hurt and this guy didn't have the right to treat her like a dog. Then I insisted he call Beverly right on the spot and personally invite her to the suite. He told me to kiss off, and of course I couldn't let that pass, so I called him an asshole.

We fought our way off into the bathroom, which was about the size of the house I was living in, and continued the argument. Glen got so mad he pulled his belt off and said he was going to spank me. I yelled out, "Well, let's just see you do it." I was buzzed and, as in Travis Tritt's song, when I drink or do drugs, I always think I'm ten feet tall and bulletproof. Right about then Glen's nephew walked in, leaned up against the wall, and watched. And in another second, my dad stomped in.

My dad's face turned beet red when he saw Glen holding me by the arm with a belt raised over me, and he demanded to know what was going on.

Then Glen's nephew said an incredibly dumb thing to Dad: "Oh, it's nothing. Glen's just going to spank Tanya."

Dad grabbed the belt out of Glen's hand and got up in his face. "Nobody spanks my little girl but me, Glen, and you better get that straight."

Glen turned. "I thought you were a man, Beau," he said. "A grown-up man." I flipped out at that and jumped Glen. My dad pulled me off and tried to get me to settle down. Glen's remark was such an odd thing to say to a father who was stopping you from beating his daughter. But that's how Glen thought.

All of a sudden the bathroom started filling up with people. Glen's family, my mother. Everybody was yelling, and Dad and Mother were pulling me out the door. New Year's was turning into a family affair all right, and it wasn't "The Brady Bunch Go to Hawaii."

I went back to my parents' room with them. The phone rang immediately. It was Glen, who started shouting at my dad. Dad told Glen he was going to come back to the suite and kill him. I somehow got Dad calmed down, mainly because I knew that he really would hurt Glen. Glen wasn't a fighter unless he was fighting with a woman. Dad sat there on the bed with tears in his eyes.

"Tanya, I'm so afraid for you," he said. "I think he's gonna kill you someday."

I went over and sat down and put my arm around him. "No, he isn't gonna kill me. Glen loves me."

I have thought a lot about why I put up with getting hit, and I don't know that I can explain it. Our fights usually started out as a mutual thing. We were both hot-tempered. Maybe it's like people who don't know they've been shot or stabbed because their adrenaline is so pumped. Cocaine also dulls both your physical senses and your good sense.

Our other problem besides cocaine was Glen's jealousy. Around Easter of 1981 the Merle Haggard road trip surfaced, and all hell broke loose. I had convinced Glen to let me organize a yard sale at his house. He was wanting to clean out his place and throw a bunch of stuff away. He even wanted to get rid of a pile of his stage costumes. I said, "Glen, you can't just throw all that in the trash! What a waste!" So I hauled it all out, put price tags on things, and while he was out playing a show in Tahoe one weekend, I had the sale.

Beverly Hills and I were out in the front yard trying to push stage costumes off on anyone who stopped by, when I heard the phone ring. I went in and answered it. It was Glen, and he was livid. "Merle Haggard is sitting right here in this dressing room," he shouted. "He says you jumped in bed with him like a trained monkey."

I said, "Well, you boys hold the phone, because I'll be right there." I left Beverly in charge of the garage sale—which only made $750, by the way—got a plane to Reno, then rented a car and drove to Tahoe. Merle wasn't around when I got there, and Glen and I immediately started to argue. There was grinding equipment and cocaine all over Glen's dressing room, and I started in on it, too. Once again, we both got trashed and I ended up getting the worst end of the fight.

I was bruised and mad, but drugs will do strange things to you, so I didn't leave. Willie Nelson was playing in town that night, and we went to the show. Merle was there, too. Afterward, I went over to Merle and asked him if he had called me a trained monkey, and if so, why.

Merle put his arm around me and shook his head. "You know I love you, Tanya." It wasn't much of an answer.

"I want to know if you screwed Tanya or not," Glen shouted at Merle. Merle just shrugged.

It really pissed me off, because it was male competition, pure and simple. So I said, "You two can screw yourselves, that's what you can do." And I left.

Merle told me later that he'd warned Glen not to ask him anything he didn't want to know. That's almost as bad as the trained monkey line.

THIRTY-FIVE

I don't know how I worked it into my schedule between the fighting and the drugs, but I did a couple of movies during the time I was with Glen. Film work has always interested me, and I even took a few acting classes with Lee Strasberg at Actors Studio. I auditioned along with four hundred others to get in and made it. Someone soon got my spot, though, because I only went for two weeks. I never had the same drive to act that I had to sing.

Unfortunately, I seem to prefer things that come naturally, things that don't require a lot of practice or need work put into them. I guess I'm just naturally lazy that way, and it's a character trait I'd like to change, because I'm tired of doing things by the seat of my pants. Acting certainly wasn't as easy as singing for me. One film I did was David Green's *Hard Country*, which starred my good-old-boyfriend Jan Michael Vincent, along with Kim Basinger, Daryl Hannah, and Richard Moll. Michael Martin Murphey was one of the writers on the script and the film's musical supervisor, and he and Katy Moffatt sang on screen.

Jan Michael called me about the movie. He said it was going to be about a small Texas town and a girl named Jodie—played by Kim—who was torn between wanting to go to Los Angeles and become a stewardess and wanting to marry his character, her boyfriend Kyle. Daryl Hannah, who was pretty much an unknown at the time, played Kim's younger sister. I would play Kim's high school girlfriend, Caroline, who had moved away and become a country singer. The role didn't sound like much of a stretch, so I said I'd do it. My part consisted of me breezing into a club where Michael Martin Murphey and Katy Moffatt played a regular gig, and singing a couple of songs, then going over to Kim's apartment and talking about life and love. I listened while Kim told me about her dreams of a career, then told her that the only way I could see that she could accomplish them was to move away from the little town. I told her too many men around there seemed to think they owned their wives or girlfriends.

I spent a few days in Bakersfield doing the picture, but I hadn't even read the script, so until I saw the movie I had no idea if Kim took my advice or not.

What they were trying to do with the movie and what actually ended up on film were miles apart. It was an attempt to show a small-town girl trying to escape from the good-old-boy kind of sexism her boyfriend and his buddies represented, and how, in the end, she and the boyfriend both escape to a better life. But it ended up as a string of beer drinking contests and silly practical jokes. Some not so silly jokes, too, like when they go through a mock hanging of an out-of-town music producer and almost scare him to death, or when Richard Moll's character dives off a bar stool to get a laugh and is paralyzed. So I didn't have to worry about what to wear to the Academy Awards for *Hard Country*. But on the plus side, I got to know and like Kim Basinger. She's very much her own woman, and someone I've wished I'd stayed in better touch with. As I said before, show business doesn't make it easy to sustain friendships.

I also did a movie with Dirk Benedict, of *Battlestar Galactica* fame, called *Georgia Peaches*. We filmed it in Charleston, South Carolina, and for two months, I was either flying in and out to see Glen or he was flying in and out to see me. Two memorable things occurred during the time I was working on the picture. First, Glen and I were shopping in a Charleston mall, and in the window of a pet store I saw the cutest little poodle. Glen bought her for me and we named her Lucy. She was my constant companion from that day on, and on down the road she played a role in one of the biggest fights Glen and I ever had.

The second memorable thing was meeting Dirk Benedict. He was so unaffected by his status as the star of the movie. He didn't seem to have any ego to speak of, at least not an out-of-control one, and he was one of the most mellow people I'd run into in show business. I watched him for several days and was just amazed at the positive energy he had. He was so full of life, and he really seemed to be one of those rare people who lived every minute of every day to the fullest. I soon learned why. He considered every minute he lived a gift. Dirk had been diagnosed with cancer a few years earlier, and part of his treatment involved a macrobiotic diet that he partially devised himself. My mother always believed in home remedies, and I was utterly fascinated by the fact that it seemed to have worked. There is so much that we disregard as fads or quackery, and I think if we really knew what naturally healing plants we have in this world, we'd be far better off. Dirk certainly was, and he still is as far as I know.

There were some other lessons I could have learned from Dirk during that filming. Lessons about a healthy lifestyle and a positive outlook. But either I learned them and didn't put them to work for me, or they ran right on by.

THIRTY-SIX

*W*hen I recorded my next album, *Dreamlovers*, back in Nashville, Glen came in and performed on it. We didn't get along any better in the studio than we did anywhere else. Glen chartered a jet and flew in from Vegas, and by the time he got to Nashville he was wired and was belligerent the whole time he was there. If it made Glen mad that I wasn't ladylike in front of his Hollywood friends, it made me furious that he was a jerk in front of my producer, Jerry Crutchfield. Even so, the duets, "Dream Lover" and "My Song," came off very well, but the album's hit was "Can I See You Tonight." "Pecos Promenade," the song I recorded for the soundtrack of Burt Reynolds's *Smokey and the Bandit II*, was another hit that year. *Dreamlovers* contained some good songs, and at the time I thought it was a great album. When I listen to the album now, I wish we could remix it.

In between recording, concerts, movie roles, and golf games, Glen and I continued to brawl our way through the tabloids. It wasn't all Glen's doing, either. Most of the time I gave as much as I got. Except for the time I got my teeth knocked out—and we're coming to that—I don't blame Glen any more than myself for any of this. I'm hot-tempered, and if pushed, I fly off the handle.

A decade after our breakup, I was a guest on Dr. Ruth's show and she was talking about assertiveness. I told her that when I was with Glen, I was probably as much at fault as he was for a lot of the fights, because I had the tendency to lash back at him when he lashed out at me. Dr. Ruth laughed that throaty cackle and said, "Aggression! You were using aggression, not *assertiveness*!"

I did start quite a few of the big fights myself, including the one at the 1980 Bing Crosby Golf Tournament, a big one among the Tucker/Campbell Cross Country Battles. Nat Crosby was running the tournament, and according to Glen, everybody who was anybody was going to be there. By that he meant movie stars. George C. Scott, Jack Lemmon, Clint Eastwood—the kind of men Glen thought I wasn't "ladylike" enough around. The tournament was held in Carmel, and Glen was already there, so he arranged for me to travel from L.A. to Carmel with Trish Vandevere, George C. Scott's wife. We were flying in the "wives' plane." What a concept.

I wasn't quite ready when Trish got to my house, and in fact, I was talking on the phone and still in my bathrobe. She got extremely angry and started laying into me about it.

"I absolutely will not wait around on you," she snapped. "I guess you don't understand that I've got a Learjet waiting."

Not, "Hello." Not, "How are you?" Nothing. Just a bawling out. Of course, even though I knew I shouldn't have been running late in the first place, I copped an attitude.

"Well, you can just stick that Learjet up your rear, lady," I snapped back. "I'll get to Carmel on my own."

She walked out, and I phoned LAX and booked a flight. My attitude didn't get any better, either. I phoned Glen, who was getting ready to perform at the stag show, an annual pretournament tradition. When I told him I wouldn't be arriving on the "wives' plane," and why, he was livid. "How could you do that? Don't you know she's George C. Scott's wife? *George C. Scott?*" Like George was God. "You've got to act like a lady around people like her," he said, pushing that button. It really pissed me off, and I told him I wasn't about to suck up to somebody just because she was married to a movie star, and if he didn't like it he could stick the "wives' plane" right up his rear, too.

Then I slammed the phone down and went to get ready. I was already in trouble with Glen, and I decided I'd just as soon it be big trouble as little trouble. I'd show him and all his movie pals a "lady." I put on the raunchiest outfit I could find, a maroon spandex dress that fit like skin and was see-through up both sides. Then just to make sure I looked ladylike enough, I slapped on a pair of boots and added a wide belt cinched up tight around the dress.

When I got to Carmel, Glen was already on at the stag show. The "no women allowed" rule made it even more fun to slide right out onstage behind Glen while he was singing. A kind of rumble went through the audience, and when Glen turned around and saw me and my getup, I thought he was going to choke. Well, what could he do except introduce me and let me sing a couple of songs for the men? Later, when Glen told the story of that night, he said about fifty pacemakers went off when I walked out on stage. But he didn't find any humor in it that night.

When we left the stage, Phil Harris took the microphone and thanked Glen for bringing his daughter along. Glen wasn't thrilled by that comment, either.

People have asked me through the years if I thought that Glen represented a father figure for me. Well, I always thought a woman who wanted another father in her life didn't have one in the first place. Believe me, I had a father right there. Many times he was there whether I wanted him to be or not, looking right over my shoulder.

But there are some similarities that I've considered. Glen Campbell and Beau Tucker were both born into poverty situations and eventually fought their way out. I've talked about Dad's childhood, and a lot's been written about Glen growing up dirt poor in Arkansas. They both have an edge, and they even share certain physical characteristics. But there the similarities end. Dad is a very strong-minded family man whose children have always been his priority.

I stayed in Carmel to watch Glen play golf the next day. I wasn't supposed to be riding on the cart, though. Like the stag party, it was a "men only" event. I think only Kathryn Crosby, Bing's widow, was usually allowed out on the course. Clint Eastwood and Jack Lemmon were in Glen's foursome. Clint is funny in a low-key way. He's very soft-spoken. Actually, everybody talks low on the golf course, which is why I don't like being out there much. I noticed people played to Jack Lemmon, because he is so witty himself. Jack is kind of the Roger Miller of Hollywood.

"Tanya, do you know what 'coyote ugly' is?" Clint asked.

"No, what is it?" I bit, even though it's an old joke.

"That's when you take a girl home, and the next morning she's so ugly that instead of waking her up, you just gnaw your arm off."

From the way Clint looked at Jack Lemmon while he was telling the joke, I'm sure that's where he'd stolen it from. So I stole it from Clint, and I've told it a hundred times since.

Not long ago someone said, "Yeah, well you know what 'double coyote ugly' is, don't you?"

I bit again.

"That's when you gnaw both arms off just to make sure you never do it again."

I flew back to Los Angeles a day or so later to appear on a couple of television shows. I was scheduled to tape Merv Griffin's show, and later on that night to perform on Bert Sugarman's *Midnight Special*. Glen stayed on in Carmel, and I wondered why because the tournament was finished. What I didn't know was that he'd met a girl there before I even arrived, and he was romancing her again the minute I left. That's probably why the guys came up with the idea of a "wives' plane" in the first place.

I was disgusted with Glen after Carmel and decided to see if I could be attracted to another man, so when Bert Sugarman invited me to come over to his house after I did *Midnight Special*, I hopped into his Rolls-Royce and away we went. When we got to his house Bert immediately started coming on pretty strong, and I realized what a mistake it had all been and asked to go home. Somewhere along the line that night, a photographer took pictures of the two of us walking together. Bert was really attractive to me—smart and talented—but underneath it all I am usually a "one love at a time" woman.

Unfortunately, while we'd been kissing and messing around, my lace dress got torn, and I took it back for repairs to the designer in Los Angeles. She fixed it, and that should have been the end of the story. But as it happened, a few weeks later, the woman was backstage at a concert of Glen's. He said she told him the condition of my dress made it look like somebody'd tried to rape me. The next week Bert and I were on the cover of the *National Enquirer*, and I was wearing the lace dress. It didn't take Glen long to make the connection, and he got so mad he phoned Bert and threatened to kill him. Of course, Glen and I had a huge fight over it, but I didn't feel guilty anymore, because by then I knew about Glen's girlfriend in Carmel. She even showed up at one of his concerts later and I ran into her backstage. She practically broke the door down getting past me and out of there. I was so shocked I didn't even throw a fit. Glen denied everything, of course. Oddly, I went and ironed Glen's shirt for the show. I'm not sure why I did that, but it gave me time to think about things. Miss Tiny, the woman who was sort of a second mother to Glen, came in while I was ironing.

"Glen's running around on me," I told her. "That girl was in Carmel with him."

She just shook her head and said, "Honey, you know how men are."

If I didn't know, I was learning fast.

In spite of the fact that I was trying to act nonchalant about Glen's running around, I desperately wanted to cry on somebody's shoulder. I knew that Dottie West had flown in from Nashville to play Vegas. I'd known Dottie for a long time, so I called her up and asked if I could come talk to her or maybe stay in her suite while I decided what to do.

She hesitated. "Well, honey, I don't think that's really up to me," she said, and handed the phone to her husband. Dottie had recently married a guy who was working in her show.

I repeated the story to him and he didn't hesitate at all. "No. I don't want you around Dottie," he told me curtly. "Don't come up here and don't phone again. I don't want her involved in you and Glen's problems."

I couldn't believe that, and it hurt my feelings terribly. I don't blame Dottie, though, because she was the kind of woman who was always under the thumb of the men in her life. If any man told me what I could or couldn't do regarding my friends, I would have told him to kiss my butt.

I'm sure that being friends with Glen and me during those times was tough on people, because things could explode at any minute, and it didn't take much to set off the bomb. Burt Reynolds was a good friend to Glen and me, but he also unintentionally caused one of the biggest rows we ever got into, and the fight that marked the beginning of the end for us. Glen told this story in his book, but he got it wrong. Glen and I had been to Hal Needham's wedding, and on our way home, we stopped by Burt's house.

Burt had just broken up with Sally Field, but because I didn't know it I immediately stuck my foot in my mouth. "Where's Sally?" I asked, looking around to find a young blonde lounging by the bar. Burt shot me a look and ignored the question. We had a couple of drinks and got ready to go. Glen and I planned to stop by my house and pick up Lucy, the dog Glen had bought me in Charleston, then head out to a friend's beach house.

As we were leaving, Burt kissed me. I don't remember if it was on the cheek or on the lips, but I do know it was a very quick, very platonic kiss. Glen didn't see it that way. He got so mad that on the way back to my house he abruptly announced that Lucy the poodle wasn't going to be coming with us. When I asked why, Glen said he didn't want to take a dog to someone else's home. But I knew he was just paying me back for letting Burt Reynolds kiss me.

We fought all the way to my house, and when we got there, I told him to go on alone, that I didn't want to come. As soon as he drove off, I changed my mind and decided to drive my own car out to the beach house. My mother was at my house, and I should have listened to her when she begged me not to go. I was driving a Porsche, and floorboarding it, so I nearly beat him there. When I did walk in the door, without Lucy, by the way, the fight started all over again, getting more physical by the minute. We did take a break from the arguing and fighting to do some cocaine from time to time. At one point, Glen started chasing me, and I ran outside and jumped over a fence and ran down the beach to see if anyone was home at Johnny Carson's who could hide me. Can you imagine what Johnny Carson would have thought if he'd been home? That gave Glen just enough time to lock me out of the house.

In Glen's book he said I kicked out a glass pane and cut my foot. Yes, I did, but it was to get back inside the house for my purse and car keys. It was actually a very bad cut, but I was too messed up and pissed off to notice. The fight raged on, and finally Glen reared back his arm and brought his elbow down in my face, shearing my two front teeth off right at the roots. I hit the floor, and all I could see on the carpet was blood. I reached my hand up and felt my mouth, and there was a gaping hole where my teeth should have been. I went completely around the bend, then. I was crying and screaming and crawling all over the room looking for my teeth. I don't know what I thought I'd do with them if I found them, but for some reason, I was frantic to find those two teeth. They didn't turn up, and I begged Glen to take me to a doctor. He refused. He said in his book that he was too messed up to get me to a doctor for my cut foot. It wasn't the foot that was causing me the pain and that I was asking for help with, it was the broken teeth.

Finally, I called my mother to come get me. I can't tell you how much I hated to do that. She'd warned me not to go out there. She knew that both of us were mad and ready for a fight. But Mother isn't one to say "I told you so." She just told me she'd be there as soon as she could. When she got there she was horrified. I was cut up, and my mouth was still bleeding, and I was crying hysterically. She whisked me out of there and to a hospital in about two seconds.

I was without front teeth for a week, and from that time on, I've had dental problems. My jawline is off now, and I started grinding my teeth at night, finally developing TMJ. Thinking back on it, I guess I was lucky that all I ended up with were jaw problems. That night and many others could have ended in real tragedy, a car accident or an overdose. Worse yet, we could have had car accidents that hurt someone else. So many things could have happened. It scares me to think about it.

The real end of our relationship came in late September of 1981, when Glen flew to my show in Bossier City, Louisiana, came to my room at the Le Boss'ier Hotel, and accused me of sleeping with one of the guys in my band. The accusation was laughable. The band I had then was a very spiritual, religious group, and none of them would have done such a thing. It wasn't enough that Glen was raising hell with me, either. He soon dragged the astonished band member in the room and started raging at him, too. I started yelling at Glen, and that really set him off. He completely trashed the hotel room, and one of my band members finally called the police. But before they could arrive, he hit me, knocked me down, and I ran to the phone and dialed my bodyguard, who was staying at the same hotel.

"Please help me," I whispered, and dropped the phone, because Glen started coming at me. I don't know where I found the strength, but I picked up a chair and broke it on him.

He just went insane, and he started yelling that he was going to kill me. By then I was so beat up, all I could think was that Daddy had been right. Glen was gonna kill me. Right then my bodyguard burst into the room and went for Glen. "Don't hurt him," I said. "Please don't hurt him. Just don't let him hurt me anymore."

The police arrived while my bodyguard was trying to restrain Glen, and they informed him they'd arrest him if he didn't stop disturbing the peace. No mention of beating me up, although I probably wouldn't have pressed charges. I never did. "You can't arrest me," Glen shouted at the cops. "I'm Glen Campbell." They didn't arrest him, either. They just took him to another room and calmed him down. Rumors flew around the music business that one or both of us had been arrested, but we weren't.

I didn't see him again that night, and I seldom saw him after that. Glen had already met the woman he later married, anyway. His banjo player, Carl Jackson, had introduced him to her in New York at a James Taylor concert. So the last big fight didn't really make any difference in the outcome of the relationship. It had already burned out.

I tried to be honest about the breakup when people asked me about it. I admitted that I hadn't wanted it and that I'd have taken him back in a minute. The only thing I tried to cover up was the violence, and I told any journalist who asked that we hadn't fought very much, that all those wild stories they'd heard were exaggerations. I guess I was trying to hang onto the fantasy a little longer.

When you are in your early twenties, big loves and big heartbreaks hit hard. Following our breakup I went into a downward spin that almost cost me my career and my sanity. I was about as sorry a case as anybody would ever want to see. My downtime was not Glen's fault, though. People are responsible for their own actions and reactions, and I take full responsibility. If there is any reason to talk about this aside from the fact that it was a portion of my life, it is the lesson I learned. No one except my children will ever again take precedence over my music. I let a relationship with a man almost destroy my music, the thing I'd loved and worked for all my life. I've come close to doing it since, but not like with Glen. And there's a lesson in that for anyone in a detrimental relationship.

I'm not sure I've ever trusted love since.

*M*y dad, Beau Tucker, at age 11 with his younger brother, Boots, and the family's first dog. This was taken in Wasson, Texas, where the Tuckers and Mother's family, the Cunninghams, lived in tents and worked the oil fields. *Tanya Tucker Collection*

*M*y parents, Juanita and Beau Tucker, in 1949. They've been married over fifty years now, and I always hoped to find a relationship as strong and lasting as theirs. *Tanya Tucker Collection*

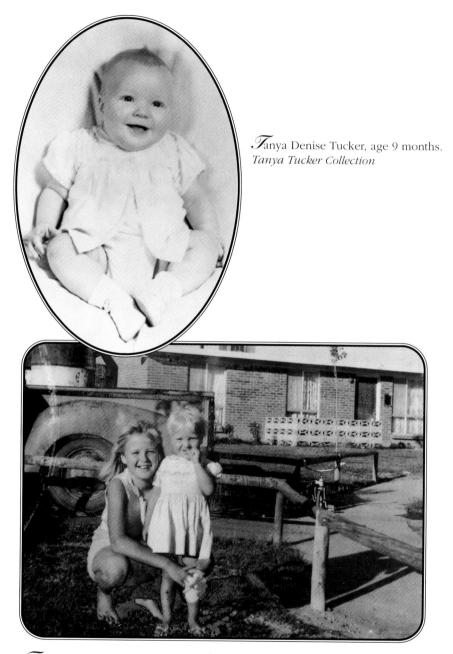

*T*anya Denise Tucker, age 9 months.
Tanya Tucker Collection

*T*his snapshot of La Costa and me was taken when we were living in Willcox, Arizona, in 1961. Even with an eight year age difference, we were always very close. *Tanya Tucker Collection*

*D*on Tucker, holding his squirming new baby sister, Tanya, at our trailer in Denver City, Texas. *Tanya Tucker Collection*

*A*ge 5 on Airport Road in Willcox. Money had been pretty tight that year, so Dad sold his tape recorder for parts and bought me this bike and a puppy for Christmas. *Tanya Tucker Collection*

*O*ne day we heard that a professional photographer was coming to Willcox to set up shop for a week or so at one of the hotels. The Tuckers got dressed up and went down for a family portrait. Don was already off studying aviation, and missed getting in this one.
Tanya Tucker Collection

*T*his was our first band, the Country Westerns. That's me and La Costa in front, with Jerry Hart, Darryl Hart, and Carl Morris in the back. Brother Don was back from school by this time and acting as our manager.
Tanya Tucker Collection

Terry Tinney and I performed at the Miss Willcox pageant in 1967. My personal pick to win, La Costa Tucker, was second runner-up. *Tanya Tucker Collection*

This time La Costa took home the title. She'd come home from college during the summer of 1968, when we were living in Phoenix, and I kept after her to enter the Miss Country Music Phoenix contest. Here I am congratulating her the night she won first place. *Tanya Tucker Collection*

*B*ill Sherrill, me, and Delores Fuller signing my contract with Columbia Records.
Photo courtesy of the Country Music Hall of Fame

*S*ome people at Columbia wanted me to appear older than my actual age in publicity photos, but Billy didn't want anyone turning me into a Lolita figure. So they compromised and came up with a 1940s starlet image.
Columbia Records

This photo was taken at a show in 1975, after I'd found this Elvis-style stage costume.
Tanya Tucker Collection

*M*CA Records rented an amusement park in Little Rock, Arkansas, and threw me a 16th birthday party to celebrate my signing a 1.4 million dollar contract.
Tanya Tucker Collection

This was taken in 1972, when Dad and I flew back home to Las Vegas after recording "Delta Dawn" in Nashville.
Tanya Tucker Collection

At age 17, MCA sent me to London on a promotional tour. I was starting to like the idea of a flashy image by then. *Tanya Tucker Collection*

*T*his 1980 shot has always been one of my favorite photos of Glen Campbell and me.
Photo courtesy of the Country Music Hall of Fame

*T*his was taken the night I met Andy Gibb at Cafe Central in New York. We wrote out song lyrics on the tablecloth that night, and although we never had the big romance the papers reported, we remained friends until his tragic death.
Tanya Tucker Collection

*R*elaxing between shows on the
bus, sometime in the mid-1980s.
Tanya Tucker Collection

*T*his shot was taken during the time I was dating Glen. Things
must have still been going smooth right then, because I sure look
happy! *Hope Powell*

*A*ccepting the Academy of Country Music's 1993 Video Award from James Brolin and Kathy Mattea for "Two Sparrows In a Hurricane." *Glenda S. Paradee*

*J*erry Crutchfield and Mae Axton came to my 33rd birthday party on October 10, 1991. This was a little over a week after I'd won the Country Music Association's Female Vocalist Award on the same day I gave birth to my son, Beau Grayson. Mae is Godmother to my daughter, Presley. Jerry has produced nearly two-thirds of my recordings. *Pamela Scoggins*

*W*hat can anybody say about George Jones, except that he's the best!
Tanya Tucker Collection

I invited Travis Tritt to Meridian, Mississippi, to perform at the Jimmie Rodgers Festival in 1993. I was going through a rocky time right then, and couldn't have asked for a more supportive friend or gracious performer.
Tanya Tucker Collection

*M*ichael Tovar and Paul Primo, in Las Vegas to do my hair and makeup in 1992. *Tanya Tucker Collection*

*D*eer Park Ranch, my home near Nashville. Sometimes it's almost overwhelming when I stand in the kitchen and realize I could probably park a couple of the trailers where I lived as a child in that one room. *Tanya Tucker Collection*

*L*iberty Lady, the bus of my dreams, finally rolled into my life. *Slick Lawson*

*C*oloring Easter eggs in 1995 at the ranch with Ben Reed, Presley, and Beau Grayson. Ben is a steady and constant presence in his children's lives. *Tanya Tucker Collection*

We played a fair in Ohio in 1996, and I took Presley and Grayson on a little shopping spree to the local WalMart. Then I snapped this shot of them in their new clothes. Don't they look great?
Tanya Tucker Collection

Ben, Presley, and Grayson relaxing in Hawaii in 1994.
Tanya Tucker Collection

This photo was taken for a piece in *Redbook* magazine. It's me and my two favorite bubble bath companions.
Mark Tucker

*T*he 1992 Celebrity Cutting Championship in Fort Worth. I was the returning champion and thought I might come home a winner again. *Don Shugart*

*T*his was a big show for me, singing at the 1994 Super Bowl in Atlanta. *Phil Gersh*

*I*t seems that nickel dreams are worth more than they used to be! I feel very lucky that some of mine came true, because they've allowed me to finally kick back once in awhile and enjoy life out here in the country. *Harry Benson*

THIRTY-SEVEN

I felt like I was snakebit for several years. I flipped back and forth between hanging around the house and running around to clubs. I spent too much money, and since I had cut back on performing, I wasn't bringing much in. It wasn't like I was completely underground, though. There's no end to the events celebrities get invited to, and I hit quite a few of them. A lot of the new romance-type pictures you see in tabloids are snapped at these events. When those stories about me and some man get into print, I always think, "Oh, Lord, I hope he doesn't think I had anything to do with that hitting the tabloids." For example, I'd known Clint Eastwood from the Glen days, when he played golf at the Bing Crosby Tournament and told me the coyote ugly joke. I ran into him again at the 1982 World Cup ski races in Aspen. He walked into one of Aspen's country bars and I yelled, "Hey, asshole." He laughed, and we talked a few minutes then played Donkey Kong until dawn. That was it. A tabloid reporter heard about it, and when we happened to be standing together on the slopes the next day, took our photo. By the time it made the papers, I'd broken up Clint's long-term love affair with Sondra Locke. I heard he sued the *Enquirer* for $10 million over that story, but I never heard if he collected a penny.

I was still jet-setting around, flying to Fort Worth to check out the action at the Stockyards, flying to New York to see what was going on at Studio 54. I did meet a good, and lasting, friend at Studio 54 in 1982, with whom I had a strictly platonic relationship that the tabloids reported as a romance. Christopher Atkins was a regular in *Dallas* and had starred in *The Blue Lagoon* and other films. When we met we talked for a while about the music business and about his career and how he sometimes wanted to get away by himself. Although I was spending most of my time in L.A., I was still at our ranch in Nashville a lot of times, so I invited him to come visit. I said, "Well, when you get to feeling that way, come on down and stay and listen to some music." When I left the club we exchanged phone numbers. Chris did call a few months later, and we met in Nashville and I took him around town for almost a week. My parents really liked him, and they were probably glad to see me doing something they considered normal, like sightseeing. People thought Chris and I were sleeping together, but nothing could be further from the truth. He was dating an actress named Cindy Gibb, no relation to Andy, and he was crazy about her. I am very capable of having men in my life who are strictly friends. Chris was one of those.

Perhaps it was because of the stories coming out about Glen and me, or because of not touring, or maybe the recordings weren't up to par, but my singles weren't being played much. You could still hear me on the radio, but it was the earlier releases. I recorded another album for MCA, *Should I Do It*, but there were no hit singles. The sessions were pure hell, because I was not in a good frame of mind.

MCA brought Snuff Garrett back into the picture for what would be my final recording for the label, a 1982 live album made at the Nugget in Vegas. Snuff never mentioned the fact that we'd dropped him as my producer after the first MCA album, and I didn't, either. We concentrated on the country songs, and the album is full of energy, but no singles were released. Dad decided MCA had stopped promoting me and asked the label to release me as an artist. They didn't kick about it, either.

Those were bad days professionally all around for the Tuckers, because La Costa's career was in trouble, too. Even with that amazing voice, Costa had been having difficulty chartwise. She felt that a change of producers might help, so she made her next album, *Somebody on a Rainy Night Lovin'*, with Jerry Crutchfield. It was a strong album, but after the title cut hit the top-twenties, singles started to falter again. Costa didn't have any real management. Bill Carter was trying to help, and Dad stepped in when he could. Dad may have been devastated when Costa fired him, but when she needed his advice, he was right there again. But with my career also in a weird state, he couldn't do much. She asked Capitol to release her from that contract in 1980, and she signed with Elektra. About the same time I was making my *Live* album, Costa was in the studio recording what she hoped would be an album. Elektra released one single in 1982, "Love Take It Easy on Me."

One positive thing that came from the breakup with Glen was that I decided to try my hand at songwriting. Not long after we split, I played a show in New Orleans with Eddy Raven, and while I was there I talked to Eddy about some lyrics and a melody line for a song about life passages in general and Glen in particular. I wanted it to be titled "Changes." Eddy and I threw around some ideas, and then we both went on our way. It didn't get finished until I was in the studio recording my next album on a new label.

In the spring of 1982 I received a call from an old CBS contact. Clive Davis, who headed CBS Records when I was on Columbia, was running Arista Records by then, and he was very interested in starting a Nashville-based division of the company. He wanted to sign me as his first Arista country artist and have David Malloy produce the record. David was a guy who started out in the business at a very young age and was considered a sort of "wunderkind." When David produced my Arista album, he was still in his twenties. I flew to Nashville and met with my new producer, and I should have known from the beginning that, like the line in *Cool Hand Luke*, we had a lack of communication.

"Clive believes you're a torch singer at heart, Tanya," David told me right off. "That's the direction he wants you to go."

"Well, I'm planning on making a country record," I told him. I'd already tried to change my music once, and it hadn't worked. I could see how little torchy touches could enhance certain songs. But not all of them.

"I'm feeling like I'm in a very peculiar position," David admitted. "Because as far as I know your musical heroes range from Elvis to George Jones, and you want to make a country record. Clive's wanting a torch-flavored album. We may have a little problem with creative direction here."

"We'll handle it," I laughed, thinking, despite all my experience, that things would work themselves out once we got in the studio. I've usually got enough confidence for two or three people.

I recorded over a period of several months during 1982. I flew in and out of Nashville for the song selection meetings and actual recording sessions. The album took longer to make than any before or since, and a lot of the reason is my fault. It didn't take long to find out that I didn't need to be in L.A. to find a party. Nashville still had plenty of people running wild, and I was soon hanging out with the musicians and songwriters who considered themselves hell-raisers. Things have straightened up considerably in Nashville now, but back in the mid-1980s liquor and drugs were everywhere. And if you're an entertainer known to live on the edge, many people will do anything to see you out there. Club owners, promoters, musicians, songwriters are only too happy to get high with you. Sometimes it's because they want to curry favor, but I think it's usually just for the show of it. I think people liked to say, "Oh, yeah, George Jones—I got drunk with him in San Antonio." Or, "Man, Tanya and I did some blow the other night and she is one wild woman!" That's not an excuse for the way I behaved, it's just the way things were. Back then, I did try to excuse some of my behavior by saying it was the liquor or drugs. I'd do something dumb and say, "Oh, man, I was just high." That doesn't fly anymore. I don't try to lay the blame on anything but the fact that I've stumbled again.

When I came in for sessions or song meetings, I stayed at the Spence Manor, rather than out at the ranch. I used the excuse that I needed to be close to the studio, but I really just wanted the freedom. The Spence is a Music Row hotel I refer to as the S&M, since a lot of weird people came in and out of there, including me. That place has seen it all. They tell about the time Mickey Newbury, a legendary writer and rowdy, was walking along Seventeenth Avenue toward the Spence and saw George Jones stagger out of a car and into the lobby of the hotel. George hadn't closed the door of the car and he'd left a paper bag filled with money lying open on the seat. Mickey shot up to George's room and handed him the bag.

"What the hell is this and why're you throwing it around your car seat?" Mickey asked.

"Oh, yeah," the Possum says. "I forgot about that. Waylon loaned me fifty thousand dollars last night."

And then there was the time David Allan Coe checked in with his wife and kids and two chimpanzees. The chimps went crazy and tore up half of the third floor before they got them under control. I'm sorry I missed both of those shows at the S&M.

I met two of my main running partners of that era, Dean Dillon and Gary Stewart, at the Spence during one of my first sessions. Lorrell, a girlfriend of mine, was with me, and we were kicking back one night, lying around in our bathrobes and watching television. Suddenly there was a big commotion that sounded suspiciously like a party out in the hall. Lorrell ran over to the door and looked through the peephole.

"There's some guys in rock-and-roll jackets out there," she whispered.

That aroused my curiosity, so I got the switchboard to connect me with the room across the hall, called them up, and asked if they had any beer.

"Well, I don't know," some guy said with a drawl. I didn't know who it was at the time. "Are you good looking?"

"We're okay," I laughed.

"That'll do," he said.

I hung up the phone and told Lorrell we better put on some makeup or we'd make me out to be a liar. It took us a little while to get dressed and fix our faces, so by the time we walked in the door Dean, Gary, and another songwriter, Frank Dycus, were picking guitars and working on a song. They didn't even introduce themselves right then, just handed us a couple of beers. Gary Stewart turned out to be the one who'd answered the phone. I recognized him immediately. He's one of the greatest singers and stylists in the business, with hits like "She's Actin' Single (I'm Drinkin' Doubles)" and "Out of Hand." I've always loved his music, so I was excited to meet him.

It was exciting just to look at Dean Dillon, because he's a fox. I didn't know who he was, although he was so cute I didn't know how I had missed him around town. He'd had several records out on RCA, and in 1981, *Billboard* voted him "Singles Artist of the Year." Dean and Gary brought a duet album out in

1982, *Brotherly Love*, and they were working on a new project, *Those Were the Days*. The two were as well known for their wild streaks as for their musical talents. Just the kind of guys I needed to meet.

The song they were working on was about Natalie Wood, who had died recently. I listened to the line they were singing and said, "Nah, that's not the best line you could come up with. Try this one." We sat around drinking beer and writing songs all night. The first song I completed with them was called "Leave Them Boys Alone," and it was all about the music business trying to control artists' lives and careers: "Leave them boys alone and let 'em sing their songs."

By the next morning we were all still up and all still trashed, but we were all still singing and thought we'd written a hit, so I wanted to tell the world. Of course, if I did that, I'd also be telling the world that Tanya Tucker was in the bag. I didn't care, but I didn't want to stagger down the alley to Tree Publishing to announce that I'd written a hit song, so I had Dean and Gary roll me over on a luggage cart. I rolled in looking like God knows what, and shouted, "Hey, guys, I wrote this song!"

I'd heard that Hank Williams Jr. was in town, so we demoed the song, tracked him down at a local club, and pitched it to him. He liked it and said he was going to record it as soon as he could. I thought, "Damn, this is easy." The next thing we knew, Hank called up and said he'd changed some words, and if we wanted him to cut the song, we'd have to give him part of the writer's credit. I started bitching about it to my dad later that week, saying I wasn't going to let him do it. His reaction was, "Are you crazy? A Hank Williams Jr. cut is the big time. And he's just doing business. That's why people like him have money."

Hank got his writer's credit, and he cut the song with guest vocals by Waylon and Ernest Tubb. I couldn't believe that I'd not only written a song but Hank, Waylon, and Ernest had recorded it! I followed that song up the charts as intensely as I'd followed "Bartender Blues," the song I'd pitched to George Jones back in 1977. This time I also had a financial interest. It made it up to number six in *Billboard*, but because we had so many writers, none of us got rich.

I continued to get caught up in Nashville distractions. One night David Malloy and I were in the studio and I got a phone call.

When I answered, a man said, "Hey, Tanya, I'm in town and wanted to get together and play some songs," this guy said. "I can't sing, but I can hum."

"Man," I thought. "Who is this weirdo and how'd he get this number?"

Then he started laughing. "This is Jim Garner, and I'm out at Ed Bruce's house listening to some fairly good songwriters. Why don't you come on out?" I love Jim Garner, and he likes me, even if Glen did think I wasn't ladylike enough around him. Jim was in town to help Ed and Patsy Bruce make their escape from "Hollyweird," where they'd lived while Ed co-starred in the remakes of *Maverick*. When the show finally wrapped, and the Bruces could return to their home in Fernville, Tennessee, they were two happy country music folks. That night they even tied a big yellow ribbon around an old oak tree in their front yard and a sign that read "The Fernville Frolic-Off."

I wrapped up my last vocal and called Dean Dillon, who ran right over with a six-pack and a guitar. When we got to the Bruces' house, I had to laugh because those "fairly good" writers were the best in the business: Sonny Throckmorton, Red Lane, Dave Kirby, Whitey Shafer, and the dean of them all, Harlan Howard. I'd met most of these writers in passing during the first years of my career. But this was the first time I'd had a chance to really spend time listening to them talk about their craft. Jim had always been a country music fan, and he got involved with writers over the years through playing golf at Willie Nelson and Darryl Royal's annual tournaments in Houston.

Every time someone played a song I'd say, "I want a hold on that! Don't you play it for anybody else." One of the best things about that night was that the writers took me seriously, too. They didn't treat me like a chick singer who didn't know her place if I had the nerve to say something about a song's lyric or melody. This was the part of the music business I most wanted to be a part of. The creativity flowing through that house energized me almost as much as being onstage.

Ed Bruce told a great story that night about receiving a phone call from Billy Sherrill late one night in 1973. "I'm cutting Tanya Tucker tomorrow, and I need one more song for the session," Billy said. "Have you got anything?"

"Sure," Ed told him. "I'll be at the studio before you are." But in fact, he didn't have a song that he thought was just right. So he sat down with his guitar, wrote all night, and by morning, he was at the studio with a guitar/vocal demo of "The Man That Turned My Mama On," which turned out to be the sixth hit of my career.

Dean was putting the big rush on me that night at the Bruces' party, but I was so excited about the songs being sung I didn't pay much attention to it. That night, at least, music had priority. When the gathering finally started breaking up, and Dean and I were getting ready to leave, Harlan Howard paid me a tremendous compliment when he said, "Tanya, I think you're a writer trapped in a singer's body."

A funny thing happened that night, and I thought it was proof positive that "Hollyweird" can affect anybody. A lot of songwriters are notoriously unbusinesslike. But anybody who knows Patsy Bruce knows that while she and Ed were married, she was the business head of the household, and she did a hell of a job, too. She is also a very straight-arrow kind of lady. That night, Jim Garner needed to talk in private about a business deal that he and Ed had going, so Jim and Patsy went into the master bedroom. Well, Patsy only had one chair in there, and a huge bed, so the two of them just stretched out across it and started talking. All of a sudden Jim says, "Patsy, you aren't going to believe this, but look out your sliding doors."

People in Fernville had found out James Garner was coming to stay at the Bruces' house, and there, peering through the glass doors, were two little old ladies with their mouths dropped wide open. Jim and Patsy came out of the room laughing, and Patsy said, "Hollyweird followed us back here and it's ruined my reputation in one day!" I thought it was great to go to a party where somebody else got into trouble.

One afternoon Eddy Raven and his guitar player, Frank Myers, showed up at the studio and said they had a first verse and a chorus for my song idea. We arranged to meet at the Spence and finish "Changes." I think the thing that makes a song work is when you say something that you really mean, something that is your truth and somebody else's truth, too. The specific and the general. I wrote a line about a man rejecting the part of a woman's personality that makes her most proud. How many men have been attracted to a headstrong woman, admired her for it, and then despised that part of her in the long run? Unfortunately, too many times, women change themselves instead of changing to another man.

I wish I'd continued to write like I did during those months with both Eddy and Frank, and with Dean and Gary. I did work on songs from time to time during the next few years, but more often than not, I just went to clubs to hear established writers perform their material.

My recording of "Changes" was Frank Myers's first cut, and he got his second cut because of coming to the studio that day. While he was there talking to me, he handed David Malloy a tape for some sessions he was getting ready to do with Eddie Rabbitt and Crystal Gayle. The song turned out to be "You and I," a number-one country hit, and a top-ten pop hit. He's now one-half of the duo Baker & Myers and, with Gary Baker, wrote "I Swear," a song that was recorded by both John Michael Montgomery and All 4 One and took home almost every award the business has to offer. But he got his start with me, so I figure he ought to be writing another one of those blockbusters and sending it my way.

Despite the interruptions, we finally got *Changes* finished. It produced one top-ten hit, "Feels Right." "Changes," the song I'd written about Glen, only went to number forty-one in *Billboard*. But I still think it's a good album. Certainly not as technically advanced as the CDs we make today, but it holds up. Somehow all those styles—the rock-edged sound, the country, the torch—worked together. Unfortunately, the album didn't do well commercially. Arista wasn't set up to market and promote country product, and the competition for chart space was stiffer than ever. Barbara Mandrell, Dolly Parton, Crystal Gayle, the Gatlins, the Oaks, Willie Nelson, Waylon Jennings—all those people were superstars, and they were recording on powerful country labels where people knew exactly what wheels had to turn to keep an act on top. It would be several years before Clive hired Tim DuBois and Arista's country division got its machinery oiled.

I hadn't helped things. In fact, I put David Malloy through a lot of crap, and although it took me a few years to understand it, my going as public as I did with my partying through those months did me untold damage in Music Row's executive boardrooms.

THIRTY-EIGHT

*D*ean Dillon and Gary Stewart soon learned that having me for a friend ain't always a walk in the park or a roll down the alley. In the summer of 1982, after *Changes* was finished, they came to L.A. and invited me to go with them to New York for a show Gary was booked to do in a little club on the East Side. I was in the process of moving from my house on Linnington to a big four-bedroom home. The rent was three times what I'd been paying on Linnington. I don't know why I moved, because I loved that little house, and I still drive by to check it out when I'm in Los Angeles. Maybe I just wanted to feel like a big shot.

I must not have been too big a shot, because I couldn't find anyone in Los Angeles to help me unpack. I'd packed everything up, rented a truck, and loaded a lot of things myself. I hired people to load the refrigerator, the washer and dryer, and the heavy furniture. The men I hired drove the truck to the new house, but they had another job to go to, and I didn't have anyone to unload. So I loved it when Dean and Gary called and asked me to go to New York. I told them I'd go if they'd help me unload a couple of things. Dean Dillon and Gary Stewart are not muscle men by any means. But they came out to the new house, and after they got over the shock of seeing what I'd meant by "a couple of things," they unloaded the whole truck. Then we flew to New York.

For the show I got dressed up in a black-and-red corset-type top and tights, and we limoed over to the club. Gary, of course, did his usual killer performance, and by the time it was over our adrenaline was raging. We ran into a country music journalist named Patrick Carr at the show and took him back to the hotel with us. We were drinking tequila straight from the bottle at the show and we didn't slow down. I was dancing all over the room, and they were playing guitars and trying to write something. We were all just wrecked. We roared all night, and by around nine the next morning I got the idea I'd go visit the record label that wasn't promoting my record worth a damn. Since the three guys were all in as bad a shape as I was, they didn't try to talk me out of it. It wasn't what you would call a good career move. We got the limo back and went to Arista.

"I want to see Clive," I told the receptionist.

She was a very New York type, sophisticated and a little uppity. She looked at us like we were from outer space, which, of course, we were. On the other hand, you'd think that through the years a rock and roller or two might have shown up there drunk.

"And who are you?" she inquired.

"I'm one of your artists," I responded, getting ticked off.

From her expression, I knew she didn't have a clue as to my identity. And if my record label didn't know who I was, I was in trouble. Clive never did come out and say hello. He was either gone, or wisely hiding behind his executive doors. We cooled our heels in the reception area for ten or fifteen minutes and then left. That was the kind of dumb stunt you pull when you party all night.

On the way back to the limo, Patrick Carr said, "What's wrong with these people? Even if they don't know who their own recording artists are, haven't they seen you in the tabloids? Don't they buy groceries?"

Moving from Linnington into the four-bedroom house in Los Angeles was another dumb stunt, because it gave me a place to invite people to come and live with me. I have always been bad about dragging home strays, and it got to a crisis point in that house. One guy turned out to be a drug dealer. I didn't know he was a dealer when I said he could stay in one of my guest rooms. I thought he was just one more Hollywood rich kid on the outs with his parents. Then one day I needed something I thought I'd stored in the closet in his room, and I discovered a huge stash of cocaine. There wasn't any question about it then. I knew he was dealing and probably using my telephone to do it. So I helped myself to a little of his dope and kicked him out. Luckily, he went peacefully.

I should at least have been charging rent to him and all the other people who came and went through my doors, because I was running out of money fast supporting a lot of losers. I don't know why I did it, but my folks think they do. They tell this story about me, and even though I don't remember it, I'll take their word for it. They say when I was in the second or third grade I started coming home famished and raiding the icebox the second I hit the door. Finally my dad asked my mother and me what in the world was going on.

"Has she been taking a lunch, Juanita?"

Mom told him I'd wanted to buy lunch at school for the past several weeks.

"Well, then, they aren't giving her enough food," he said, ready to call the school and complain.

Finally they got the story out of me. I wanted to make a new friend at school, and I had been giving my lunch money to the girl.

"Why?" Dad asked.

"So she'll like me," I explained.

My parents say I still do that, give people things to make them like me. I prefer to think I do it because it makes them happy, but I'll be the first to admit that I've always wanted to please people. Show me an entertainer who doesn't.

My parents had given up their house in Los Angeles by then. Dad had traded Tuckahoe for a bigger ranch, which they named the Double T. They kept calling and asking me to come home, but I wouldn't even discuss it. The beginning of the end came when La Costa flew in to stay with me for a few days. When she saw the collection of weirdos and misfits who were living at my house she was afraid to sleep in the guest room, which had no lock. She made a pallet on the floor of the walk-in closet and curled up on the floor, hoping if some drugged-up man came in the room, he wouldn't find her. I never took any drugs in front of Costa, but she knew I was doing them. After several days of agonizing about my living situation, La Costa phoned Dad and told him about the people she'd seen and her suspicions about me. She was scared that if I stayed out there, I was going to wind up dead.

As it happened, I wound up nearly broke. I had a good friend, Diana Venegas, a clothing designer who had a little shop in Los Angeles. A girl who had been working at her shop had cancer, and she had been hospitalized for months. Diana was the only person the girl had to turn to as the hospital bills mounted up. Diana had the shop, but although she tried, she wasn't making enough profit to pay the girl's bills. One month, I had just received a check from an episode I did on *Fantasy Island*, and Diana told me that she didn't know if the hospital would keep her friend any longer unless she could pay something more on the bill. I endorsed the check over to her. I was behind on my rent, I had all sorts of unpaid bills, and I desperately needed that $7,500. It was like I was drowning and threw away the life preserver. I don't know what I was thinking, except that Diana's friend needed help, which at that moment, I could provide. And maybe I could book some quick gigs to bail myself out.

My dad was quicker than me. He knew I was supposed to be getting a check, and just a few days after it had arrived he phoned from Nashville and asked me if I had paid my rent. I had to admit I hadn't. Dad called and convinced me I needed to come to Nashville and sign some contracts. We probably crossed paths in the air, because while I was flying East, Dad was in a plane headed West. He rented a truck, got some of his friends together, packed up my stuff, and moved me out. Just as he was pulling the truck out of my driveway, the rental agents showed up with an eviction notice and locks for the doors. Dad hated the thought of more bad publicity, and if they went to the papers with the story, it was going to be one more nail in my career's coffin. He climbed down out of the truck and went over to talk to them. They didn't like it, but Dad convinced them that he'd make it right with them. Unlike that time when we got kicked out of that trailer in St. George, Utah, the agents believed he could do it, and they allowed him to leave. He'd have driven off no matter what they said. I know my dad.

It seems like my dad has found himself in situations where he had to rush in and scoop me up my whole life. I said earlier that I was a climber when I was a kid. One morning after we'd just moved to Willcox, Dad was having coffee at the kitchen table and staring out the window, when he spotted a small lump up on top of a fifty-foot drilling rig he'd bought to repair and sell. All of a sudden he shouted, "My God, Juanita! That's Tanya!" He ran out, hoping to get underneath me so that even if I fell before he could climb up to me, he could still make the catch. That time I climbed down before he could even get to the rig. When he moved me out of L.A. in 1983, I think he knew I wasn't going to be able to climb down on my own.

I was ready to say good-bye to Hollywood. There were too many temptations for a girl who liked to party, and it had never felt like home, anyway. Mother and Dad had plans to build a home at the Double T, but at the time they were staying in a two-story house they'd wanted to remodel for a caretaker. I piled as much of my stuff as I could into the second-floor bedroom. When I got settled in, I decided the thing the room needed was pink. Lots of pink. I painted the walls pink, bought an antique iron bedstead and painted it pink. I shopped for new rugs and curtains. I wanted my new world to be bright and cheery and pink and happy. I extended my new pink stage to the concert stage and put together a pink ensemble. I bought a hot-pink tank top, hot-pink earrings, a hot-pink bracelet—even hot-pink socks. I'd wear that with a little pair of gray shorts—I didn't want to go completely overboard—and a print bandana. I looked bright and pink and happy up on the stage belting out my songs.

But I was far from happy, and it showed. Between the parties and playing gigs, I was wearing down. I looked older than my years, and I was exhausted a lot of the time. Even the fans started worrying. One night in Fort Worth I was signing autographs after the show, and an old lady came up to me and took my arm. "You gotta start takin' care of yourself, child," she said. Nobody knew that better than me, but I wasn't taking the good advice.

One of the first things I did after I got back to Nashville was to make a trip to New York, where I planned on staying two days and wound up staying a month.

THIRTY-NINE

I received a call from Chris Atkins, who asked me to come to New York for a couple of days for the premiere of *The Pirate Movie*, a film he'd just done. I loved the idea of seeing him and, more important, having the opportunity to check out the action in New York. My parents just couldn't believe I was going, but they really couldn't do anything about it. I phoned a friend from the Mike Chapman days, Mark Fleishman, a co-owner of Studio 54, as well as of the Executive Hotel, and he offered me a free room. Well, that meant room service, so even though I didn't have much money, I knew I could get by. It's a funny thing, this celebrity business. Sometimes you get stuck with the check because everyone at the table figures you're rich. Other times you pick up perks every time you turn around. That New York trip was basically a perk.

I missed the premiere but got to town just in time for the parties. I couldn't have planned it better if I'd tried. I saw Chris briefly, then took off on my own to check out what was happening. The place to be was Cafe Central, an actors' hangout frequented by people like Robert Duvall, Danny Aiello, Joe Pesci, Christopher Walken, Robert de Niro, Liza Minnelli, Debbie Harry, and Andy Warhol. One person that I particularly remember from that scene was John Cassavetes. He was one of the most alive, intense men I'd ever seen. You'd watch him talking to people, and they were just mesmerized. He was totally in control of any conversation he was in. Danny Aiello and Joe Pesci were big laughers, big jokers, and didn't take anything but their craft very seriously. I liked the crowd a lot, and since the price of my hotel room was right, I decided to stick around.

I had the time of my life for about a month at Cafe Central. Andy Warhol would bring a little Polaroid and snap pictures of me, and I kept wondering when I might see myself up on the wall of a museum. I probably wouldn't have understood the answer even if I'd asked whether he was planning on painting me. He talked so softly that his words seemed to float through the air and disappear long before they got to your ears—what little I could make out. It might have been him, and it might have been the drugs we were all taking, but his conversation seemed a little airy, too. I loved looking at him, even if I missed most of what he said.

One night Danny Aiello told me he'd heard Robert Duvall was having a stag party at some Irish restaurant, and he thought we should go. We took a cab to a little place in a basement that looked kind of like a mob hangout, and the place was filled up with Cafe Central types. Robert Duvall was getting ready to film *Tender Mercies* and was obsessed with country music, especially Merle Haggard. I knew as much as anybody about the Hag, so even though I'd crashed the party, Duvall cornered me and asked questions all night.

"What about this idea?" he'd say, and talk about a song he'd like to do for the movie.

"How does this sound?" He'd sing a line or two.

This man was really trying to get into his country music character for the film. He wanted to be Merle Haggard. When everybody had partied out and the sun was coming up, the soon-to-be-wed Robert asked me to go home with him. I guessed he was really going the whole nine yards for the *Tender Mercies* role, but I told him I wasn't into being his prewedding one-night stand. He just shrugged it off. The two of us may not have ended up in bed, but I've sure sat in bed and watched his movies many nights. Robert is one of my all-time favorite actors, and *Tender Mercies* is one of my all-time favorite films. And not just because I helped him get into character.

I also met Andy Gibb, yet another man who started out as a

flame and ended up as a buddy at Cafe Central. He was handsome, but his eyes were particularly striking. They were so open, trusting, and friendly. We sat at the restaurant and talked until the wee hours of the morning, and then we went to his room at the St. Moritz and talked some more. Andy was one of the most fragile men I've ever met, very sad and hurting so much over his breakup with Victoria Principal. From what he said, she must be one cold human being. I don't think she even looked back when she walked, no matter how much pain he was in. We lay there on his bed for hours comparing breakups, and I had to admit that his sounded worse than mine. Andy was such a gentle, fragile soul. He was whipped. I tried to toughen him up, but didn't get very far.

"Hey, you gotta get over this and get on with it, Andy," I said. "You're too talented to let a woman get you down like this." Like I was in a position to be giving advice, since I was doing so well with my own love life.

He didn't respond to anything I said, just kept on about Victoria. Of course, he was so heavy into drugs right then that I don't think anything got through the haze. I regret that I scored him a gram of cocaine that night. If I'd known how serious his problem was, I wouldn't have done it. But then, if I'd known just how much physical and psychological damage cocaine can do to anyone, maybe I'd have wised up and cut myself off.

In addition to his pain over Victoria, Andy was crushed about having been dropped from the Bee Gees. I could understand why they couldn't trust him, though; he was doing a ton of drugs and was just too unreliable. Andy and I ran around town off and on for several weeks, made the tabloids, and even though our conversations mainly consisted of our ex-loves, everyone thought we were having a big romance. We had a little romance, and it turned to friendship quickly. That's par for me.

Andy Gibb and I talked on the phone once in a while after I finally tired of the scene in New York and came back to Nashville. The last time I talked to him was just a few months before his heart gave out on March 10, 1988. The long years of drug use had taken their toll. Ironically, I was in drug and alcohol rehab at the Betty Ford Clinic when I learned the news.

FORTY

I was a grown woman before I realized that one of the things I'd missed out on by being a child star was the opportunity to develop close, long-term female friendships. I always felt like an adult, I was around adults much more than children, and my dreams were adult dreams about a career. Through my teens I was on the road, surrounded by my family and band members, and then it seemed like the minute I got to be a grown-up woman in my early twenties, my world was dominated by the fast party life I found in Los Angeles, and Glen Campbell. I never seemed to meet anybody normal.

I felt the void clearly once, when I traveled back to Little Rock to go to a Barry Manilow concert. I left Nashville a day early, and all the way to Little Rock, I kept thinking of Jan Carter's fried chicken. It seemed to stand for that whole time when things seemed simple, when the Tuckers and the Carters were one big extended family. I stopped at a pay phone on the outskirts of town and called Jan.

"I'd like one order of fried chicken," I said. "That'll be to eat in, not to go."

Jan was shocked to get a chicken order from out of the blue. Then she figured it out. "Tanya! Is that you?"

"It's me, and I'm on my way to your house."

"Then I'm on my way to the kitchen," she laughed.

By the time I got there the chicken was sizzling in a pan. Both the Carter daughters, Joanna and Julia, were there. Joanna was in high school and Julia was home from college with a group of her sorority sisters. After we ate chicken, Julia and her friends took me along with them to a local honky-tonk. I sat at the bar nursing a drink and watched these girls sharing laughs and inside jokes. They were looking forward to the next week's college dance, talking about their current boyfriends, discussing whose heart was broken and whose was on the mend. Tears came to my eyes. Julia sat down beside me and asked me what was wrong.

"Nothing," I reassured her. "I just wish I had some sorority sisters."

I don't know if that episode was the reason, but around that time I started finding some friends who have lasted a lifetime. I didn't specifically set out to gather this group of friends around me. Maybe for the first time, I just had the opportunity to find them, or for them to find me.

Actually, I'd met Barb Shipley back in 1977, when I flew to Steamboat to meet my rodeo guy, Bobby Brown. I used to visit her in Steamboat, and we'd get up early and cook scrambled eggs, watch television, maybe hit the slopes in the afternoon. When I first met Shirley Porter at a party at songwriter Hank Cochran's house in 1983, she was married to songwriter Royce Porter. T. Martin is married to songwriter Glen Martin, and she works in his publishing business. Tracy Johnson was a single girl from Minneapolis, just out to have a good time when I met her in 1984. She's married now but she still loves a good time. We all got along well and started calling ourselves the T-Birds, since so many of us have names that start with "T."

For the T-Birds, a good time doesn't necessarily mean a wild time. We usually hook up out on the road when I'm playing shows. Sometimes it's just a few of the girls, and other times we can all make it to the gatherings. What we like to do is check into a big suite at a hotel, shop or swim in the hotel pool during the day, and spend our evenings having a few drinks in the clubs or at the hotel having a pajama party.

I think I like the pajama parties best. One of my favorite things to do is to sit around and watch television and talk with the T-Birds. We're just like a bunch of junior high girls. We gossip, talk about guys, and try on each other's clothes and makeup. I can't stay out of other women's makeup bags. They'll be putting some kind of cream on their face and I'll say, "What's that for?" Then I'll end up trying it out, along with their eye shadows or blush.

The T-Birds are happy women, with normal lives, and I cling to those kinds of people. I know it's unrealistic, but I always imagine what it would be like to have a "normal" life. One where things are organized and people don't pull you in all kinds of directions. Sometimes I feel like I have so many things going on that I might explode in a million pieces. I'm sure they all feel like that at times, too. But for me, the pulling comes from so many places. But I don't feel that way at a p.j. party with the T-Birds. They couldn't care less about my being a celebrity, either. If I couldn't sing a note tomorrow they'd still be my friends.

For the most part, their husbands seem to understand this female bonding we need. Tracy's husband, Jim, gets a kick out of us. And when we are out running around, he just trails along with an amused look on his face. I played a concert in Minneapolis, and Tracy, her husband, Jim, and a friend of his came. After the show we got on the bus, and I was trying to think what we should do next, whether we should go to this or that club, or go to a late dinner. It's always that way after a show. Me trying to think what to do next. This was very confusing to Tracy's husband's friend, and he asked Jim what he should do. Jim laughed and said, "When you're with Tanya, you've just got to hang on." That's how it's sometimes felt to me, too.

FORTY-ONE

*J*ournalists have often referred to the three years from 1982, when I made *Changes* for Arista, to 1985, when I signed with Capitol, as my "downtime." But even though I didn't have a recording contract, I never felt like I left the music, and the music never left me. I was playing shows. I went to music events like I always had. I was living out at the ranch with my parents, hanging out around Nashville, and in general, having a hell of a time. When I wasn't on the road, my routine was to sleep in as long I could up in my second-floor room at the Double T, then go out and saddle up one of the horses and take a ride, or maybe read the *National Enquirer* to see what I was up to, until I got bored. Then I'd head for town and see what was happening on Music Row. There were lots of clubs where songwriters and musicians hung out, and one of my usual haunts was the Third Coast. Its nickname was the Rock & Roll Hotel, because the place had rooms to rent, and when rock musicians came to town, many of them stayed there. Some stayed at my old stomping grounds, the Spence Manor, but the Spence doesn't have a bar and that was sometimes an inconvenience. Staying at the Rock & Roll Hotel meant you could party all night, then crawl up to your room and crash. It saved on hassle and DUI arrests.

Many of us were drinking too much during those days, but not all of the nightlife involved getting crazed. Just hanging around the bars with songwriters can be great, and I had a lot of those times. I still do, as a matter of fact. Unlike Hollywood, where everyone is posing and imaging when they go out to clubs, Nashville's night places are filled with writers and singers and industry people who mostly just want to have a good time. I suppose there's some posing, but it's not the norm. I had a lot of fun during that time.

As I mentioned earlier, being an entertertainer sometimes means people will pick up your tab, and other times it means you get stuck with it. One night at the Third Coast, I was sitting with a girlfriend talking and having some drinks. It seemed like every writer and musician in town stopped by the table. They'd order drinks and appetizers, talk a while, maybe pitch me a song. Then they'd head on down the road. I never thought much about who was paying what. I guess I thought they were paying their tabs on their way out. After about four hours and fifty guitar pickers, the crowd dwindled down to just me and my girlfriend. When my friend got up to go to the bathroom, the waitress thought she was getting ready to leave the bar. She flagged her down and started adding up a huge pile of tickets. My friend looked down at them and about fainted. Nobody had paid for anything. When she came back to our table, she was shaking her head.

"I guess you know those guys stuck you with their bar bills," she said. "I bet that bill is three hundred bucks."

About that time Harlan Howard came in. Harlan has this great mane of white hair and would have been perfect for the role of God in the movie, if George Burns hadn't grabbed it. He is one of my favorite people to be around anyway, because he loves to laugh and have a good time. He's also one of the few of the old-time songwriters who is still writing as many hits as ever. That makes him not only one of the most talented guys in the business but one of the richest. Harlan sat down and ordered a drink.

He sat there awhile doodling on a napkin. Then he said, "You know how to pitch a song to a producer, don't you?"

I knew something good was coming.

"You find the song in your catalog that's the very best one for that producer's artist, and you put it on a tape. Then you find two or three other ones that would work, but they're not perfect, like the first one. You put those on a different tape. Then you make your appointment and go in and play him the two or three that would work. He might hear something or not, but he'll probably keep the tape. Then you thank him for his time, and start to leave. When you are just about through the door, you pause and say, 'Oh, by the way, here's something I just wrote, maybe you could tell me what you think of it.' Then lay it on him. He'll shake his head and say, 'I can't believe you didn't play me this in the first place. I got to have this one.'"

I can just picture Harlan doing that, too. He's not only one of the best writers to ever pick up a pen and a guitar, he's one of the slickest.

He kept on sipping his drink and doodling on his napkin.

"You got a song idea, Harlan?"

"Not yet," he said. "But before the night's over, I will."

He thought that over a minute, then turned to me and said, "Tanya, you know what a songwriter's life is, don't you?"

I had to admit I didn't.

"It's just one big bar napkin."

He finished his drink and asked the waitress for his bill, and mine as well.

I tried to protest and explain about my bill, but Harlan wasn't having it. He insisted he was paying and that was all there was to it.

So I winked at my friend and waited for him to hand it straight back to me when he saw the amount. But when Harlan saw it was over $400 he didn't flinch. He just handed her a credit card, and said, "Had a couple of drinks tonight, haven't you?"

I laughed and said, "One or two."

My drinking was only one of several painful subjects that I joked about. I still didn't have the whole Glen breakup in any better perspective, but I was trying to cover up the hurt and appear Tucker tough in public. I started making jokes about it all during some of my shows. I'd sing "Changes," with every bit of pain the song deserves, then when the applause died down, I'd say, "Yeah, I'm missing some front teeth from a little ruckus we had a while back. But you should see *his* face."

It seemed like when I wasn't joking about my old problems, I was stirring up new ones. When I first got back to Nashville I was still running around with Dean Dillon. Our romance had heated up after that night when I ignored his rush at Ed Bruce's house. Once I moved back, Dean and I started blazing a trail all over Nashville. We went public with both the relationship and the lifestyle. We were doing drugs and a lot of people in town knew it. Everybody, it seemed, except one of the tabloids, who printed a story about clean-living Dean saving me from my bad habits. They called him a good old Tennessee country boy and said I was looking for my roots in him. More likely both of us were looking for toot. But Dean and I didn't last. Dean was looking—or thought he was looking—for a permanent partner, and I wasn't.

One person I met while I was out rocking around town back then not only became one of my lifelong friends but also played a major role in my return to the radio airwaves by writing some of my biggest hits. When Paul Davis moved to Nashville from Atlanta, he already was a pretty successful pop music singer/songwriter with top-ten hits like "I Go Crazy" and "'65 Love Affair." He told me he decided to move here because of the familylike feel that existed among the country songwriters. One of his first successes in Nashville was "Meet Me in Montana," which was a huge hit for Dan Seals and Marie Osmond. Paul's one of those nonjudgmental people who doesn't have an unkind bone in his body. He's a tall, gentle man with a Mississippi drawl, and he's full of humor and wisdom. I loved being around Paul because even though he likes to party and have a good time, he has a calming influence on people, and I could use one every so often.

I lived at the Double T for eight or nine months, then bought a small, rustic two-bedroom home near Hickory Hollow Mall in Antioch, a suburb of Nashville, from songwriter Hank Cochran and his wife, Suzy. I called it the Song House, because Hank wrote a lot of hits there. It was always a great gathering place. There's a big stone fireplace and the inside is paneled with barn wood.

I decided to buy the Song House at the Cochrans' 1983 Super Bowl party. Suzy showed me through the house, and as I went from room to room I fell more and more in love with it. I liked everything from the rugs to the kitchen table. Hank came up to me later and mentioned he'd been thinking about selling the house. I told him I'd not only buy the house but everything in it as well. "Pack up your underwear and your song awards, Hank," I said. "I can move in next week!" It happened almost that fast, too. Hank and Suzy moved out, and I moved in within the month.

I met Shirley Porter at that Super Bowl party. I didn't have a date for the party, and Shirley's husband, Royce, was out of town, so she and I were both on our own that day. The place was full of writers and musicians—sports fans—and Shirley seemed so stable among all the crazies and rowdies. We spent the Super Bowl getting to know each other, talking about everything from music to men to her job as a hair stylist. We were all drinking a lot, and the more I drank the more I wanted Shirley to cut my hair. I'd been wearing my hair long and had been thinking about doing something different with it, anyway. I kept badgering Shirley about it, until she finally said all right. We grabbed a pair of Suzy Cochran's scissors, and in the midst of this raging Super Bowl party, Shirley went to work on me. Four different times I went to the bathroom and checked the length, and four times I came back and told her to cut some more.

"Tanya, you're gonna hate me tomorrow," Shirley said, after the final cut. My hair was about two inches long.

"Nah, keep on cuttin', Squirrely Bird," I urged with confidence.

The next morning, I crawled out of bed and took a look at myself in the mirror and almost died when I saw what I'd made Shirley do. I knew she was probably wondering what my reaction was going to be, so I called her up.

"I do hate you for the haircut," I said. "But I love you as a friend, Squirrely Bird." That was thirteen years ago, and we've stayed friends through a lot of good and bad times. I've seen her through her divorce from Royce and a move to Dallas, where she now lives. She's seen me through men and babies, as well as through personal and career highs and lows. I've been there for her, too, and I like to think I gave her some good advice on occasion. After her divorce and her move to Texas, she called me and said she had met a man and was going to marry him. "Well, do one thing for me Squirrely Bird. Wait one year just to make sure." After a year she was sure. They're now very happily married. But I think that year was important, because by the time it was over there were no questions in her mind.

I regretted getting my hair cut so short at that party, but I never once regretted buying Hank Cochran's house. I wanted to make the Song House into a place where writers and musicians still came around and wrote. I couldn't seem to soak up enough of that creativity. One of my first guests was Paul Davis. I'd lure Paul out to the house and make him enchiladas and tacos and

FORTY-TWO

I was ready for Nashville by 1985, but some of Nashville wasn't ready for me. Many people on Music Row thought I'd lost my fan base because of all the bad publicity about Glen Campbell, and I'd never be able to get them back. Between me rocking around in bars right on Music Row and the experience with Arista, a lot of people in Nashville figured I was through. It's amazing to hear that you're a has-been at the age of twenty-four, but that was the buzz on the street. I shrugged it off. I figured I'd rather be a has-been at twenty-four than forty-four. I had a better shot at coming back.

Dad was more afraid about my career than I was. I should have seen that I had some fences to mend and something to prove, especially when my dad couldn't seem to get anyone to believe I could, and more important, would, still make hits.

One reason I didn't take being without a record label more seriously was that I was back out on the road so heavily. I didn't tour much for a couple of years after Glen, but between 1983 and 1985, when I signed with Capitol, I was back out on the road a lot. It was crucial that I start bringing in money. We'd gone several years with very little coming in, and we were starting to feel a financial crunch.

Promoters usually shy away from booking artists with no new product on the airwaves, so in some ways I was lucky that the tabloids had kept my name out there. My name still sold tickets, even though it didn't command the big prices I'd gone for in 1980. I went from $25,000 a show down to $10,000 or $15,000. That sounds like a lot of money until you start taking away things it has to pay for, like percentages for the booking agency, bus rental, band and crew salaries, and the daily expenses of the road; the money dwindles quickly.

Once again, my dad hit the streets to tell producers and label heads about his daughter. Unfortunately, the ones he spoke with thought they knew everything they needed to know about Tanya Tucker. Even Billy Sherrill passed. Completely frustrated with trying to find me a recording home, Dad phoned Jerry Crutchfield and set up a meeting. Jerry had always treated my dad with complete respect. The two liked and trusted each other, so they were completely honest and up-front about the hole they believed I'd dug for myself. Dad told Jerry he was afraid I'd lost all my credibility on Music Row, and that label heads wouldn't even talk to him about me. Jerry said he didn't have any doubts at all that we could make hit records again, and he believed, as I did, that my fans hadn't turned their backs on me. But he knew getting me a record deal wasn't going to be easy, and he and Dad even talked about starting their own label if worse came to worst.

The first place Jerry went was PolyGram, and while they did agree to let him cut a record on me, they offered only about half of what he needed as a recording budget. So he went to see Jim Fogelsong, who headed Capitol in Nashville.

Jerry didn't tell him who he was pitching at first. He sat down and said he had a young woman who was one of the most exciting acts he'd ever seen, that she had the talent to make hit records and to make the label proud, not to mention a lot of money. Jim raised his eyebrows and said, "Well, this young lady must be something. What's her name?"

"Tanya Tucker," Jerry said.

Jim didn't jump for joy. He'd heard about my lifestyle, and he'd been told that I was unreliable. Jim said he'd think about it, and the two men spoke on the phone at various times over a period of several weeks. One day Jim seemed like he was ready to sign me and the next day not.

My dad kept trying to find out what was going on, and

the news that Jim was waffling scared him. But Jerry had a plan.

"Now, Beau, don't let this get you down yet," said Jerry, in that slow, laid-back way he has. "Jim's going to Los Angeles tomorrow, and I've bought a ticket, too. He won't be able to get away from me, and I'll have six hours to change his mind."

Once the two got settled on the plane, Jerry started his sales pitch. He told Jim that he didn't see why artists should fit into stereotypical molds, and that my having a wilder image than most of the women in the business didn't affect my ability to make good records. And for my misbehaving, he explained I was a lot like a colt, just a little too frisky at times. That killed me. Pretty damn frisky is more like it. He reminded Jim that I was still younger than many of the new female acts, and that I had a very contemporary sound.

"She's a blue chipper," Jerry finished.

"I believe you're right," Jim said. "You go make a hit record."

At the time, I was playing a three-week gig with Ray Stevens at the Desert Inn in Vegas. I was happy about the news, but not relieved, like my dad. I figured there was a deal floating around out there somewhere. When I got back, I met with Jim and signed the contract. Such as it was. I signed a one-album contract, with not a penny of up-front money. Dad was thrilled to get that.

Now it was up to Crutch and me to make the record that could put me back on the charts. I still wasn't scared, though. Only after we had the first hit on Capitol did I realize how close I'd come to blowing it.

The other thing I wasn't ready to do was settle down. My poor dad. He'd spent the first half of my career trying to keep management under control, and now he was going to have to try to do the same with me.

He gave me one of his heart-to-heart lectures after I got the deal with Capitol. He told me about the record labels and producers who wouldn't even take his calls. He told me about Billy Sherrill turning me down. He told me Capitol Records was my last shot, and if I blew it, everything we had could be gone. "You know, Tanya, the only way a star can stand still and stay a star is if they're rich," he told me. "Eddy Arnold will always be a superstar whether he has an album out or not, because he's rich. You aren't rich, and you've been standing still so long those record people are trying to bury you." I promised him nobody was going to bury me.

The first thing I told Jerry was that I wanted to play a major role in song selection. I'd said that before to producers, but this time I felt like I had a better handle on the material Nashville had to offer. I told him I'd spent the past couple of years hanging out with writers, going to songwriters' nights, and I really wanted to play a role in what we recorded. After I wrote and recorded "Changes," I knew what it felt like to sing my own song. I wanted to find songs that sounded so much like me that I would have written them if I'd had the chance. I wanted to look for songs where people would know more about me after they'd listened to them than they knew before.

"I want you to take responsibility, Tanya," he said. "Your input is crucial if we are going to make the kind of album we need to bring you back."

"Well, then," I smiled. "Let's go out there and find them."

I love Jerry Crutchfield, because he listens to me and respects my opinion. As I had learned, many producers have their own agenda and don't pay much attention to what the artist wants. But Jerry listened, and the first two songs I brought him ended up on the album. "Just Another Love" was written by Paul Davis, and "One Love at a Time" by Paul Davis and Paul Overstreet.

We missed a couple of songs during those sessions. We didn't cut that Paul Overstreet song I loved, "I Won't Take Less Than Your Love," and there was a Paul Davis song that Jerry and I both sang around the studio, and even at dinner during breaks, "Love Me Like You Used To." It is so odd that we waited to record both of those songs on the second album. When we finished recording *Girls Like Me*, we looked at each other and said, "Now why didn't we cut 'Love Me Like You Used To' and 'I Won't Take Less Than Your Love'?" "Next time," Jerry said.

Jerry and I were full of confidence when we started work on *Girls Like Me*. When I say we were confident we'd succeed, I don't mean arrogant, nor do I mean I never have any self-doubts. I've had plenty of them, and more so as an adult than when I was a child. When I was fourteen or fifteen years old, I was fearless. I never paid any attention to how I was singing a song. I just did it. As I got older, there were times I thought, "God! I don't know how anybody could think I could sing." I knew I could sing okay, but sometimes I felt like I wasn't special or different. So then I'd have to say to myself, "Well, what can you do to make yourself believe you're special? What kind of a song can you do?" That's why, when I look for songs now, I try to find ones that are great enough to push any self-doubts I have aside.

One of the songs Jerry brought to the table was "Girls Like Me." The song is about women who keep looking for but never finding the right man. Despite the fact that I ran around Nashville with an ever changing entourage of pals, I wasn't really dating anyone special. That permanent relationship I wanted always seemed just out of reach. It's like Tracy Johnson's husband, Jim, said: If you're around me, you've just got to hang on, and not very many men seem to want to do that for the long haul. But that didn't stop me from wanting to find the man of my dreams, and I related to the song so much that we titled the album *Girls Like Me*.

Another song that fit the bill was titled, "I'll Come Back As Another Woman." There again, the song said a lot about me. Even though the song is about a woman who plans to come back around and break her ex-lover's heart, it also fit my career situation, since I was hoping to come back to the charts after a three-year hiatus. There's another, deeper, level, though. I've always felt I was several people traveling around in one body. All these different "Tanyas" make it difficult for people to stick with me, since my moods change a lot. I'll be up and down and all around within a matter of hours. I remember once when I was on tour in Europe a few years ago, and Jerry Lee Lewis happened to be staying at the same hotel. I'd done my show and was about ready to go to bed when he called and wanted to come to my room. I thought, "Oh, man, I've got to sleep." But Jerry Lee is pretty hard to say no to, so I said, "Well, come on." I lay there on the bed half the night listening to him talk everything from music to his cousin, Jimmy Swaggart, whom he said wasn't quite the religious icon he seemed. That comment almost put an end to the whole conversation, because that was before Jimmy's bad press, and I wouldn't listen to any hurtful talk about him. Jerry Lee paced around with all that excess energy, energy he couldn't seem to focus anywhere but onstage. He had so many personality types going at once that it flat wore me out, and then I got to thinking that I must wear people out some, too. They could have titled that song "I'll Come Back As Several Different Women."

The label released the first single, "One Love at a Time," in February of 1986, and it moved up the charts as if I'd never been gone from the airwaves. I don't believe the deejays cared one way or another where I'd been for three years. Of course, I had the complete support of my record label, which was something I'd been without for several years. The second single from *Girls Like Me*, "Just Another Love," was released in July, and it became my first number-one record since "Here's Some Love" in 1976. We had two more hits from *Girls Like Me*, "I'll Come Back As Another Woman" and "It's Only Over for You." It was after "Just Another Love" took off that I really understood how close I'd come to blowing my career. It took a hit to remind me what I'd nearly lost.

It's amazing what a big record will do. All of a sudden the label was flooded with requests for interviews, television appearances, and signed albums to give away at benefits. Booking offers doubled and then tripled. And I was out on the road with a five-piece band and a vengeance to promote the record. After a couple of hits, I was back up earning in the $25,000 range. It's possible that being away from recording those couple of years was the best thing that could have happened. I'd taken a short vacation from the studio, and I was ready to come back in and kick some butt.

Things were going great for me, and some news from Tovar added to the excitement of the time. He'd moved from Jon Peters's salon to working for Jose Eber, and he had finally put together the backing to open his own salon. "Tovar's" was under construction on Wilshire Boulevard in Beverly Hills. His clientele was expanding to include film stars like Barbara Carrera, Heather Locklear, Tina Turner, and Erin Gray. I put the word out in the country music industry, and soon he'd added Dolly Parton and Emmylou Harris to his client list. I was as proud of Tovar's as if it were my own, since we'd talked about his dream of owning his own salon ever since we'd met.

I didn't have much time to bask in the glory of this so-called comeback. That summer, in between show dates, we were already looking for songs for the follow-up album. I knew that to show everybody we meant business, they had to be as strong as, if not stronger than, the ones on *Girls Like Me*. Jerry and I already knew two songs we wanted to do: "I Won't Take Less Than Your Love" and "Love Me Like You Used To." Paul Davis's "Love Me Like You Used To," the song Jerry and I had sung around the studio during the *Girls Like Me* sessions, became the title cut and the first single.

"I Won't Take Less Than Your Love" is about unconditional love, and it has three distinct situations in the verses. The first verse is about the love between a husband and his wife, the second about a mother and son, and the third is about the Lord's love for us. We decided the song called for a trio and that we should ask Paul Overstreet and Paul Davis to sing on the record. Paul Overstreet was a natural, since he'd written the song, and I wanted Paul Davis because I love his voice.

"What verse do you want?" Jerry asked.

There wasn't any question about it. I wanted the verse about the mother and the son. Even though the first verse doesn't specify what the husband's occupation is, the scene I pictured was that of a farmer and his wife working side by side. I knew that Paul Davis had always wanted to be a farmer.

"How about the one about the husband and his wife for Paul Davis, and since Paul Overstreet is so spiritual, he can sing the one about the Lord."

Once again, we found a song that suited me perfectly, "If It Don't Come Easy." I like things to come easy, even though I've made them difficult for myself many times, like I did during those crazy months when I'd recorded *Changes*. *Love Me Like You Used To* had one thing in common with that album. It seemed like it took forever to record. This time, however, it was my tour that got in the way. I'd come in from the road and cut a couple of sides, then hop on the bus and head out again. Sometimes the bus was pulled up at the studio door, waiting for me to finish recording so we could take off on the next gig. The first single, "Love Me Like You Used To," was released in July, and within a couple of weeks we knew we had another hit. Even though we were happy with the results, and the album turned out to be one of my best efforts to date, I decided to do something different when I recorded the next album. I wasn't sure what, but I knew I wanted to record in peace, instead of piecemeal.

One way I hoped to make my life more peaceful was to cut

back on club work in 1987 and do mostly the fair circuit. I love playing fairs, even the little county fairs, because they are family-oriented events. If I walk into a club I immediately want to party, and that's just what I had been doing. What's more, I brought the lifestyle home with me when I'd get back from a road trip. I'd come in off the road and be so tired I was about to die, and so I'd sleep for a day or so, then hit the streets looking for a good time.

I'd try the Third Coast or the Tavern on the Row to see what was going on. Sometimes I'd run into the party crowd and sometimes not. I still wasn't really dating anyone. So my social life in Nashville centered around clubs where I could hang out with writers and sometimes listen to them showcase their songs. A lot of those times were just simple get-down, drinkin' guitar pulls. But there was also the underside of the Nashville nightlife. That involved cocaine, which was still everywhere in the late 1980s. You'd be out drinking, and a guy would hand you a tape over the table and a hit of cocaine under it. A lot of us were doing it. I'd be hard-pressed to say who wasn't. But I was one of them, and that fact did not escape my dad, who kept hearing horror stories about my party life both out on the road and in town.

A lot of the things I did during that time were just other examples of me trying to shock somebody, just an updated version of smearing my body with blood and pretending the family Doberman had attacked me. One night not long after *Girls Like Me* was released, I went to the Third Coast, got coked up, and pulled my shirt up over my head just for the hell of it. I didn't have a bra on, so that story hit the Row fast. I can't deny that I'm an exhibitionist at heart.

Another night when Barb Shipley was in town, we went to dinner at Faison's, a trendy little restaurant close to Music Row, and I was doing my usual, drinking and cutting up and laughing real loud. I got pretty drunk. When we left, I saw a cop standing there, and because I was feeling fresh, I turned around, stuck my rear in the air, and flipped my skirt up at him. He laughed and we left. I didn't think anything about it at the time.

I knew I was partying too much. I talked about quitting everything from smoking on up to booze and drugs. But I didn't do it. And by August of 1987, my dad was so worried about my lifestyle he was taking steps to clean it up. Even though he lectured me every chance he got, I had no hint he was thinking about sending me away for help.

But I did know we'd somehow lost touch with each other. Maybe it was the fact that he was so worried about me, but I'd felt a distance growing between us, and I felt like I wanted to address it with him. For me, beginning that kind of conversation is the hardest thing in the world, so I did it in song. As I said, Dad has been a big Jimmie Rodgers fan ever since I can remember, so when I was approached about doing one of Jimmie's songs for an album titled *The Superstars Salute Jimmie Rodgers*, I immediately accepted. Because I felt I had some things I wanted to tell Dad, I chose a song called "Daddy and Home," which talks about a father who is also a best friend.

Dad appreciated the sentiment of the song, and I believe it probably strengthened his resolve to straighten me up. The only way he could see to bring me home was to force the issue. But that year was so busy, I probably wouldn't have recognized a Mack truck heading right at me, which was kind of what was going on. I played over 175 dates in 1987, a lot of them in clubs, and sandwiched in between them, I was doing other work.

I spent six months planning the Twenty-Fifth Anniversary Celebration in Steamboat Springs, Colorado. It seemed like I was always showing up for other people's ski races or golf tournaments, and I'd wanted to host a celebrity event for a long time. So when I learned that Steamboat would be celebrating its Twenty-Fifth Anniversary in '88, I decided that would be the perfect time and place. I'd been coming to Steamboat since 1977, when I flew in with Bobby Brown for the Cowboy Downhill Ski Race, and I loved the town. Steamboat is not a show business–type place like Aspen, even though celebrities do come there. It has a feel of the Old West, which made it a natural place for me to hang out. Barb Shipley lived there, and I had other friends as well, including Billy Kidd, the world-class ski racer who is now the director of skiing in Steamboat. Billy agreed to co-host the Twenty-Fifth Anniversary Celebration, and during the summer of '87 we started planning the event.

One thing I wanted at the Twenty-Fifth Anniversary was a songwriters' show, since so few people outside the music business ever have the opportunity to hear these great talents do their own music. I invited a group of my favorites, Paul Overstreet, Paul Davis, Dean Dillon, Royce Porter, Glen Martin, and Red Steagall, and they all accepted. I could picture a big finale to the writers' show, where I came up and joined the two Pauls on "I Won't Take Less Than Your Love." I also invited a lot of celebrities, stars such as Hank Jr., Kathy Mattea, Lacy J. Dalton, Lorrie Morgan, and Keith Whitley.

I started carrying a notebook around and frantically jotting down ideas. I've always been that way, wanting to make things happen. The closets in my bus, and at my house, are full of notebooks with lists of things I wanted to try. But so many of the things that crossed my mind never became realities, because they would have taken time, money, and somebody to carry through on the details. I had none of those things. I was on the road, and my dad was trying to keep my career going. So the ideas just flew on out the bus window. In the months between my signing with Capitol and starting this new phase of my career, I had even more ideas. The more I had on my plate, the more I seemed to want to stack. Part of that was because of the time I spent out on the road, rolling across America promoting the record. I'd be too excited to sleep right away after a show, and when the bus pulled out, I'd start thinking about new businesses I could start. A lot of my ideas during that time were good ones, too. I wanted to start a publishing company. I'd been wanting to do that ever since I'd listened to Al Gallico and Billy Sherrill talk about the money there was to be made in song publishing. My dad was dead set against it. My parties always seemed to involve writers, so he didn't want me having any more contact with them than was absolutely necessary.

Another idea I got after eating one too many lousy road meals was a chain of Tanya Tucker Truck Stops, where people could count on quality meals. I even envisioned becoming a real estate developer. The idea of the Tucker Building on Music Row sounded pretty good.

I never did get any of those ideas off the ground, but a lot of my developer energy went into the ski event. That August, I flew to New York to hold a press conference about the Twenty-Fifth Anniversary, and I played a show at the Lone Star to help generate some publicity. Then, American Airlines, which was sponsoring the Hall of Fame Race at Steamboat, asked me to come to Dallas during the week of October 9 to meet with their executives and work out the details for the Hall of Fame Race. The timing could not have been more perfect, because an old friend had approached me about helping him launch his new Dallas nightclub during that same week. Tommy Allsup had been a buddy since he played guitar on my first sessions, and

I wanted to help him if I could. The tenth of October is my birthday, so Mother and Dad came along.

On the afternoon of the tenth, we met with the airlines people at American's headquarters in Dallas, and I brought in a demo of a jingle I'd written, hoping they'd use it for the promotion spots. They were all very businesslike and polite, and when I left the meeting I had high hopes that my jingle was going to be used. Then, driving back from the meeting, I saw the car of my dreams in a Dallas car lot: a Mercedes-Benz 560 SEC. We stopped and looked at it, then went to Tommy's club. A group of the T-Birds were there for my birthday. When I came out for the second performance, five hundred fans stood and applauded and sang "Happy Birthday." Then, after the show, I was escorted outside, where Mother and Dad were waiting with their present to me, the Mercedes I'd seen that afternoon. I grabbed the photographer who was taking pictures for the grand opening and asked him to get a shot of the T-Birds on the Mercedes. I made everybody pile onto the hood and roof for the photo opportunity, and while we were up there, we heard a groan, followed by a thud, as our combined weight dented the roof of the car. The look on my dad's face should have told me that he had about had it with my kind of partying.

With all my bookings and plans for the ski event taking up a lot of my time, I started to grow concerned about the next record. I talked to Dad and we scheduled a week in December when I could come in off the road, then I called Jerry Crutchfield and asked him if he thought Capitol would allow us to go somewhere else, where we could have some solid recording time, without any of the interruptions we had in Nashville. Jerry saw no reason why we couldn't do that.

"Listen, Crutch," I ventured. "How about we go someplace warm? Someplace with a beach."

"Well, there's Compass Point Studio in Nassau," he said. "They've got good equipment. Are the Bahamas warm enough for you?"

"The Bahamas are perfect for me," I told him. "Book it."

It was that simple, and we spent the first week of December in Nassau, making *Strong Enough to Bend*, which contained three more hits: the title cut, "Highway Robbery," and "Call on

Me." We took along a group of outstanding musicians, James Stroud, Mitch Humphries, Don Potter, Kenny Mims, and Bob Wray, along with two engineers, Scott Hendricks and Chris Hammond. When I say these guys are outstanding, I really mean it. In addition to being great in the studio, Scott Hendricks and James Stroud went on to head record labels.

We'd work in the mornings, then in the afternoons we'd snorkel the waters around Nassau or lie on the beach. All but Jerry, that is. Jerry wasn't much on snorkeling, and he covered for us in the studio when we were out playing. I played more than the rest, I might add, because the nightlife in Nassau is wild. I'd hit a few of the clubs, and I know I wasn't always in great shape when I got to the studio the next day. But nobody can deny that *Strong Enough to Bend* turned out to be a great album. When we finished work and got ready to go home, I called all the guys together and presented them with Heuer diving watches. Crutch got a watch, too, but it was a "land" watch.

In January, I flew to Colorado for the Twenty-Fifth Anniversary Celebration in Steamboat Springs. I'd decided I wanted my hair shoulder length for the event, so Shirley Porter also flew to Steamboat, bringing hair extensions. All my writers were there for the songwriters' show, and all the folks from Capitol Records came.

Two of the things that stand out in my mind had nothing to do with the actual running of events. One evening Barb Shipley, Shirley Porter, Paul Overstreet, Paul Davis, and I went to my cabin at the resort, and I slipped into my sweats, removed my makeup, and lay there on the couch while the two Pauls sang. I'd join in on songs I knew and just lie there being a fan when they sang new songs they'd written. Those times are among the best in this business. Among the most embarrassing in this business are the unexpected disasters that you have to laugh at yourself for. At one presentation Barb Shipley, Shirley Porter, and I were all standing together. Barb, who is a tall, strong, blonde ski-type, prone to bear-hugging people, grabbed me around the shoulders to congratulate me on the way events had gone thus far. I felt a slight tug and saw Shirley Porter's hand shoot up behind my back. The cold wind on the back of my neck told me all I needed to know. Barb's hug had pulled off the hair extensions on the back of my head. Shirley walked beside me all the way back to the cabin, with her hand at the base of my neck holding up my hair and my dignity.

Just like I'd dreamed, I had my Songwriters' Night at the Top of the Gondola in Steamboat and joined Paul Overstreet and Paul Davis for "I Won't Take Less Than Your Love" as a big finale. The ski events went like clockwork, and my big show on the final night turned out great. American Airlines decided not to use my jingle, but even that didn't lessen the pride I felt over the event.

My only disappointment was that some of the people I'd invited, like Kathy Mattea and Hank Jr., couldn't make it. But Lorrie Morgan and Keith Whitley came. I didn't see much of those two, though, since they were taking a second honeymoon and stayed in their cabin much of the time. One night we had a sleigh ride, and I'll never forget how happy Lorrie and Keith looked bundled up against the cold Colorado winter. Just a little over a year later Keith was dead of alcohol poisoning. It was a heartbreaker not only for his family and friends but for all of country music.

When we wrapped up the event and I flew back to Nashville, I felt like I owned the world. I'd partied a lot, so I was hungover and tired, but I couldn't imagine anything but the best for the first part of 1988. I had finished a new album, my concerts were sold out, and I'd successfully pulled off a fantastic country music event in Steamboat. I was on a roll.

FORTY-THREE

I'm from the Betty Ford Center, and I'm here to help you."
A stranger spoke those words to me on the morning of February
2, 1988. I had just walked into the living room of the president
of my record label. My dad had told me the night before I was
expected at a planning meeting at Jim Fogelsong's house the following morning at 9:00 A.M. I don't even breathe at that time of
day, but for some reason, I hadn't questioned it. I'd gotten up
early that morning, dressed up, styled my hair, and put on
makeup. At least I had the image going for me. I'd even arrived
on time.

I looked around the room and saw a small group of my
friends and family. Besides Jim, there were my parents, my
brother Don, Jerry Crutchfield, Royce and Shirley Porter, Barb
Shipley, Paul Overstreet, Dean Dillon, and the stranger, who
turned out to be the facilitator. I knew exactly what was coming
down. An intervention. Something inside me closed down. From
the expressions on people's faces, I knew that everybody was
afraid I was going to say, "Screw you," and take a hike. But I
saw tears in my dad's eyes, and the hurt look on my mother's
face, and I said, "Well, let's hear it."

The facilitator went on to ask me please to understand that

these people were there because they loved me and to remember that as they each spoke. I thought, "Oh, man. This is it. I'm busted." I'd heard about these things, and I knew that people were going to dredge up things I'd done when I was drunk or doing drugs. All I could think about was what my parents would think. I was aware they knew about some of the things I'd done, and they saw it right up close and personal with Glen Campbell. I didn't want them to know anything more.

Then, one by one, people started telling me about my behavior and why I had to straighten up. Jim Fogelsong didn't have any specific stories to tell, just observation and hearsay evidence. "I've been hearing around town that you're an alcoholic, Tanya," he started off. "And your appearance does make me wonder about it. Your face has been puffy, and you look tired a lot of the time." I sat there listening and thinking, *Damn it, of course I'm tired. I'm working my butt off.* Jerry Crutchfield talked to me about my talent and said I owed it to myself to respect that talent enough to take better care of myself.

I couldn't believe Paul Overstreet and Dean Dillon were there. They'd been two of the biggest hell-raisers in Nashville when I was hanging out with them. Paul had quit drinking in 1985 and become a born-again Christian, though, so I guessed he was there as an expert witness. Dean was, too, since he had been to Betty Ford and cleaned up.

Paul Overstreet gave me a generic sermonette about turning my life over to God, then gave the floor to Dean. I held my breath, because I certainly didn't want him telling my folks we'd done drugs and had sex. He started out by telling me that his time at the Betty Ford Center had saved his life. He admitted that we'd done a lot of drugs together. My dad had been sitting there with his head down, and it suddenly shot up and his mouth dropped. He'd had no idea Dean was one of my drug pals. Dean went on to say how much he cared about me, then he got real nervous and tried to lighten up the mood of the room by adding, "Tanya, see my new hat? You can buy things when you get off drugs." I doubt that it was the facilitator's idea of a great antidrug lesson, but Dean probably thought it was a perfect pitch at the intervention of a world-class shopper.

My parents were the most devastated people in the room, but Royce and Shirley Porter were the most uncomfortable. Shirley never thought she or any of the T-Birds would be involved in something like this. I later learned that they hadn't wanted to come at all, but they had been made to feel that if they didn't and I overdosed, it would practically be their fault. I also found out that there was a no-show. Paul Davis had gone underground the minute he returned from Steamboat Springs. When it came around to Shirley, she stammered and finally said, "Well, you know, Tanya, you got drunk that one time and made me cut your hair too short. I told you it wouldn't look good." If I hadn't been so sick to my stomach I would have laughed.

Barb Shipley reminded me that when I was drunk I'd mooned a cop. That is not technically true. I had bent over and flipped my skirt up that time at Faison's, but that's not a moon. A moon is when you pull your pants down and show your whole ass. But I wasn't in a position to point that out just then.

My brother Don just said a lot of brotherly stuff about loving me and not wanting to lose me. La Costa hadn't been able to come from Phoenix for the event, but she sent a letter that Mother read. Costa didn't have any stories. She just reminded me of all the good times we had growing up and how the Tuckers were strong people, and if we stood together, we could get through anything. She later told me she thought if she could remind me of where I came from and how far down the road I'd made it, I'd straighten up. My parents said very little, my dad just kept tearing up. Mother would look at him and then at me. Even though he'd set it up, Dad can't discuss it even now.

I thought about a lot of things while I was sitting there. I was told that Dad had planned this for a long time, and that everybody had known about it for months. Mother and Dad had known in October, when we were in Dallas for my birthday and they gave me the new Mercedes. Crutch had known when we were in the Bahamas. Barb, Paul, Dean, and Shirley had known during the Ski Event. Jim Fogelsong had known, too. He said Dad had approached him months earlier and said that, like it or not, the label was going to have to accept the fact that I needed thirty days to clean up. Jim said he'd told Dad the label would stand behind whatever decision the family made.

I thought about Dad chasing all over the country and working his butt off to get me into the music business. I thought about the fact that half the guys in Nashville were doing drugs, and I was the one they wanted to send up the river. I know that's beside the point, but that's what I was thinking. I knew I got out of control sometimes, but I didn't think I needed to go to a clinic because of it. I sat there staring into space, and once again I caught my dad's teary eye. He looked like his heart was broken. Suddenly, he came over to me and dropped down on his knees.

"My God, Tanya, please get help. Your mother and I love you so much, and we're sick from worrying over you."

"Your bags are already packed," the facilitator said.

I knew I was beat, so I looked at my mother and said, "Let's go."

Mother, Shirley, Royce, and Barb accompanied me to the airport, and I don't think anybody said much. Shirley Porter offered to keep my dog, Lucy, while I was gone. I stared out the car window and just kept saying to myself, "You can get through this, Tanya." I didn't believe I needed to go, but if that was what everyone wanted, then I'd damn well do it. Just like always, I'd try to do what made them happy. Mother came with me on the plane, and again, there was no conversation. She couldn't speak and I didn't want to. I just wanted to get to the clinic, do my thirty days, and get out.

⚜ ❧ ⚜ ❧

I got to Rancho Mirage and the Betty Ford Center and checked in late that night. It was a very nice place and certainly didn't look like a prison, but I felt like jail was where I was headed. I knew that for the next thirty days, I'd be under supervision. And even though I knew I could leave at any time, I knew I wouldn't. Not after seeing my dad on his knees in tears. They checked me in, then searched my luggage for liquor and drugs, including nonprescription drugs. You can't even have most kinds of mouthwash because of the alcohol content. I ended up with three other women in the Swamp, the room where Elizabeth Taylor had stayed when she was there. They explained that every room had a Granny, meaning the woman who'd been there the longest, and that she was in charge of the day-to-day details connected with our living arrangements. I was told that my middle name, Denise, was what I would be known as, since they wanted no mention of my being a celebrity. Boy, they thought *they* didn't want it. Denise-with-no-last-name was fine with me.

One of the staff members gave me a book about drug rehabilitation to study and a journal so I could write down my thoughts every day. I had some thoughts all right. I wrote down the name of every person who ever made me mad and exactly why they were rotten to the core. The journal was probably one of the few benefits I got from being there, because I did open up in it.

The journal was the only place I opened up. It wasn't hard for me to cover up how I felt in front of the counselors, since I'd been hiding my feelings all my life. There had been so many times that the business had run me ragged, and all I did was tell everyone it was easy. I'd given the public a flashbulb smile a million times, and I'd put up a tough front a million more. I had the feeling that I was getting ready to do it again, because I wasn't about to spend the next thirty days trying to explain my behavior to strangers.

Betty Ford was packed with rich people, and if I were to bet on the one group best represented while I was there, it would be Washington wives. Maybe it's because Betty Ford travels in those circles, I don't know, but they were certainly there in force during my stay. After being around those women and seeing how severe their problems were, I know that if I had to pick a way to spend my life other than singing, it would not be as a politician's wife. At least the only reputation I have to worry about damaging is my own. These women live in a reflected spotlight, for better or worse.

Everybody there is assigned a job, and I got vacuuming. I didn't care, as long as I didn't have to clean toilets or be the one in charge of waking everyone up at 5:30. We attended group counseling sessions every morning and afternoon, then had special night classes on things like the bad effects of smoking. Graduates were always coming back to encourage us. I about fainted when a guy stood up at one meeting and said, "Hello, I am so and so, a hope-to-die drug addict, alcoholic son-of-a-bitch motherfucker." I thought, "Well, damn, I guess we know now that cussing ain't a sin."

There was no free time. You could make a few phone calls if you kept them under three minutes, and you could have visitors every Sunday afternoon from 1:00 to 5:00. Mother, Dad, and La Costa came, and all it did was make me want to leave with them. But I had decided to stick it out. Most of the time I felt like an observer, like I was watching from some faraway place.

It was just like me and Liz Taylor to find guys at Betty Ford. I noticed mine at one of the first lectures, sitting there with his short, sandy blond hair and athletic build. I also noticed that he had a nice face. Cute, but also nice, and I was in need of a nice face right about then. He didn't seem to have any deep emotional problems. He was simply a young guy who had some trouble with drugs and was trying to straighten up. The problem with meeting men at Betty Ford is that there's no "fraternizing," as they call women and men having anything to do with each other. So my rehab romance was really just a little light flirtation as we passed each other in the halls. As time went by, he started passing notes to me, and I began to think maybe when we got out we ought to get together. Of course, since you have so little free time, and you are in such a restricted environment, people never know how they'd relate on the outside. The people who run Camp Betty don't want it to turn into a pickup joint. But we both felt drawn to each other, and after a few weeks of sneaking words here and there, we made a plan. He was being discharged before I was, so when I finally checked out, he'd come pick me up and we could get to know each other away from the watchful eyes of the staff.

Every Saturday we had classes about a quarter of a mile away at the Annenberg Center, and since the counselors didn't walk right along with us, it felt like getting let out of jail. There wasn't supposed to be any talking, but I'd use that time to tell jokes, anything to lighten the mood. Actually, my mood was improving because I had decided to perform at the Academy of Country Music (ACM) Awards on March 16. I'd had a standing invitation to perform, but once I checked into Betty Ford, everyone assumed I was out of circulation. After I'd been at the clinic about a week, I used one of my three-minute phone calls to contact Capitol and tell them I would be there and be ready to perform. I planned on singing "If It Don't Come Easy," and I sometimes practiced it while we walked to the Center. It was definitely against the rules, but the other inmates loved it.

One time, when my usual counselor had been off on a week's vacation, his replacement ratted on me to him. "Every time the group walks to the Center, Tanya Tucker has been holding court," he griped. My usual counselor was an okay sort of guy and blew it off. I just thought it was a stupid thing to get up in arms about, anyway. I am the kind of person who will always hold court, if holding court means telling a few jokes or cutting up. I'm in the business of pleasing people. That's what I've been doing all my life. Of course, my name was supposed to be Denise-no-last-name, but by then people had recognized me. I thought the holding court comment probably had to do with the fact that I am an entertainer, and I had to wonder if rehab centers really are all that good if you are a public figure. I know it's worked for a lot of them, but I wondered, just the same.

I was busted another time when the guy I'd been carrying on my little flirtation with tried to pass me a note. The counselor grabbed it and read it to the class. "Denise, I am just crazy about you," the counselor read with sarcasm. It made me feel like I was back in grade school.

But in grade school, girls weren't sneaking out to the Pavilion to have sex with some guy, and they weren't doing cocaine, and those things went on at Betty Ford. I have to believe that they go on at any rehab center, because if that many people who have drug and alcohol problems are rounded up together, somebody is going to find a way to cheat. I know that when I was there some of the women did cocaine, several were meeting men, and one even attempted suicide. I am very proud to say that even though I knew how to obtain drugs while I was there, I did not do it. I felt it would be like cussing in church. My standards may not be all that high all of the time, but I've got 'em, nevertheless.

Amazingly enough, even with the note passing, the joking around on our walks to the Center, and the negative attitude, I made Granny of the Swamp room! I outlasted everyone else and was in charge. Maybe life is like that. Just be the last one standing. I wasn't having a good time at the Center, but I was proud to have made Granny.

I was twenty-nine years old, and most of my roommates were much younger. I felt close to them. It's so different for young girls who get into bad habits. They can't think past the next boyfriend. At least I had a career to look forward to, and that was what kept me going. One night a couple of the girls were talking, and one said she just didn't see how she could survive if her boyfriend didn't really love her.

"You ought to quit worrying about boyfriends and start worrying about yourself," was my advice. "'Cause I'm here to tell you, men are gonna come and go in this life, but you're gonna have to live with yourself forever."

The girls listened, but I always felt like I related to their problems better than they related to my answers. I knew firsthand that counting on a man to make your happiness for you doesn't work.

In many ways, the younger girls in the Swamp had the same problem as the Washington wives. Men dominated their lives, and not always good men.

One of the worst times for me was the "hot seat" part of group sessions, when people got to ask you anything they wanted and you had to answer. One of the things that got your rear up there in a minute was to start crying, and you can bet I didn't do it. I might like the edge, but I dreaded the hot seat. Actually, it was pretty funny when they called me up one day. Everybody looked at me, and I waited for whatever horrible and personal question someone would ask. This one woman shot her hand up, and the counselor called on her. She looked really intense and I thought, "Oh Lord, here it comes."

"What's it like to know Don Johnson?" she inquired.

When I knew him it meant having to fill his Volkswagen with gas because he was a mostly out-of-work actor, but I didn't say that. I said he was a nice guy.

"What's it like to be up onstage all the time?"

Before I could even think of an answer, one of the counselors turned to another staff member and asked, "What's this sound like to you?"

"Merv Griffin," the other guy answered.

That sort of threw a cog in the works of that session. Who'd have thought that Don and concerts would get me off the hot seat? During my stay I was on the hot seat several times, but I wasn't one of the ones who ever really said anything. And since I'd quickly figured out that the fastest way to get there was to cry or run your mouth, I zipped my lip and kept my emotions in check at most sessions. In some ways, the counselor wasn't thinking straight when he shut down the questions about performing. Maybe we were on the track of something, because being onstage my whole life has definitely affected me. I know this—it's very hard to have thousands of people screaming for you and then go back to a hotel room alone. I think that's why I'm always looking for a party after a show.

I am almost incapable of spilling my guts to somebody who's watching me like a hawk and wanting me to break down. Maybe if the staff hadn't kept saying things like, "Quit fighting us" or, "You have to surrender," I would have felt more at ease. I couldn't relate to that kind of talk. Another thing that made me crazy was all the talk about "feelings" this and "feelings" that. Hell, I didn't even like the song. They also kept after me about the reasons I'd done drugs and drank. Nobody would accept the fact that I'd had a happy childhood. They kept trying to get me to say I'd been abused or that somebody'd raped me somewhere down the line. I told them I did the things I did mainly because I liked to party. People do drugs either to get an edge or get rid of one, and I've done both. They didn't buy it. I shut down, evaded questions, and bided my time. So as the weeks crawled by, the staff became convinced that none of the classes or therapy sessions or meetings were working.

They were only half right, because the classes and sessions were not in vain. I learned about the physical effects of drugs, and it scared me. For the first time, I heard just how dangerous chemical substance abuse is. I didn't think I had a serious problem, so I didn't relate to most of what they said. Call it denial if you want, and maybe it was. But I did start to think about the effects drugs and alcohol had on my body. They could make me feel like I was having a good time, but they could also depress the hell out of me. On the other hand, I did not think Betty Ford was the answer. I was there to please my mother and dad, not because I felt I should be in rehab. After three weeks or so, the counselors decided I wasn't ready to be released and added two weeks onto my time. I didn't like it, but I agreed. I just kept telling myself I had to prove I could stick it out. I didn't want the tabloids calling me a Betty Ford dropout.

The counselors there were also very concerned about my plans to sing at the ACM Awards. They believe that you should stay away from your old environment, the one where you had done drugs, for about a year. They tell you if you don't want to slip, don't go around slippery places. I didn't see how I could do that and still make a living. March 16 was the big day. I would get out of jail and go to the ACMs. Since I was cutting it close, I called Shirley Porter and asked her to bring me a dress. Then I phoned Tovar and told him to set Shirley and me up with hair and makeup appointments at his salon on the afternoon of the sixteenth.

Not long before I checked out, I learned something about first impressions from my girls in the Swamp. By this time everyone knew who I was, and one of the girls in the Swamp had brought in a tape player and one of my tapes, which we sometimes played. A new girl walked in who looked like a rich, snotty Beverly Hills brat. She had the $500 haircut, the designer clothes. I figured we'd never get along and that she'd hate the idea of some country girl being her Granny. She looked around the room and down at the tape player. "Can I borrow this Tanya Tucker tape?" she asked. Country music must be the greatest icebreaker in the world. I shot a look at my girls and shook my head, mouthing out a silent "no." So we didn't bring up who I was, and since I didn't have stage makeup or costumes around the Center, it took her several days to realize it was me. In those few days, I saw that what I had mistaken for arrogance and a spoiled rich attitude was fear and insecurity.

In so many ways, knowing her and some of the other wealthy women made me thankful that I'd had to work hard when I was a kid. At least I knew what the world was like, and that the tougher it gets, the tougher you'd better be. When I was packing to go, the new girl came over and sat down beside me. All she said was, "I know who you are, and I just wanted to say I love your music and I like you." I liked her, too.

On March 11, about a week before my release, the counselors called me in to an office and had me sit down. I don't know what I expected, but it wasn't this: "Andy Gibb is dead." No one prepared me for the news. There was no "We have bad news about a friend of yours." They just dropped it like a bomb, and then added that drugs had ruined his heart. Inside I was shaking and getting sick to my stomach. I know they were trying to break me down, thinking that maybe if I broke down over Andy I might pour my guts out to them. I was sitting there, but I was also out there in that faraway place, watching to see if Tanya Tucker was going to fall apart. So I didn't do it.

I just said, "Are you through with me?" and stood up.

Then I went back to my room and felt like shit. Barry Gibb later told me that Andy had been trying to get hold of me. But Barry didn't know why.

I flunked Step 12 at Betty Ford. I was told to report to the office of one of the women counselors the day before I checked out. "Step 12 is the final portion of your treatment," she explained. "I want you to think about this carefully and confess the worst sin you have ever committed. It's very important that you be honest with me."

I couldn't believe it. I thought priests were the only ones who heard confessions. And, to be honest, I couldn't even think of the worst sin I ever committed, so I made up some little jive sin and let it go. Instead of ragging me about it, she told me about a line of beauty and health products she sold and asked me if I wanted to buy some, or had any entertainer friends who did. I guess she had to sell me on something. But it showed me that I'd been right. Celebrity status changes things even at Betty Ford. Not only did I feel like people were looking at me differently, they were hawking lipsticks and vitamins.

One of the things they do each night is gather all the counseling groups together around several bonfires, and the people who are leaving throw their journals into the fire. It symbolizes leaving all your anger and hatred behind and starting fresh. I hadn't taken those bonfires any more seriously than anything else that was going on. I didn't throw my journal in the bonfire on my last night; I kept it and threw a cigarette lighter in the fire, instead. I didn't mean to be disrespectful, but sometimes I felt like I just had to do something to stir things up. I like big entrances and big exits. The lighter exploded, of course, and now I realize that I hadn't changed all that much from the days when I was setting off firecrackers in Glen Campbell's living room.

One thing got me at that last bonfire, though. Each night, the various groups sang, and sometimes throughout my stay I'd sing "I Won't Take Less Than Your Love," since it was playing on the charts then. One night, I was standing there and heard another group start those familiar lines. By the second verse every group standing at each bonfire was singing it. On the last night, when all the groups started singing, I felt I had seldom experienced such an outpouring of love and acceptance, even onstage when tens of thousands of people applauded. It was the closest I came to losing control of my emotions, and I was glad it was dark, because I might have ended up in the hot seat.

The day I was sprung I had only one regret, and that was about leaving my girls in the Swamp. I hoped somehow they'd learned something from our talks about making your own life. I believe that for many people the counseling and classes make all the difference in the world. But not me. I just didn't relate to people lecturing me. I lecture myself enough as it is. I didn't have much of a chance to reflect on it, anyway. I had get to L.A. to play a show at the Academy of Country Music Awards.

FORTY-FOUR

$\mathcal{M}$y potential boyfriend, the note-passer, came to pick me up and take me to Los Angeles for the ACMs, but by the time we arrived I knew we had nothing in common. Neither one of us had much to say. For better or worse, we were both back in the real world. I think the little flirtation had been mainly a diversion for me, something to make me feel better and to take my mind off the counselors' constant attempts to probe into my thoughts and feelings.

I had him take me to the Beverly Wilshire Hotel where my world was waiting. I checked into my suite and looked around. I could make all the telephone calls I wanted. I could smoke all the cigarettes I wanted. Even though I didn't want to, I knew that I could even order a drink from room service. I didn't believe I had a serious problem with drugs and alcohol, but I did know I liked the way I felt. I felt positive, and happy, and rested.

The first thing I did was call an actor friend of mine, Billy Long, and ask him to be my escort for the show. I wanted a friend on my arm when I walked in the lobby of the Universal Amphitheater. Billy said he'd be honored. So the first day of the rest of my life involved a date with a gorgeous man. I had that going for me.

There was a knock on the door, and when I answered it, there stood Shirley and Royce Porter.

I threw my arms around their necks. God, I was glad to be at the Beverly Wilshire instead of Camp Betty. Shirley and I ran off to Tovar's. When we came through the door, Tovar went nuts. He kept telling me over and over how glad he was to see me, and he showed me the book he'd just had published. It was about the classic beauties he'd worked with, and he included me. I said, "No! You're kidding!" But I loved it. Shirley and I had him autograph our copies and then got down to the business of being pampered for the rest of the afternoon.

After we left Tovar's, we went back to the Beverly Wilshire and put on our dresses. The music business offers women the great opportunity to play dress-up as often as you'd ever want. Shirley had brought my dress, which had a black, backless fitted top with a short, ruffled white chiffon skirt. Shirley wore a blue sequined gown. With our new hair and makeup, we both felt like classic beauties. One problem, though. Shirley'd forgotten to bring a pair of shoes for me. I panicked and called Capitol's publicist, Bonnie Rasmussin, who was also staying at the hotel, and she sent her niece, Noreen Markel, off in a limo to shop for a selection of heels.

By the time the four of us, Billy and I, and Royce and Shirley, arrived at the show, I was very nervous, and not just because I was shoeless.

"Shirley, I don't know how people are going react to me," I said.

"They're going to love you like always," she reassured.

"Man, I don't know which I'd hate the worst," I went on. "People looking at me and knowing I'd been in the tank and talking behind my back, or people smiling and saying, 'Oh, I'm so glad you got help.'"

I'd have hated that because I didn't think I had really needed all that much help. It would seem too much like sympathy, and sympathy is something that's easier for me to give than to take.

"It's going to be fine," she kept saying. "Unless you have to go barefoot."

When we got there, I immediately went to the dressing room area where I waited, watching the clock tick away toward show time. I was the show opener, set to walk down through the audience singing "If It Don't Come Easy," so I didn't have time to waste waiting on shoes. I had a picture in my mind of Noreen stuck in L.A. traffic and me waltzing down the aisle in my stocking feet. Finally, minutes prior to my going on, Noreen came running down the hall waving a shopping bag. I slipped on a pair of shoes just as the opening strains of music began. When I walked down through the audience, the applause was deafening.

I started singing "If It Don't Come Easy" and was feeling on top of the world, when all of a sudden, I forgot the words to the song. It wasn't coming easy at all. God, of all the times to do that. Usually when singers like me, or George Jones, or Hank Jr., or Waylon, blow lines, folks figure they're on something. Or at least they did back when everybody was crazy. Here I was, fresh out of Betty Ford, on nationwide television, and I couldn't remember the words to my hit song. I kept my chin up, kept waving to people, smiling, and just repeated a line and hoped nobody would notice. If they did, nobody seemed to care.

After the show everybody kept crowding around, telling me how good I looked and congratulating me on my performance. I knew what they were really saying was, "We're glad you're back." I especially remember how kind Dwight Yoakam was. He said what I'd done took a lot of strength, and it was an inspiration to other artists.

We left the show and went to a record label party at Le Dome. I'd talked so much about the place that Capitol decided to welcome me back to the world by holding their post-awards gala at my old stomping grounds. If they'd asked the counselors at Betty Ford about it, I'm sure they'd have been told not to. But drinking wasn't on my mind that night. Everybody else was drinking, but I didn't even consider having one. I was on a natural high.

After I got back to the hotel and got to bed that night, I lay there thinking about the past six weeks of confinement and how much I'd like to ride to the beach and feel the wind in my hair. So the next morning I phoned the concierge to arrange for a rented convertible, then phoned Shirley and said, "Get ready to hit the road, Squirrely Bird. We're outta here." We picked up the car, which turned out to be a BMW convertible, and headed for the beach, where we sat for hours, while I got used to the feeling of being able to do exactly what I wanted. We didn't talk about Betty Ford. I'd kept in touch about my stay through phone calls and letters, and I was all talked out about it. Instead, she caught me up on Nashville and her family, and the fact that her daughter, Angel, was turning sixteen in less than ten days, on March 25.

"Let's take her somewhere," I said. "Let's take her to Panama City and we'll fish and sail and go out to dinner—we'll do everything. I need a vacation before I head back out on the road." Lord, it felt good to be able to make plans without checking with a counselor.

The label needed an album cover for *Strong Enough to Bend*, so Bonnie Rasmussin and I stayed in Los Angeles for the next week. We shopped and went to lunch every day and dinner every night. We bought new clothes and spent one day with a photographer. On one of the first nights we went to dinner together after the awards, Bonnie seemed like she had something on her mind. She toyed around with her salad, and since she loves to eat as much as I do, I knew she wanted to say something.

"Okay, what is it?" I asked.

She looked relieved. "Well, before I came out here for the ACMs, your counselor at Betty Ford phoned me and said if we were going to stay out here, I was supposed to take you to Alcoholics Anonymous meetings every night."

It didn't make me mad, although I'm sure she thought it would.

"No way," I said. "I do not need an AA meeting."

What I needed was a trip to Florida with one of the T-Birds.

⚜ ⚜ ⚜

The five of us piled into my new Mercedes and headed south— me, Shirley, Angel, and two of her friends. We had rented a beach house in Panama City, Florida, and we kicked back for almost a week. We sunned ourselves, we rented a boat and fished, we ate ourselves silly, and we ran up and down the beach laughing like the teenagers we were with. I guess the only wild thing we did was to go to one of those places that makes personalized license plates and get one made for the Mercedes that said "Ms. Bad Ass." That license plate made the papers many times over the years, as proof of what a wild child I was, and maybe people thought I'd been drunk somewhere and bought it. But it was just me and Squirrely Bird, sober as judges and in Panama City for Angel's sixteenth birthday. We never even thought about ordering drinks. One day we went to Captain Anderson's, where you roast your own coffee. That was the extent of our drinking.

It all ended too quickly; in fact, the very day we drove back to Nashville. I was sunburned, a little fatter, and a lot happier than I'd been in months. I left on the bus that very same night to play a show.

I was back in Nashville for Easter Sunday of 1988, and Shirley invited me out to her lake house in Hendersonville for an Easter egg hunt. La Costa came with me and brought her kids, three-year-old Kali and five-year-old Zach, and the adults hid eggs all over the property. For a year or so I'd been hearing the faint ticking of my biological clock. It wasn't something that over-whelmed me, but I kept thinking that time was going by and I was starting to want to have children. Over the last several years, I'd turned my mothering instincts toward Costa's children and Don's kids. But being there and watching so many happy kids chasing after the hidden Easter eggs, I turned to Shirley Porter and said, "You know what? I want to have a baby."

FORTY-FIVE

*W*ell, thank you, Jeff," I thought as I stood looking at the man Jeff McKay had just introduced as Ben Reed. It was May 26, 1988, a little over two months after I'd checked out of Betty Ford, and I was playing a show at a Tulsa honky-tonk. I'd met Jeff several years earlier, taping a show called *Downtown* in L.A., and I continued to run into him at golf tournaments and other celebrity events. He was an actor with a good list of credentials, including about forty episodes of *Magnum P.I.* Jeff spent a lot of time in Tulsa, since it was his hometown, and on this visit he'd come to my show and brought a friend.

I couldn't believe what I saw. Ben Reed was tall, handsome, and looked like he could be a movie star. He was dressed in stark contrasts—a pair of white Levi's and a black shirt—and he dominated the room. Ben Reed was a doll, so I made a conscious effort not to appear too interested that night. I figured a guy who looked like that already had more women chasing him than he needed. I wanted him to think he was the pursuer, not me. He appeared to be a little aloof on the surface, but it didn't take long to see that he was genuine, friendly, and a nice guy.

He told me he'd just graduated from West Virginia University, and when I said he looked like a football player, he explained that he had planned on going pro until he suffered some shoulder injuries. And he told me he planned to study acting in Pasadena, California, having auditioned and been accepted to the American Academy of Dramatic Arts.

We talked about Jeff's career, Ben's hopes for getting into films, and what it took to break into acting, or any part of the entertainment business. Ben believed perseverance was a key factor, and he was prepared to go to L.A. and keep plugging away until he made it. I'd been through the L.A. mill, too, with Far Out, *TNT*, and all the imaging and hype that went with it. Ben hadn't seen the underside of the business, and I hated to be the one to burst his bubble, so I didn't have much to say about his career plans. But we danced and talked. And I sneaked a few drinks at the bar. Because I was a recent Betty Ford graduate, I didn't want to flaunt the fact that I was drinking. That's one thing Betty Ford's counselors hit right on the head. If you're around slippery places, you'll probably slide. I was out playing clubs, and when I came through those swinging doors, I wanted to swing. When I left that night, I told him he should come to Nashville and visit sometime, and we exchanged phone numbers.

A few weeks later, I played a gig in Oklahoma City, and Ben brought his parents to the show. We all went to a late dinner, and I was very impressed with both of them. They were very gracious, and while they said they loved the show, they didn't seem to be affected by the whole star trip. I liked the fact that Ben seemed so close to his parents. It felt like the beginning of a wonderful relationship with someone who had the same feelings about family that I had. For the next month, Ben and I talked on the phone almost every other day.

I also spent a lot of time on the telephone calling the T-Birds about my new boyfriend. "He is the most gorgeous guy," I'd tell first one and then another. "He's got a great personality, and he's kind, and I'm just wild about him." I hated the fact that we were going to be so far apart.

Ben went to Cancun on a graduation trip with a couple of his friends that June, and while he was there, he sent me a postcard that read: "Hope the invitation still stands. I'm coming to Nashville and would like to see you."

The day I got the card, I was working out the details for a video that would help promote the title cut single from *Strong Enough to Bend*. We'd decided to shoot the clip in Nashville and give it the backyard, hometown, family kind of feel. The song's writers, Beth Nielsen Chapman and Don Schlitz, had used the image of a tree that's "strong enough to bend" to portray a love that lasts because the partners are willing to give. I saw the song as meaningful to all family relationships, not just that of a husband and wife. I wanted a family reunion kind of theme for the piece, with the young couple on a picnic, surrounded with what would appear to be cousins, uncles, aunts, parents, and grandparents.

Ben visited during the week we shot the video and appeared as an extra in the piece. Billy Long, my actor friend who escorted me to the ACMs earlier that year, was also staying at the house, since I'd asked him to play the male "lead" in the clip. Ben was positive Billy had a big crush on me, which was funny since in the entire time I'd known Billy we hadn't even kissed. Ben stayed at the house for four or five days, but he kept talking about moving to Los Angeles to get his acting career started. As soon as the video shoot was finished, Ben and I headed out to Shirley and Royce Porter's house on Old Hickory Lake. We fished, boated, and had a wonderful, relaxing time. Shirley said, "You undersold him, T. He's better than gorgeous!" Before he left, I invited him to be my date for the Country Music Awards that next October, and he said he'd love to come. When he got back to Tulsa, he packed all his things into Old Blue, his Blazer, and headed to Hollywood.

※ ※ ※ ※

One night while he was driving to California and I was out on the road, I started looking at this huge moon through my hotel window. I started writing on a scratch pad, and these lines just rushed out: "By now he's as far as Winslow, he can't wait to see where his name will be on the Hollywood Walk of Stars." I couldn't come up with a chorus at that time, but I held onto the scratch pad and scribbled down verses over the next few weeks.

Then, in July, I played a show in Fort Pierce, Florida. "I'm sure happy to be in Gary Stewart country," I said from the stage. And when I came off after the show, there stood my old songwriting friend from the Spence Manor. "Man, I am so glad to see you," I said. "I've been working on another song."

I told him all about Ben and how much I missed him. I told him about Ben's plans, and I showed him my verses. Gary and

I sat down and worked out a chorus that ends like this: "If Hollywood don't work out, and all your dreams fall through, there's a Tennessee woman who'd love to share her dreams with you."

"I want to demo this now!" I said, when we'd finished.

Gary knows me, and he knows that patience isn't one of my virtues. He knew of a little studio there in town, and we went over at 6:00 A.M. to demo the song. "'Tennessee Woman' is going to be the title of my next album," I said before the bus pulled out for the next show.

My feelings were torn over Ben and his move to Los Angeles. I felt like I was just getting to know him and knew how difficult trying to build a relationship was going to be if I was on the concert trail and he was hitting the streets of L.A. looking for his big break. There was a part of me that didn't want him to even pursue the film thing, and another part that understood completely. Nothing and nobody could have stood between me and my ambition all those years ago. And I respected him for going after the career he wanted.

While I was out on the tour promoting *Strong Enough to Bend*, I spent a lot of lonely nights on the bus thinking about Ben and wondering what was going to happen between us. We were on the phone constantly. Ben had arrived in L.A. and rented a little apartment. He was starting his acting classes, and he was waiting tables and working construction to stay alive. I missed him terribly.

July was booked tight, and I was in emotional pain missing Ben for a lot of the time, and then I added physical pain as well for quite a few of the shows. I played a concert in Virginia Beach, Virginia, and since I had a day off I decided to go jet-skiing. Jet-skiing is a rough sport, and one slip can take you out, which is exactly what happened to me. I hit everywhere at once. I was in bad pain in the water by the time they dragged me out and took me to the hospital. The doctors suggested I take some time off, not so much because they were afraid of permanent damage, but because of the pain. Right. You don't cancel shows because you're sore. By the next show I had a bruise across half of my back.

Two days later, I walked out onstage in Webster, Massachusetts, feeling like I'd been beaten up. Performing is always a crapshoot, anyway. You rely on sound and light systems up and down the road and hope your guitar player didn't have a fight with his girlfriend or the keyboard player hasn't broken a finger. Then, every time you want to do something normal, like jet-ski, or roller skate, or ride a horse, you know in the back of your mind that you could be gambling away a few shows. Or else you'll walk out onstage hurting like hell.

That's how I felt that night in Massachusetts, until a fan approached the stage. Nothing helps a performer forget physical pain like a loyal fan, and after I did a few songs, a little girl walked up and handed me a 45-rpm copy of "Delta Dawn." My back pain faded like Delta Dawn's rose from years gone by. I remember thinking that back then, when I'd made that record, I couldn't believe it was happening, and how it had taken years for me to understand I was a star. I just rocked for the rest of the performance. It was sweltering in Massachusetts that July, and I bet I dropped four or five pounds up there. Like after any high, the pain returned soon enough. The rest of the month was more of the same, and it took several weeks before my back didn't ache every morning after a show.

In August, when I had a few days off, I went to see Ben in L.A. We had a great time until we made the mistake of heading to the bar at the Howard Johnson's and starting to drink. That led to an argument about some stupid thing that I can't remember. It's no good to argue with me when I'm drinking, and Ben wasn't even going to try. Finally he said, "Go on back to Tennessee, Tanya." In a very un-Tanya Tuckerish move, I apologized and said, "Look Ben, let's make up. We can make this thing work." He just shook his head and told me he didn't want to see me again. Needless to say, I left Los Angeles and hit the road again in anger. I doubted I'd ever see him again, and I almost convinced myself I didn't care.

I had decided to attend the CMA Awards alone, or with friends like T. and Glen Martin or Royce and Shirley. I was nominated for Female Vocalist for the first time in fourteen years, and the two Pauls and I had a Vocal Collaboration nomination for "I Won't Take Less Than Your Love." I didn't expect to win, but being a nominee again was exciting. About ten days before the awards show, Ben phoned. I almost fainted when I heard his voice.

"Do you need an escort for the show?" he asked.

"I thought you didn't want to see me again," I said.

"Well, I'd like to take you to the awards and see if we can't get back together."

It took me about two seconds to say "Come on."

The Country Music Association Awards are always held at the Grand Ole Opry the first week of October, during what is called Country Music Week, and that's when I celebrate my birthday with my friends. It's hard to schedule personal celebrations into your tour timetable, so we sometimes have to readjust events to suit the industry. So that's what I'd been doing with my birthday, celebrating at a time when I knew people would be around. I'd have my birthday party either early or late, depending on the exact day of the awards show. We'd celebrate twice. Once on a riverboat or at a local restaurant, and also at the Opryland Hotel the night of the CMA Awards. I always rent a huge two-bedroom suite at the Opryland Hotel so my friends can all gather there after the show. The second bedroom is for any of the T-Birds who come to town and want to hang with me at the hotel. I believe in keeping my friends close at hand.

I was flying high for the ten days after Ben's call. In my mind, every problem between us was handled. I was so confident that we were going to make it as a couple that I even hoped I'd get pregnant while he was in Nashville. Having a child had been in the back of my mind for so long, and after meeting Ben, I felt I wanted him to be the father. I just knew we'd make the perfect child. I can't explain why, but I believed it.

Ben flew into Nashville the night before the awards, and I picked him up at the airport. He was even better looking than I'd remembered. We had a birthday party at Merchants restaurant that night, and about fifty people came. We opened presents, and I showed Ben off to everyone. I could see, though, that he was getting overwhelmed by all the hoopla and the rowdy country music types. Ben is reserved, and I don't think he was quite ready for Country Music Week and Tanya's birthday all at once.

The next night topped the birthday party. I wore a dress that Diana Venegas had designed for me. My folks were at the suite, and when Mother saw that dress, she decided the dress she had on wasn't good enough to wear to the show. Well, Shirley Porter insisted on taking her gown off and missing the show so Mother would have a nice dress. Shirley said she'd just as soon hang around at the suite in a housecoat, anyway. My limo picked us up, and we felt on top of the world, the perfect couple. It felt good to have Ben on my arm, too, because he is definitely a head-turner.

The night started out great, even though I lost Female Vocalist to K. T. Oslin. Randy Travis walked away with Male Vocalist, and George Strait won his first Entertainer of the Year award. The Pauls and I lost out on Vocal Collaboration to the Trio: Dolly Parton, Emmylou Harris, and Linda Ronstadt. Mary Chapin Carpenter stole the whole show that year with her hilarious song titled "Opening Act," which detailed the many indignities show openers sometimes live through. Everybody in the audience knew exactly what she was talking about, and the crowd went completely nuts over her.

After the show, we all went back to my suite at the hotel for another party. It was one of the suites that have a balcony over-looking the Cascades, a huge enclosed courtyard filled with tropical plants, fountains, and sparkling lights. Some people were a little put off because my dad had issued a "no alcohol" edict, but most went along with it. The ones who didn't go along with it sneaked their liquor in and drifted off to the extra bedroom to take a swig away from Beau Tucker's eagle eye. A rock-and-roll promoter came to the suite, and he kept talking about his company headquarters in Hawaii. "I want to go to Hawaii," I said, nudging Shirley Porter. "We both want to go."

"You got it," he said. "As soon as you're ready, give me a call and I'll book the tickets and the rooms." I logged that informa-tion in the back of my brain.

Even though I'd already had my birthday party, more people had sent things to the hotel, and there was a stack of presents on the table waiting to be opened. I started opening things, and each time I'd pull something out, everybody applauded. Everyone, that is, except Ben. I kept glancing over to where he'd pulled a chair off to himself, and he'd be yawning or star-ing off into the distance. I could tell he was bored to tears by the party, by my friends, and I didn't know, maybe by me.

Soon it was obvious to everybody in the room that my date was less than enthusiastic about my post-awards show party, and I was afraid it was making people uneasy. So I took a break from opening presents and went over and sat down on the arm of his chair.

"I guess you're ready to call it a night," I said.

He shrugged.

"Well, I'm ready to go to bed any time you are," I went on.

"I'm ready right now," he said, and stood up.

That was the end of my thirtieth birthday and post-CMA Awards party. I told people we were too tired to stay up any longer, and that I'd open the rest of their gifts the next morning. Everyone left, except for Shirley Porter, T. Martin, and another T-Bird, Pam Scoggins, who were staying in the second bedroom of the suite. Ben and I went into our bedroom. He handed me a little wrapped box, my present from him. It was a sexy little black nightie, far too small for me, but I wore it anyway. I stood in the bathroom and looked at myself in this nightgown that was halfway down my front and up my backside. I was griped about the party and Ben's attitude, and I thought I looked goofy in this too-tight bit of satin and lace, but I still had an unbelievable feeling of anticipation. I might have been mad at him, but I still wanted the child I believed I'd conceive that night. Like most men, Ben turned over and went to sleep as soon as we'd had sex, but I was too excited to sleep.

I went out onto the balcony of the suite and looked down on the Cascades Courtyard. I felt more alive in that moment than ever before, feeling like life was beginning to form inside my body. I looked up and said, "Lord, if this is your will, I've conceived a child tonight. Please, God. I want to have a baby girl, and I want to name her Presley." This may sound like fiction, but it's the true story of my daughter's conception. I stood out there a long time, charged with excitement, but also feeling a deep peace, as if my life were moving on to another level. I wanted to be a mother.

The next morning, I went down to the bedroom where Shirley, T. Martin, and Pam Scoggins were sleeping. I got them up and said, "Thumbs up. It's a winner." That's how confident I was that Presley was on her way.

Things remained strained between Ben and me the entire day. Ben acted like he would rather be anywhere than with me, and when a man acts that way around me, I start to turn off any feelings I might have had or thought I had for him. By the time I drove him to the airport, I figured whatever relationship we thought we had was over.

It wasn't over, of course, because I was pregnant.

Weeks went by, and when I didn't hear from Ben, I knew I had to make a decision. I finally decided not to tell him or name him as the father. After all, we were finished as far as I could

see, so why drag him into it. I certainly didn't want him thinking he owed me anything or that he was somehow obliged to
me because I was having his child.

I look back on it now, and see that I shouldn't have been
worried about telling my parents, but I was nervous as the devil.
I was anxious about everything. I figured my relationship with
Ben was over. I didn't know what the record label would say.
And the intervention and Betty Ford were still heavily on my
mind. That whole period of my life seemed like "let's everybody
worry about Tanya" time.

I sat down with Mother and Dad and told them I was pregnant. I told them that it was Ben's child, but we were no longer
a couple, so I was not even going to name the father once news
of the pregnancy got out. My parents did not fail me. Dad just
said, "Well, we've got to go down to Capitol again." So he and
I made an appointment with Jim Fogelsong. Jim must have
thought, "What now?" It had been just a little more than a year
since Dad called him and told him he was sending me to Betty
Ford. Now we were on our way to tell him I was pregnant, and
that I was not getting married. It was impossible to know what
might happen, with the label, country radio, and the fans.

I felt horrible when we all sat down in Jim Fogelsong's office.
Everybody was lined up, with me sitting there in a chair across
from them. It was like, "Well, here's this pregnant woman, and
what can we do about it?" My answer was "deal with it," but I
kept my mouth shut except to say I wanted this baby, and
career or not, I was going to have it. "What about the father?"
Jim asked. "He is no longer in the picture," I said.

Well, what could they do? Finally, everybody congratulated
me and wished me and my baby well. As he had done with the
drug intervention, Jim promised that Capitol Records would
stand firmly behind me. When we left his office, my dad was
one relieved manager, and he was wondering what we should
do about informing the public.

To make sure we examined every angle of the PR that would
have to surround the news of the pregnancy, Dad enlisted Paul
Moore, who in turn called in a friend of his, independent publicist Cathy Gurley. After batting several ideas around, we decided to simply issue a press release, do very few interviews, and
let the chips fall. I, of course, couldn't let it go without adding
my two cents. So I issued a quote that said the baby was a girl
and I was naming her Presley, after Elvis. I also mentioned that

I thought it was too bad Elvis hadn't left some sperm in a sperm bank, because I'd sure like to have his child. Imagine my surprise this year when Alanna Nash's new Elvis book mentioned that at one time he considered doing just that, leaving sperm in search of the perfect woman for him to father another child with. Hey, he wouldn't have needed to look any farther than my house.

The rock promoter who'd come to my post-CMA party phoned me around the first of December and invited me to bring my friend and come to Hawaii to meet with his company's executives. In mid-December, Shirley Porter and I were on a plane for Hawaii.

"What's Presley's middle name going to be?" Shirley asked, once we were in the air.

"I've been thinking about that," I said. "I want to somehow name her after my mother and me.

"Tanya and Juanita," Shirley said slowly, and that's when it hit me.

"Presley Tanita! That's it. Presley Tanita Tucker." And so she was named on an airplane headed for the islands.

We checked into a suite at the Hyatt Regency on Oahu. I thought going from a cold and dreary Tennessee winter to the sunny skies of Hawaii was just what the doctor ordered for this three-and-a-half month pregnant woman. All I wanted to do was kick back on the sand, look at the ocean, and think about the child I was carrying. I didn't want anything but peace and relaxation.

As soon as I got there, I called Jim Nabors's home to see if he'd allow us to use his private beach for sunning. Jim was away, but luckily his house manager remembered me and gave us carte blanche use of the property. We hired a cab and took off for Jim's place. We put down our blankets and lay there looking out at the waves. I got out a cassette player, strapped the earphones on my stomach, and played a Julio Iglesias tape for Presley. I had a terrific crush on Julio Iglesias for a long time. "Crush" isn't the word, actually. I was hot for him. But then, when I finally met him I saw that he was almost my size. In fact, I'm positive his behind is smaller than mine! That kind of cooled me off. But I wanted my baby to hear beautiful music long before she was born, and I couldn't think of a voice more beautiful or soothing than Julio's.

Beautiful and soothing came to a screeching halt when

Shirley and I decided to take a walk along the beach. Weird people and incidents seem to pop into my life at any given moment. We were strolling along, just looking at the beautiful scenery and not talking. That's one thing I love about being with the T-Birds, we don't feel awkward about lulls in the conversation. I was looking at the beach, and Shirley had her head turned toward the ocean. All of a sudden I spotted a man standing on the beach ahead of us. He was stark naked with his penis at full salute.

"My God, Shirley, don't look now, but there's a naked man over there," I whispered. Shades of Glen Campbell all those years ago in Las Vegas.

Of course, Shirley's head jerked around right away, and when she saw him she was speechless. He had a lewd grin on his face as he stood there staring at us. Even though he didn't make a move, we figured we better get gone. We walked a little faster, then started trotting, and by the time we got to Jim's house to call a cab to come get us, we were running at top speed, scared to death, but unable to stop laughing. When we got to the house, I stood there trying to catch my breath, and Shirley said, "Can you believe that?"

"No," I said. "His thing is every bit as brown as the rest of his body!"

I guess he was a trespasser, because later nobody seemed to know why he'd be running around naked on Jim's private beach, but he sure livened up the trip for these two Tennessee girls. Nobody was home at Jim's, so we trudged on up the beach to look for a phone.

We saw a big estate on a hill about a mile from Jim's and headed up there. The sign said "Open House," and there was a big new Mercedes parked in the drive, so we walked up and opened the door. A very primly dressed woman looked at us very disapprovingly. Shirley and I had on matching neon green bikinis, neon green thongs, and big neon sunglasses. We were flat neoned out, and when Shirley realized how the woman was looking at us, she immediately got defensive.

"Are you two brokers?" the woman asked.

Shirley misunderstood the question. "We most certainly are not hookers," she shot back. "This is Tanya Tucker."

I was just dying. Here we were, trying to have a peaceful afternoon on Jim Nabors's beach, and suddenly we're running into naked men and Shirley's thinking we've been mistaken for hookers. The realtor did recognize my name, and I guess she figured I might be a prospective buyer, since she invited us in to see the place, neon bikinis or not. I was only half listening when she was talking price, and I thought she said the cost of the house was $500,000, which sounded like a hell of a deal for a house that overlooked the beach. A deal so good even my dad would want me to make it. He'd even be more proud if I got a car thrown in, so I said, "Well, for that money, would you include that Mercedes?" The agent assured me she would, and even called us a cab so we could go back to the hotel and consider the purchase. I took her card, and we headed back.

"Man, that's a great price," I said, looking at the card. "Right up from Jim's place and everything."

"How much did you think she said that house cost?" Shirley asked.

"Well, she said five hundred thousand, didn't she?"

"Try five million," Shirley said, shaking her head.

I looked back at the place as we drove down the long drive to the highway. "And it's not even beachfront property!" But that's an example of why my dad's in charge of our land deals, and not me.

That week was the end of any rest for me for the whole pregnancy. I was booked solid, and I stayed out on the road until I was eight months along and could barely waddle across the stage. It was hard. At one point, the baby turned, somehow rested on a nerve, and I couldn't get out of bed. It just knocked me to my knees. Once that pressure eased, I still had trouble standing for long periods of time, and I often had to try to do part of my show sitting on a stool in the middle of the stage. My feet and ankles swelled up, and I started getting that same deep itch on the palms of my hands and the soles of my feet that I'd had all those years ago when Delores Fuller had me out on the "Delta Dawn" radio tour. It was pure stress. And I did the same thing at thirty-one that I'd done at thirteen. I started scratching my hands and feet with a hairbrush until I'd rubbed the skin so raw I needed bandages. I finally found a medication that put an end to the itching, but the swelling continued.

I opened for Hank Jr. that March, and I honestly didn't know if I could make it through the show. In addition to my feet and legs killing me, Hank's crew was completely uninterested in my sound or lighting requirements, and they couldn't be bothered to help my band get a sound check. Mary Chapin's song

"Opening Act" nailed it. When you open for someone, sometimes you feel like grabbing them by the throat and saying, "Hey, you, could I possibly get one little tiny bit of respect over here?" I don't know where Hank was, or if it would have made any difference if I'd found him. He was such a big star that he helicoptered into venues at the last minute a lot of the time. In the back of my mind I was thinking, "Do you suppose Hank knows I'm pregnant, and he's holding it against me?" My pregnancy press release had been sent out, and I'd made a public announcement on *Entertainment Tonight* just a week before the concert. One side of me didn't believe Hank could care less about my unwed mother status, and the other side wasn't sure.

I made it through the show, and by the time I finished performing I was ready to get as far away from Hank's people as possible. The experience drove home one thing about an artist's employees. If your staff treats people rudely, it reflects on you. If some big old roadie shoves a fan out of the way, or talks rough in front of someone, or your secretary gets snotty with someone on the telephone, it's the artist who is remembered for it, not the employee. And although I haven't always succeeded, I've tried to drum that into the heads of anyone who is representing me on any level. You have to be able to rely on your staff, band, and roadies, because they can make or break a show and endear or alienate a fan base.

Because I was pregnant, I especially needed people to rely on during those times. There was one band member in particular. We had hired a new guy, and I noticed more and more that I turned to him to see that the tour ran smoothly. It's not that the others were inconsiderate but that this particular fellow seemed willing to take charge. He was a gentle, kind man who seemed to understand that I wasn't the old hell-raising, self-sufficient Tanya, and I needed some help out there on the road. Little by little, he became more important to the road show and to me as a friend. I thought he was very cute, too, but not only was I pregnant, my dad had an ironclad rule: Do not date band members.

FORTY-SIX

I better go to the hospital, Mother," I said.

"What! Are you in labor?"

"I'm real close," I said. "But I'm not gonna have her until tomorrow. I'll bet every one of my doctors is home watching fireworks with the kids, and I don't want the second team!"

Mother, La Costa, her two kids, and I were sitting in Dad's Jeep watching the Fourth of July fireworks in Brentwood, Tennessee, when I started feeling like this baby was on her way. We got to Vanderbilt and I checked in, then we started the countdown. The next morning I was in labor, but not making much progress, so they decided to speed things along and broke my water. They'd given me an epidural, so the full impact of the doctor's words didn't hit me like it would have if I'd been completely alert.

"Her heart rate's down to sixty," he said. "Tanya, she's healthy right now, but I think the cord's wrapped around her. I'm going to do a Caesarean section."

"Well, get after it," I said groggily.

The next thing I knew, Presley Tanita Tucker was lying on my chest. She was fabulous. There's no way for a mother to really describe the feeling that comes over her when she first sees her child, except maybe that she feels a fulfillment and a completion that couldn't be equaled in any other way. Looking back, I wish I'd not had the epidural, because I wish I'd had the full impact of giving birth and seeing the new baby the second it came into the world. Even though you know it's gonna hurt, I think you always want to be fully there, to fully comprehend what you've just done. And looking at Presley made me know what I'd just done was right.

"Honk if you're the father of Tanya Tucker's baby," a Nashville deejay announced on air on July 5, 1989, as soon as he learned that Presley'd been born and we were at Vanderbilt. According to friends of mine, dozens of wise guys cruised the hospital area and blasted their horns.

Speculation about the baby's father went even more wild after Presley was born than it had before. Billy Long made the tabloids as a candidate for Presley's dad. Poor Billy was stunned by the rumors and told reporters he didn't know anything about my being pregnant and he certainly wasn't the father. There were plenty of men who were willing to take credit for Presley, though. A lot of my friends joked about it. Every time I ran into George Jones he'd say, "You can't deny it any longer, Tanya. You know that kid is mine!" Charley Pride was always saying, "Be sure and keep our secret. Don't ever let on the baby is mine."

I opened a show for Lee Greenwood in Cleveland when Presley was five months old. La Costa and Presley were both with me, and as usual, La Costa came out and sang a couple of numbers during my show, and then Presley and I joined her onstage just prior to my final number. Lee was standing backstage after my portion of the show and said he wanted to talk something serious over with me. I agreed, and we sat down for a heart to heart. La Costa was there with me at the time.

"Look," Lee started. "What would you think about this? I'd like to take credit for Presley."

I thought he was joking around, and started laughing.

"No, I'm serious," he said. "We could call a press conference and announce that I'm the father, take some photos of the three of us. It'd be great for both our careers."

I about died. "It wouldn't be that great for Presley, though, would it?" I told him, and ended the conversation. Hey, I love publicity, too, but that was a little over the top. Makes you wonder if he'd have been willing to pay child support.

Later his road manager swore it had all been a joke. Was he serious? You've got me. It sure sounded like an earnest suggestion.

I went back out on tour three weeks after Presley was born. I was a little unsure how taking a baby along would work, but the few times I went out without her I couldn't stand it. I'd lie awake at night while the bus rolled down the road, thinking of Presley at home. Maybe waking up and wanting to be fed. I knew Mother was taking good care of her, but I felt it should be me there with her. So we put a crib on the bus, and La Costa and Mother came out on the road, too.

When La Costa came out with us, she always participated in the show, singing "Love Train" and one or another of her favorite releases. The crowds seemed to love the idea of the sisters back together, and then, when I'd bring Presley out toward the end of the show, the crowds went wild. I saw immediately that my fans didn't think less of me for wanting to have her. Only once that I know of did a fan at one of the shows comment negatively about my single mother status, and all that involved was a woman who bought a La Costa T-shirt. She explained that if Tanya hadn't had a baby out of wedlock, she might have bought one of hers, too. So I lost a T-shirt sale. So be it. I did hear that some preachers brought up the fact that I should be a role model, and I was an example of how country music was getting as bad as rock and roll. But since I wasn't there when they were saying it, I didn't know if it was true, and I didn't worry about it.

My mother hated having Presley out on the road, because her schedule was always changing. Sometimes she'd be in bed by 8:30, and sometimes by midnight. I hated the schedule problem, too, but I just couldn't stand being out there for weeks at a time without her. I'd have given anything to have been able to take time off to stay out at the Song House and just be Presley's mom. But I was a single mother and I knew I had to get out and work as much as possible to support my family.

It's the little details of taking care of an infant out on the road that get you. Making sure you have enough formula, baby food, diapers. Anyone who's ever taken a baby on a long trip knows what I mean. You have to think ahead all the time, because you can't afford to be a hundred miles from nowhere and run out of baby food. So we were continually double-checking our supplies, anticipating Presley's needs, then checking the time and miles between truck stops. I couldn't have done it without Mother and La Costa, because we left a trail of nannies all over the country. Some were too old to take the road show, some were too young to take on the responsibility, and others were just along for the ride. Any mother will tell you that child care is one of the hardest things to find, and if you're an entertainer on the road, your problems are magnified. A lot of the most reliable people won't want to be away from their own families that much, and a lot of starstruck girls might be attracted because they think it'll be glamorous. Believe me, it ain't even glamorous for the star, let alone the staff.

My life settled down a great deal because of the baby. It was partly because I was feeling the responsibility of motherhood, but partly because I seldom felt lonely or in need of a party after a show. I could go back to the bus and head down the road, cuddling with my little girl. I was tired some of the time, simply because of Presley's feedings and schedule, but on the other hand, I didn't have any hangovers to sleep off. There were definite benefits as far as my lifestyle was concerned.

Presley and I spent a lot of hours together rolling across America when she was a baby. She was too little to remember any of it, but she had a lot of experiences out there on the road. She even went to prison once. I played a fair in Lucasville, Ohio, on August 9, and while La Costa, Presley, and I were having breakfast at the local Bob Evans, a woman approached me.

"Aren't you Tanya Tucker?"

I said I was, expecting an autograph request. But instead, she said, "Did you know that Johnny Paycheck is right down the road at the Chillicothe Correctional Facility?"

Johnny's legal battles over a bar shooting in Ohio had gone on so long that I didn't know for sure when he'd finally been sentenced or where he'd gone to prison. I did know that I disagreed with the decision, since from everything I heard, the man he took a shot at later admitted he was at fault in the incident. We went back to the bus, and I'm sure that my bus driver never expected me to say, "Head on down that road, Lee. We're going to the prison in Chillicothe."

I called the prison from the bus, and when I finally got through to the warden, I asked if it was possible to speak with Johnny Paycheck. "Do you mean Donnie Lytle?" he asked. I guessed prison was a lot like Betty Ford. You don't get to use your stage names. The warden didn't act like he believed it was Tanya Tucker, but he said to come on to the prison and he'd meet with me, anyway. When I got there, he just shook his head and escorted me to the infirmary. I offered to do a show at the prison if it would help get Johnny out any quicker, and it didn't occur to me until later that the warden could probably have slapped me with bribery charges.

Johnny couldn't believe it was me, either. And I still can't believe he lived through those several years he spent in prison, because he was very sick with emphysema. I asked him if he needed anything, and he said just extra pajamas. Then he thought about it a few minutes and asked me if I'd mind singing on an album called *Jailhouse Rock* that he'd recorded with Hank Cochran right before he was sentenced. I promised I'd call Hank as soon as I got back to Nashville, and I headed on toward my show. On the way, we stopped at a store, and I ran in and bought a pile of p.j.'s and slippers for the bus driver to deliver to the prison while I performed the concert.

When I got back to Nashville, I went straight to Hank Cochran's house and sang on *Jailhouse Rock*. I don't think anything ever came of it, though. I thought then, as I do now, that it would have been a million seller if it had been advertised on television with an 800-number. The music business is one that's full of unfinished projects and finished projects that are lost because of a lack of follow-through.

We'd had three hit singles from *Strong Enough to Bend*, and Capitol decided that was all they'd release from the album. "Strong Enough to Bend" went to the top of the charts, and the label followed that with two more hits, "Highway Robbery" and "Call on Me." But I balked at only three single releases, since I wanted "Daddy and Home" to be a single and a video. When the word came down that they'd go ahead and send it out to radio but not waste money on a video, I hit the fan. I insisted the label release the song to radio, and I decided to make the video myself. I hired a video crew, and we shot the clip with me sitting in a motel room waiting on the tour bus to be repaired and thinking about the home fires. I put together a series of old photographs and home movies of Dad and me. I thought it was a beautiful, touching video, and it meant so much to Dad that I made it. If the song had contained an important message when I was out running completely wild, it meant twice as much now that I was a mother.

The single stiffed at number twenty-seven. This didn't have a thing to do with the fact that I'd had a baby out of wedlock, it had to do with what I call, "Lesson number 38 in Recording Artist 101": Never force your record label to release a song it doesn't want to release. You're laying yourself wide open for a big "See, we told you so." If the company ain't the pilot, your record ain't gonna fly.

❧ ❧ ❧ ❧

I got my first big chance to show off my daughter to the industry at my birthday party that year. I held it at the Magnolia Room at the Opryland Hotel, the night after the 1989 CMA Awards, where I lost Female Vocalist again. Me and Susan Lucci, oh well. I wore a simple, floor-length black gown, with my hair up, wanting this to be a classic, elegant birthday gala. The party was strictly a no-drinking and no-smoking affair, this time by my orders, not Dad's.

But even without alcohol, my parties can get crazy. There in the Magnolia ballroom, where over four hundred guests, including Marie Osmond, Garth Brooks, Highway 101's Paulette Carlson, the Nitty Gritty Dirt Band, and a crowd of industry executives stood in elegant attire, Mother and Dad presented me with three miniature horses. Dad led the horses out, and they promptly dumped several piles on the ballroom floor! Then when we got them on the hotel elevator, they performed a couple of encores. It reminded me of one time when I was around twenty, and I drove my Porsche to Denver City, Texas, to visit some of my relatives. While I was there, one of the family offered me three ducks and two geese for Tuckahoe. I didn't want to wait to have them shipped, so I loaded them right into the Porsche and we headed back to the ranch, ducks quacking and geese honking all the way. You can dress me up and take me out, but I can turn into a hillbilly real quick.

I felt so lucky through those first six months of Presley's life to have the backing of my record label. With the exception of my wanting "Daddy and Home" to be a single and video, Capitol couldn't have been more supportive. Over the years, I had learned many times over that unless your label considers you a priority—one of the artists whose releases are carefully planned and pushed hard both at radio and retail—you will probably be left standing in somebody's dust. On December 11, 1989, a bomb dropped on Music Row when EMI, Capitol's parent company, named Jimmy Bowen the new president of Capitol Records in Nashville.

Man, I thought, here we go.

Bowen had the reputation of being one of the toughest men in the business, an executive an artist had better not push if he or she wanted to keep a career going. He fired all but two or three people at Capitol within his first week. Fogelsong was out, of course. Bonnie Rasmussin was out. It was the second time around for Bonnie and Jim. Bowen had taken over MCA Records a few years earlier and they had been caught in that corporate housecleaning. Being a record executive is as chancy as being an artist.

Bowen always did that; he'd go through the label like a steamroller and replace everyone with his own handpicked staff. He did it to ensure loyalty, and I knew that a new company president has to have complete loyalty. But knowing it didn't make me any less nervous.

Bowen was a noted record producer, and he was also known to force artists to change producers, even when they had a long-standing relationship. I didn't want to leave Jerry Crutchfield, and I didn't want to lose my priority status. The label's new kid, Garth Brooks, was making waves on the charts, and Bowen was bringing acts like Eddie Rabbitt, Lacy J. Dalton, and the Gatlins from his previous gig at Universal Records. He could very easily turn all his attention to them and forget Tanya Tucker, no matter how well my records were charting. I had no idea what he thought of me as an artist or of my single mother status, so we didn't know what to expect when Bowen called for his first meeting with us. He said we needed to talk about career direction, as well as go over the photo shoot I'd done for *Tennessee Woman.* One hopeful sign was that Bowen had hired Cathy

Gurley's company to represent the label's public relations. She'd been a part of our initial Presley press release plans, so I figured she was in my corner.

We took the whole family to the first meeting. I carried Presley in the office wrapped in a fluffy blanket, and Mother and Dad accompanied us. Presley was only six months old, but in her pink dress and matching headband, she looked like a star, too.

I was surprised at how cordial and laid-back Bowen was. He fussed over Presley a bit, then we got down to business. From the moment he started talking, I knew everything was going to be okay.

"Tanya, you are one of this label's top priorities," he said. "I want to see you selling gold, winning awards, and taking your rightful place as one of the industry's most important female artists. That's my job, to see that it happens. Your job is to continue to make hit records with Jerry Crutchfield."

I don't know if he could hear me say "whew" under my breath.

Bowen went on to explain that the new regime wanted me to have a more uptown, classy image. Forget the wild country party girl, and forget the sexpot. I was a young mother and an adult woman, and everything from my publicity pictures to my album covers to the clothing I wore for televised interviews should reflect this new class. A photographer showed up about then to take a shot of Bowen and me for the trade magazines.

"All right!" I yelled, and then ran and jumped right in Bowen's lap and shouted, "Here's your photo op!" I couldn't dump the old image completely.

Bowen turned red and said, "Well, make me a print of that, but don't show it to my wife."

That was my introduction to the new Capitol Nashville, and their intro to the new, much classier, me.

FORTY-SEVEN

As Presley grew from an infant to a baby with a personality and identity of her own, I began wondering if I'd made the right decision about keeping Ben out of her life. She was too young to ask any questions right then, but what would she have to say to me later? I knew that she was being denied a father during her first year, an important developmental period. My dad, of course, was the Grandpa of the Century. He doted on her. Both my parents did. But a doting grandfather is not a father, and I agonized for months over what to do.

I had no idea what reaction to expect from him. Would he deny that the baby was his? I didn't see how that was possible, given both the mathematics and Presley's face. She looked so much like him. Or would he fly off the handle and cuss me out because I'd kept him in the dark about it? The decision was taken out of my hands in March of 1990 when I took nine-month-old Presley to the Larry Gatlin Golf Tournament in Texas. I'd not heard from Ben, nor had I seen Jeff McKay, the mutual friend who'd introduced us back in Tulsa, since I'd gotten pregnant. But Jeff loves golf tournaments, and he showed up at Larry's. I attended the charity auction and the reception the night before the tournament to perform "Texas (When I Die)" and auction off some personal memorabilia to help the cause. I was standing toward the back, holding Presley, when Jeff made his way through the crowd and found me. We talked a few minutes and then right out of the blue, he said, "There's no mistaking that baby. She's Ben's."

I said, "Well, Jeff, it doesn't take a great mathematician to count the months back to the CMA Awards."

What I didn't know at the time was that Jeff had sought me out that night on Ben's behalf. Ben hadn't thought much about it when he first heard I was pregnant, figuring I'd met someone and he'd one day read all about the father of my baby in the tabloids. He'd also started a relationship with someone else, and he was busy working and going to auditions. Time slipped by. But months after Presley's birth, when I was still refusing to name the father, he started wondering. He happened to be talking to Jeff one afternoon in L.A. and asked him if he thought Presley could be his baby.

"I'll probably see Tanya at the golf tournament this weekend," Jeff told him.

"Find out if that's my child," Ben said.

The first thing Jeff did when he got back to L.A. was to call Ben and tell him he had a baby girl. Ben says he went through an array of emotions that afternoon: anger at me for keeping the pregnancy from him; fear at learning he was a parent; love for this child he'd never seen. He also says he felt a staggering sense of responsibility, because family is very important to him. He promptly called Beau Tucker in an attempt to track me down. Dad took his number, as if I didn't still have it in my book.

As it happened, I was due to appear at a telethon in Los Angeles right after the golf tournament, and Dad called me at Century City, where I was staying. In some ways, calling Ben was easier because Presley was not with me. Whatever we initially had to say to each other would not be complicated by his daughter being in the same room. I was apprehensive about talking to Ben. I still didn't know what his reaction would be. Once he saw his child and realized he'd missed almost the first year of her life, would he ever speak to me again? I called him, and the first thing he said was, "I hear I have a baby girl." I told him I thought he knew that all along. He said that only in the past few weeks had he considered the fact that he might be a father.

He came straight to Century City, and the minute we sat down to talk, we both started crying. We talked about family, and how important having a family was for both of us. What we didn't talk about was us. I think we both believed that whatever we'd once had was long since dead. I told Ben I was heading out the next day for Branson, and that Presley and the nanny were meeting me with the tour bus at the airport.

"I'm coming with you," he said.

"I know," I said.

I felt like a big weight was off my shoulders. Presley would know her father. There would be no heartbreaking scenes later on in life when she asked why I'd hidden the truth from her and from her father. For once, I was doing the right thing.

We landed in Springfield, Missouri, the following afternoon, and when we got into the airport, Ben stopped in his tracks, as if he'd been hit. Coming across the room in a stroller was his nine-month-old daughter. Once again, tears were pouring down both our faces. He stayed in Branson to get to know his little girl, and for the next few days he just poured his heart out about his feeling for her. I had some things to say, too. I made it clear that I didn't need anything from him except that he love his daughter. He made it clear to me that from that day on Presley Tucker had a dad who would be there for her.

In Missouri, we had a good, family-type week. Ben and I rented mini bikes and in the afternoons rode around in the hills while Presley napped. Ben got a picture of him and Presley taken at one of those places that puts photographs on coffee mugs. He had one made for me, one for his mother, and one for himself. He's had his morning coffee from that mug ever since.

Ben told me that since we'd last seen each other, he'd gotten his first big break. Soon after Presley was born, the Emmy Awards show hired him to film a series of national commercials. He played a star arriving at the show and getting out of his limo to the sound of the cheering crowds. Since that time, he'd had quite a bit of commercial work, but we both hoped the scenario played out on the Emmy commercial was a sign of things to come.

For better or worse, Ben and I were now a team for at least

one purpose, parenthood. On the surface, things remained the same. Ben flew back to L.A. and his acting pursuits, and Presley and I hit the road in the bus again. But everything in both our worlds had changed that day. I was still a single mother, but I was no longer a single parent.

In May, Capitol released *Tennessee Woman*. No one who knew Ben and me and heard that album should have had any question about Presley's father. I even subtitled "Tennessee Woman" "Ben's Song." "Walking Shoes" was chosen as the first single, and it hit the top-five that winter. A duet with T. Graham Brown, "Don't Go Out," was the second top-five single from the album, with CMA, ACM, and Grammy nominations in the Vocal Collaboration category. We had two other big hits from the album: "Oh, What It Did to Me" and "It Won't Be Me." The song I felt strongest about, "Tennessee Woman," wasn't chosen as a single, but I didn't push it.

FORTY-EIGHT

*I*n March of 1990 I was in Portland, Oregon, playing a radio appreciation day show. I'd been on the bus, showering and getting ready, and hadn't heard the act before me. Then, as I was sitting on the bed putting on my nylons, I heard the wild applause. It was overwhelming. Clearly, Travis Tritt was something special. I made it a point to go introduce myself, and after my show we sat around backstage talking. I had seldom met a young performer with such a clear vision of his music and his career direction. He was a Southern country rocker and made no bones about it. He knew that because his music was a little edgier than the norm, it could mean he might be overlooked for awards and that some songs might not make it to the top of the charts. But he was not going to consider changing his sound.

I like to think of myself as a rebel and as an outspoken woman who has fought to make music my way. The truth is, I have often tried to speak up and have just as often gotten scared and backed down. So I loved listening to this new artist speak his mind with such conviction. I hoped the business didn't knock it out of him. I'll get a little ahead of the story here and tell you it hasn't. I haven't heard of him compromising yet.

We decided to tour together, and one of the shows we were

set to play was at Westbury, New York, on June 27. I had the twenty-fifth and twenty-sixth off, so I came in early to do a few interviews, shop, and see the sights. Presley and Mother were traveling with me, as was the label publicist, Cathy Gurley. I'd learned that this was Travis's first time in New York, and I got to thinking about what an experience your first trip to the Big Apple ought to be. I remember one vivid picture from my very first trip to New York, clear back when I was thirteen years old and on Columbia Records. Dad and I flew in for some talks with CBS executives, and we had lunches and dinners and meetings. The thing that stands out in my mind was the fact that we stayed in a huge hotel, yet the rooms were little and cramped. I thought, if you just look on the outside, you'd think this place is a palace. But once you get past the surface, it's not what it seems. Just like a lot of things. Show business. Relationships. Recording contracts. Management deals.

I wanted Travis to have a better memory of his first trip, and I wanted him to feel like a star. So I started making plans. I got us tickets to *Phantom of the Opera* for the next night, and I planned to take him to my favorite sports bar, Mickey Mantle's. I also got Cathy to go out and buy one of Travis's cassettes, so I could plan a little surprise for him. Then I started taking care of my business. I did several print interviews. Mother, Cathy, Presley, and I shopped for some new clothes for Presley, who by this time had almost as extensive a wardrobe as I did. Then we stopped for lunch. One of the greatest things about Presley's personality is that people have always seemed to be drawn to her. Waiters and waitresses would stop by and fuss over her, and they'd always have ideas about what they could prepare that a nine-month-old child could eat. By the end of the day, Mother and Presley were ready to go back to the hotel and crash.

I was ready to take Travis on the town, so I waited in the room and then in the lobby. There was no sign of Travis Tritt's bus, so I went ahead and took Cathy with me to the *Phantom of the Opera*, since Mother insisted on staying at the hotel with her granddaughter. The next afternoon I was in my room, watching television, when Travis called.

"Man, look at this city," he said. "We're right on the outskirts of town."

"Where the hell have you been?" I asked. "I had all kinds of plans for us."

"We got held up," he said, which is the way most entertainers explain being late for anything. "Keep the plans, though, 'cause I'm on my way."

I knew we were screwed as far as getting *Phantom of the Opera* tickets. I'd had a hard time getting those, so as a last-ditch effort, I called Charlie Feldman at BMI, who had transferred from Nashville to the New York office a few years earlier. I don't know how Charlie pulled it off, but he got us tickets for another Broadway hit musical, *Grand Hotel*. I arranged to meet Travis in the hotel lobby and told him to put on his New York party clothes, 'cause I was ready to rock. So I'm waiting at the bar in a white tailored suit, and in Travis walks, wearing his leather jacket and boots and looking every inch a redneck Southern rocker. I loved it. We headed out to see New York. After we saw *Grand Hotel*, we headed over to Mickey Mantle's. Sure enough, just as instructed, when we walked in, the music blasting through the place was Travis singing, "I'm a member of the country club, country music is in my blood." Travis just fell out. From there we hit every happening club in the city, and we had cocktails at every one of them. We stayed out half the night, and by the time the limo came to take us out to Westbury, we were so hungover and exhausted we slept all the way.

Travis had been worried about the New York audiences and how they'd respond to his music. I told him he shouldn't be concerned, because Westbury draws a country-loving audience when Nashville artists hit town. And I was right; that crowd couldn't get enough of him. The folks at Mickey Mantle's couldn't, either. Travis later told me that he went back on his next trip to New York, and the fans swarmed around him like he was the biggest star in the sky. Well, I'd wanted Travis to like New York, and I wanted New York to like him. He did and it did. I love it when a plan comes together.

It was while I was touring with Travis that I got into a situation I can only categorize as one of those stupid, dumb-ass deals that goes down but that has no acceptable explanation. In midsummer we played a show in Massachusetts. The band member I'd come to rely on so heavily during and after my pregnancy was having a birthday, so I took everyone to dinner. I'd put him in charge of much of the tour planning, and he made being on the road much easier. I didn't have to worry anymore about a lot of the little details that sometimes made me crazy, things like where the equipment was and who was feeling sick and who needed guitar strings about five minutes before the show. The fact that when I had been vulnerable, this man stepped in and was supportive gave us a powerful link. My father had always been the man I counted on. And now I had another shoulder to lean on and someone I could trust to look out for my interests. I had a friend.

The whole band went out to dinner, and Travis joined us for a while. It was one of those celebrations where everybody is having a great time, laughing and telling jokes. But through it all, I was watching my band member. I didn't think I'd ever before noticed just what a sweetheart he was. Oh, I'd always thought he was cute. But because of my dad's band rule, I'd never gone past the first-glance stage. After dinner the band and I went back to my bus. My favorite musician and I started talking about the show, and one by one, the other members left, until it was just the two of us. I started feeling almost nervous, like a kid with her first crush. For one thing, I knew he was married and had kids. Because of that, I'm not going to mention his name here. He's not under public scrutiny, and I'm sure he wants it to stay that way.

"My wife and I are splitting up, Tanya," he said, as if he could read my mind.

"What's the problem?"

"We haven't had any kind of a marriage for the last couple of years. I'm only there for the kids." He put his head in his hands. "I don't know what I'll do if I lose them."

I put my arm around him, forgetting yet another of my dad's rules: Quit trying to save unhappy people. When they go under, they'll drown you right along with them, because your grip on the life raft ain't all that tight.

He stayed with me on the bus that night, and when we woke up the next morning, we were like two kids, ready to go out and conquer the world together. I believed every word he said about his faltering marriage, and I believed him when he told me he was in love with me. There's a big problem with a love affair between friends. You think you know everything about the person. You don't think they'd lie to you or lead you on, because they've been there for you on so many other levels. That's what you think, but the heart can lead the mind's good judgment astray.

That night marked the beginning of what I thought was going to be the best time in my life, and it ended up one of the worst. I understand why female artists like Tammy and Reba have husbands who play a big role in their careers. They travel together and make decisions together. The road isn't such an empty place because your partner is there with you at almost every truck stop. You also don't feel like you're out there drifting if you have someone on the bus who knows every detail of the tour, the show, and your career plans.

I didn't know why I was so insanely attracted to this man. Sometimes I thought it was my age. I was thirty-two, and I knew that women get more sexual in nature as they get older. So I kept thinking that I was just going through a stage, maybe even a midlife crisis. Except that it didn't feel like a crisis. It felt like smooth sailing.

Over the next few months, he and I became inseparable. He seemed to adore Presley, and of course, that was a priority in finding a lifetime mate. He had to love my daughter. I had no illusions of this man stepping into Ben's shoes as a father, though. From the moment Ben knew about Presley, he was a doting daddy. Ben called and came to see his daughter whenever he could, and of course, if I played anywhere close to L.A., he could spend time with her. Sometimes when I looked at the two of them together, I felt a sadness that it hadn't worked between us. I'd wonder what it would have been like to be married to the father of my child. I'd try to picture what it would be like to have another child with him, and be a real all-American family. But I thought our time had come and gone, and now was the time for my new beau and me. If Ben ever questioned or even noticed how much time I was spending with my band member, he didn't mention it.

Of course, whenever he and I talked about his impending divorce, he had one or another reason that it couldn't happen just yet. But I believed he was working on it. I started mentioning him in my shows, too. At that time, Lorrie Morgan was going out with a tour bus driver, so I'd make sly allusions to that, and wink over toward the band. Or I'd talk about how cute certain guys in my band were. I need to make it clear that the reason my dad didn't want me dating a band member had nothing to do with a band member being less important a person than me. It had to do with professionalism out on the road, and the problems that can be caused when anyone dates someone they work with.

I was dodging my dad at every turn. He has spies out on the road with me at all times. I'm never sure who they are, but they're there, and it didn't take long before Beau Tucker knew Tanya was screwing up again. I tried to be unavailable for his calls, but every so often he'd catch up with me.

"Do you have any idea what you are doing?"

"Yes," I'd say. "I'm living my life."

"You are ruining your life."

"Just because he's in the band—"

"—just because he's married!"

"I'm happy, Daddy. Isn't that what you want?"

"This whole thing is going to come to no good end."

"It's going to be fine, Daddy."

And so it went. I'd argue with Dad, make love with my new boyfriend, talk with Ben on the phone about Presley, then go off down the road to another show or another celebrity event. And sometimes those things, shows or special events, become something I focus on so hard that I ignore whatever is going wrong in my day-to-day life.

FORTY-NINE

$\mathcal{T}$he event I was most looking forward to that winter was a celebrity cutting competition in Fort Worth. Ever since Mike Mowrey had introduced me to the world of the cutting horse and cutting competitions when I was fourteen, I'd tried to practice whenever and wherever I could. I hadn't been able to afford those lessons way back then, but as I mentioned earlier, one good thing about being an entertainer is that you get to do a lot of things you couldn't do if· you had to pay! Cutting is one of those things.

I was ready to win when I rode into the Will Rogers Coliseum arena in Fort Worth, Texas, at the National Cutting Horse Association's Futurity Celebrity Cutting on December 1, 1990. The announcer knew it, too, when he said: "Ladies and gentle-men, here comes Tanya Tucker, and from the look on her face, I'd say she's here to win." It's hard to believe I had any confi-dence at all, because my musician boyfriend was tap dancing about his divorce by then, and every time I saw Ben Reed with Presley, it nearly broke my heart. I knew that most people close to the situation, friends and family alike, wanted Ben and me to get back together. I didn't know what I wanted anymore, with the exception of that cutting event, which I wanted to win.

Cutting is the one area of my life I am intensely competitive about. I don't think I'm particularly competitive when it comes to my music. Applause and knowing my fans like my records and concerts is enough for me there. Maybe it's because cutting involves a skill, rather than a talent. I love the knowledge that I'm skilled at something as difficult as cutting.

And it is difficult. You have two minutes and thirty seconds to ride from the end of the arena to the cutoff line in the middle and to cut as many cows from the herd as possible. They have anywhere from five to thirty head out there. Winning requires a lot more than skill on the rider's part, though. You need a good horse that can outmaneuver the cow, and a cow that doesn't merely run back and forth but really tries to dodge the horse. A good cutting is a beautiful thing to see.

There had been a lot of good cuttings that day. Larry Wilcox, the star of *CHiPs*, started the action with a good ride and a solid score of 219, followed by former Pittsburgh Steeler Hall of Fame member Mel Blount, who scored 217. If you judged from the applause when the participants were announced, either Christie Brinkley, Michael Keaton, or Dallas Cowboy Randy White was the crowd favorite. Christie looked beautiful that day. She was wearing a black sequined blouse, black hat, and fringed chaps, and she was riding a gray mare named Precious Playboy. She did a good job and ended up taking fourth place in 1990, with a score of 213, and winning the event the following year. Michael Keaton had finished second in his first cutting event, and the NCHA in Fort Worth was his second. He had some bad luck, though, and got a cow who wasn't going to leave the herd no matter what he did. Randy White also had a couple of tough cows, and he didn't score well enough to finish in the top four. Johnny Rutherford, the race driver, had an unfortunate incident when his horse slipped on a turn, and I think the crowd was surprised when he recovered well and cut his cattle smoothly from the herd.

I was riding a terrific cutter named Mr. San Dancer, and from the moment we faced the two yearlings, I had complete confidence. The cows were perfect, they bobbed and weaved like boxers, and San Dancer met them at each turn. I scored a 220 and won the event by one point. NCHA President Dennie Dunn presented me with the gold buckle.

You don't really get much free time to spend with other celebrities at these events, but I did get to talk a little with Christie Brinkley during practice time.

"I know Billy's got some songs for you," she said.

I loved that. You figure it'll happen in Nashville, where everybody on the street is a writer. But it seemed so strange that here was Christie Brinkley pitching Billy Joel songs to me at a cutting.

"Well, get 'em to me," I told her.

"I love your singing," she graciously added.

"Well, I love your face," I laughed. "If I'd had your face with my voice, I'd a' owned the world by now."

You never really know how celebrities are going to treat you when you're out in public. For example, I didn't get to say much more than hello to Michael Keaton that day. I wanted the chance to at least talk a little, because he seemed like such a deep person, with nothing superficial about him. But we never had any free time to talk. Then, a couple of years later we were at another cutting together, and I saw this cowboy walking across the arena toward me. When he got close enough, I could see it was Michael, and he said, "Hello, Tanya, I just wanted to come over and say hi." I was so impressed by his coming to say hello that I didn't even dig for any profound conversation. *Northern Exposure*'s Barry Corbin participates in a lot of cutting events, and he's another person who makes an effort to speak to people and who seems like he might be your next-door neighbor. The same goes for his co-star, Janine Turner.

I appreciate people like that, because meeting celebrities out in public can turn very weird, very fast. Anyone who has ever hesitated before asking a celebrity for an autograph needs to know that it's the same whether you are another public figure or not. One night a year or so ago I was out at a place in Phoenix called Stix, where a lot of pro basketball players were hanging out in back with the Phoenix Suns. I was in there with some friends shooting pool, and one of the waiters came over and said, "Tanya, Charles Barkley is in the back room and he'd like you to come back so he can meet you." Well, who'd have thought Charles Barkley knew about this country singer in the first place? But when I turned to look back there, I saw a couple of rows of what looked like bodyguards, so I stayed put. I've been in those situations before.

"You tell Charles I'd love to meet him," I said. "In fact, I'll be waitin' to meet him right here at this pool table all night."

I thought the people I was with were going to die. They kept after me to go back there so they could meet him, but I kept on shooting pool. I just didn't feel like fighting through all those bodyguards to maybe, maybe not, meet Charles Barkley. All of a sudden I felt this big hand on my shoulder, and when I turned, it was Charles. He introduced himself and then said, "I want you to know it's a real honor to meet you. I'd like you to be my guest at one of our games sometime." We talked for a few minutes until so many girls crowded around him that he had to make a fast retreat back to the safety of the bodyguards.

A few minutes later another waiter came over. "Michael Jordan is back there, and he'd like you to come back and say hi." Would wonders never cease? This time I just couldn't talk my friends out of it. They absolutely insisted. I didn't want to do it. As a matter of fact, I had a bad feeling about it.

But we wound our way to the back of the club, where a huge guy stood with his arms folded over his chest, guarding the door to basketball land. I tried to be as polite as possible.

"I'm Tanya Tucker, and Michael Jordan asked me to come back here and say hello," I said. He looked me up and down like I was carrying a pipe bomb, and disappeared into the back room. In two seconds he was out again.

"Michael don't know—uh—nobody by that name."

I could tell by the offhanded way the security guard talked that he hadn't even told Michael anyone was there to see him. For one thing, it was obvious he didn't even remember what name I'd given him. But there I am anyway, looking like a fool, just like I suspected I would. I turned around to my friends and said, "Now, do you see why I don't do this shit?"

I have enough crazy stuff going on in my regular life. I don't need to add celebrity one-upsmanship to my list of weird.

❧ ❧ ❧ ❧

And speaking of celebrity-associated weird times, I want to tell you about doing *Lifestyles of the Rich and Famous* soon after the Celebrity Cutting. When I watch those shows I always think the people on them have everything under control. On television they appear to have perfect homes, perfect careers, and perfect lives. And rich? Sophia Loren was on one of them talking about having six or seven homes, located all over the world! When I did my segment for the show, I'd come in off the road late the night before, and I was whipped. I didn't have any household help and I hadn't even had time to clean my house. I sure didn't feel like jumping out of bed that morning and hauling out a mop and pail. Presley had been staying at Mother and Dad's during that trip. The first thing in the morning on the day the show was being taped, Mother brought Presley to the house and got her ready for the shoot. Then she and one of the label's publicity representatives, Summer Harman, swept and dusted before the film crew got there. I don't care how old you get, there are always times your mother is going to have to bail you out.

Dad had watched some of those Rich and Famous–type shows, and when they panned across the front of my little two-bedroom place, it killed him. The Song House sure didn't look like the usual star home, places like Tammy Wynette's huge white home with gates that read "First Lady Acres" or Loretta Lynn's antebellum estate called "Hurricane Mills." Well, I'm sorry, but I loved the Song House. And thanks to Mother and Summer, it looked good when they filmed. At least there was no dust on the piano. But that show started the wheels in Dad's head in motion. Soon afterward, he saw a property called Hidden Valley for sale in Brentwood, and once he saw the mansion that was on it, he bought the place. Of course, as usual, he made a killer deal on the property, and nowadays he'll probably say that's the real reason he moved me, but it had a lot to do with a television show.

One day I was on the bus headed back to Nashville when I got the call. Dad told me not to go to the Song House, because he'd moved me to Hidden Valley. It was like the move from L.A. all over again, only this time it was a result of the rich and famous, not the wild and infamous.

FIFTY

*R*ight after the holidays my life took another sharp turn. Maybe it was seeing Ben with Presley on Christmas, or maybe it was the fact that my new beau had to spend time with his wife, but I started feeling closer to Ben again, and I began wondering if there could possibly be a future for us. Ben started to feel the same way, and by January of 1991, we were a couple again.

We started talking about having a life together, and even having another child. There is a fairly large age gap between Ben and his brothers, and so he believed in having children close together. And so, on January 5, we went to Santa Fe to spend a few days in Ali McGraw's condo at Rancho Encatada. We invited Shirley Porter and Roe Farone to come with us. The four of us went skiing and went to Taos to shop. We had a great vacation, and I believe that's when Beau Grayson Tucker was conceived. Ben swears it was on January 22, when I played a show in Dallas. Our entire little family was staying at the Stockyards in Fort Worth: Ben, me, and Presley. We made a big fire in the fireplace, put Presley to bed, and made love in front of the roaring fire. I think Ben just likes the romantic idea of the roaring fire, but wherever it happened, Beau Grayson was very much wanted. Ben and I wanted, planned, and prayed for a baby brother for Presley.

Ben and Presley came with me to Chicago on February 12, where I was scheduled to appear the following day on the *Oprah Winfrey Show*. We'd been at a polo match in Florida for the past several days. Ben scored three goals at the match, as a matter of fact. The theme of the Oprah show was mothers and daughters, so Mother flew in from Nashville and we met her at O'Hare, where Oprah's limo picked us up and took us to a hotel. The other guests set for the show were Ally Sheedy and her mother, Charlotte, and Lisa Hartman and her mother, Jonnie.

Oprah was picking up the tab at this hotel, and all we were to do was sign for whatever we wanted—room service, drinks at the bar, or whatever. When Mother went to dinner and found out she was Oprah's guest, she wouldn't order more than a salad, hating for Oprah to see the bill and think the Tucker entourage had been extravagant. I told her I thought Oprah could probably afford to buy her a steak, but Mother held firm.

The next morning we all went to the studio prior to the taping for hair and makeup. That proved to be as big a stumbling block for Mother as the food had been. Stylists gave her the works, heavy lipstick, lots of eye shadow, and blush. Mother was watching herself being made up, but she didn't say a word until just before we walked out to the soundstage. Then she whispered, "Tanya, I just hate for your daddy to be watching television and see me all painted up like this! I look like a floozy!" Of course, when we got back to Nashville, Daddy agreed. "A woman as beautiful as Juanita doesn't need all that junk on her face," he told us.

Mother hadn't realized Oprah was going to be talking about points of contention between mothers and daughters. I don't think I quite understood, either. I suppose the show's concept was in one of the dozens of faxes that came to the hotel in Florida while Ben and Presley and I vacationed. And since I hadn't warned her, Mother clammed up when we got around to my wild lifestyle. We aren't the kind of family to air dirty laundry, and that hour in front of the camera was pure hell for Mother. She would just as soon have told the world that I always acted like I was teaching Sunday School. Ally and Charlotte Sheedy talked about some rough times Ally'd gone through, and Lisa Hartman brought up the fact that her mother seldom approved of her choice in men. When we took a commercial break, I turned to Lisa and said, "You know who you should meet, Clint Black. He's just the kind of good guy a mother wants to see her daughter bring home." She didn't let on, but she'd already met Clint at one of his shows. I take credit as a match-maker for that union, anyway.

I wanted Ben to sit in the audience with Presley and bring her up toward the end of the show, but he flatly refused. Ben hated the idea of being considered my tagalong boyfriend who might be using my name to further his career. So he stayed backstage, and a crew member carried Presley out when the time came. After the show, Presley and I had our picture taken with Oprah, and we chatted with her for a few moments. That was our only contact with the show's star, since she didn't come back to the dressing rooms before or after the taping.

I have a huge amount of respect for Oprah. She appears to be able to balance stardom and big business extremely well. I've wanted so badly to do that myself. Harlan Howard told me that I was a songwriter hidden in a singer's body. I'm also a detail person hidden in an idea person's body. I see so many details I want handled in both my personal and professional life. When I cut an album, I start carefully planning the videos and album cover photo shoot. I think about specific promotions that might work. But I never seem to have the time to carry them out myself, or enough personal staff members to do it for me. So I end up leaving things to others. Sometimes they get done the way I'd hoped and sometimes not. I'd sure like to know how women like Oprah juggle all those businesses. Not being able to do it myself is probably the most frustrating thing about my life, and the thing that drives me the craziest. After reading this book, I'm sure you'll be saying, "No, what drives her the crazi-est is men." They'd be a close second.

On February 28, Ben and I went to Las Vegas for a show, and Ben told me he was going to ask my father for my hand in mar-riage. He was so old-fashioned about it, so proper. There we were, one child already and one hoped for, and he was going to ask my dad for my hand in marriage. Both my parents gave their approval, although Dad later told me he didn't think any-thing was going to come of it, since I hadn't come with Ben when he asked the big question. Maybe they were right about my not coming along having some importance, because in light of what happened a month or so later, it was obvious I didn't know what I wanted.

I had three days off in March, and I spent them with Ben in

his Los Angeles apartment. Ben was living in a little efficiency at
the Horace Heidt Estates. It was a very cool place. Horace Heidt
was a bandleader during the heyday of the big bands. He built
a house for himself and some bungalows for his band, then
eventually added on and made the whole thing into a little
apartment community. Most of the people who lived at Horace
Heidt were sixty or older, and Ben was everybody's grandson.
When we came and went, it always seemed like there was some
elderly couple smiling and waving to us. It served to remind me
that people could and did get married and stay together until
old age. We'd get up early every morning, and Ben or I would
fix a big breakfast with scrambled eggs, sausage, and pancakes.
I do love to eat. We'd go out to lunch or dinner and then come
back to Horace Heidt and watch television. One afternoon we
went out and bought a home pregnancy test kit, and when it
came up positive, we were two of the happiest people alive.
Those three days were probably the best we ever spent together. We lived like normal people, until I had to go back on the
road.

My plan was to tour with the musician I'd been seeing as
nothing more than another band member. I wanted to concentrate on the fairy tale world in which I married the father of my
children and everyone was thrilled about it. But once I was back
in the world of truck stops, tour buses, and a different venue
every night, I wasn't so sure. Many decisions made on the road
are not made from a realistic standpoint. The musician kept after
me about how much he loved me, wanting to talk about us. He
said he loved me first as a friend, and that he loved me just as
I was, with no changes needed. Ben wanted a wife who'd be a
lot more traditional than I believed I could ever be. Little by little, I broke down. The musician had some sort of hold over me,
and I still can't figure out what it was.

I didn't know what to do. I felt guilty about everything in my
life: over my lover, over Ben, over sneaking around with a band
member and making my dad nuts. It got so bad that when Ben
left messages at various venues or hotels, I wouldn't return the
calls. I didn't know what to say, so I decided I wouldn't say anything.

I played Knott's Berry Farm in Buena Park, California, on
March 23 and 24, and Ben drove from Los Angeles to find out
what was going on. As soon as Ben arrived, he went back to
where the buses had pulled in. I had gone with Presley and the

nanny to check in at the hotel. Right away, Ben noticed that band members were acting strange around him, and finally one of them let something slip about the one I'd been seeing again. Ben says he realized then that all those times this guy had been hanging around me had not been about band business. It was the first time he knew about the affair between the guy and me. He went to my bus and was sitting there getting madder by the minute, when he saw the guy climb down off the band bus.

When I came out of the hotel and walked across the parking lot toward the buses, my boyfriend was walking toward me holding his shoulder. He looked terrible. I rushed over and asked him what had happened, and he told me that when he'd gotten off the bus, Ben had been waiting for him. Remember, Ben is a former football player. He's pretty to look at, but he's no "pretty boy" by any stretch of the imagination. He's big and as strong as an ox. Ben grabbed this musician so hard he dislocated his shoulder. Then Ben accused him of having an affair with me while I was pregnant with his child. Ben told him he was about as sorry an individual as he could imagine. He went on to say, "If I were you, I'd get down on my knees and apologize to me. And while you're there, you might want to beg your wife's forgiveness, too."

My boyfriend said he'd dropped to his knees and apologized all over the place. When he finished, Ben just returned to his car and drove back to L.A. I was pissed at Ben, but in some strange way, I was relieved that it was all out in the open. The musician and I stayed in our insulated world of interstate highways and concerts for the next couple of months. And he continued to take care of details for me.

I was playing the Roy Clark Theater in Branson, Missouri, and was in my dressing room there when one of the crew dropped by with a woman he introduced as Tudy Clymer. Tudy was married to a friend of the guy's, Jerry Clymer, and they lived in Lead Hill, Arkansas, about thirty-five miles from Branson. She and some family members had been sight-seeing in Branson, and when they saw my name on the marquee, they stopped by to say hello to my crew member. Tudy happened to mention that she was between jobs, and as it happened, I was sorely in need of a personal assistant. So the crew member asked if she'd be interested in working with me on the road. She said she would, and he brought her back to meet me that night after the show.

Tudy and I hit it off right away. It was as though we'd known each other our entire lives. She had also worked with Jean Shepard, the Opry star, so she understood what all would be required. I hired her on the spot. She warned me she had three problems as far as being on the road: she hated to fly, she never wanted to go to California and take the chance of being in an earthquake, and she never wanted to stay anywhere above the second story of a hotel, in case of fire. I was hoping that by the time she realized she'd be doing all those things she would like the job so much she'd stay anyway. She became a great friend and another T-Bird.

The band and I were staying at a house I'd rented at Big Cedar Lodge in Branson. My musician boyfriend was still taking care of the business at hand, so I had no idea that pressure was building in him. We were all at the Lodge the following afternoon when he crumbled over and passed out. One of the other guys and I hauled him to the bathroom and held him under the shower to try to revive him while Tudy called an ambulance.

We all went to the hospital, and after the doctors examined him, I went in the room and sat with him. He had no idea what had happened. He said he just started feeling weak, and the next thing he knew, he woke up in a hospital bed. By this time his wife had phoned Big Cedar Lodge, and been told he'd gotten sick. She kept phoning the hospital, and he kept refusing to take her calls. I thought that since he wouldn't talk to his wife, they really were estranged or soon would be. I also thought he was overworked or had the flu or something. I didn't realize it was serious stress. What I didn't know was that he was catching hell from two sides: his wife and my dad. Every time Dad called about band business, he railed him up one side and down the other. If my father ever wanted to fire a band member, this was the one. But this was also one of the few times he knew he couldn't do it, since he knew I'd be standing squarely in the way. The musician's wife was doing some railing of her own. She wasn't sure that her husband was having an affair, but she suspected it.

He stayed in the hospital that day and we went straight from Branson to the Golden Nugget in Las Vegas. Meanwhile, back at the ranch, the day we left Branson, his wife paid a visit to my dad. He was working at our offices in Brentwood, Tennessee, when he was told she had walked in the door and was asking to see him. She sat down in his office and explained that she needed to see her husband, that she knew that if only the two of them could spend some time together they could work things out. The problem was she didn't have the money to get to Las Vegas.

Dad bought her a plane ticket. He now says it was her big blue honest-looking eyes that convinced him to help her. But I know exactly what it was. That's his way of handling a situation. Throw everybody in there together and see what happens after they mix it up. He knew Ben Reed was coming to Vegas to see Presley, so we had a hell of a group assembling.

My boyfriend and I had been having a good time at the Nugget. He'd come to my room and tell me how much he loved me and thank me for staying at the hospital when he was sick. I ate it up. Then one morning while I was still sleeping, Tudy answered the door to our suite and it was his wife. She brushed past Tudy, stormed into my bedroom, and sat down on the bed. She didn't stay long, and I was still half asleep while she was talking, so I don't remember her conversation verbatim. The gist of it, though, was that her husband loved her, and that if I'd get out of the picture, they could be happy again. I thought she was in total denial about their relationship. Can we talk about the pot thinking the kettle black? After she said her piece she left as quickly as she'd come. One thing I had caught. My dad had bought her the ticket that got her there.

I lay there in shock, wide awake finally, wondering what in the world the woman was up to. I didn't have to wonder what my dad was up to. I phoned him and raised hell. I told him that no matter what he did, he was not going to ruin my new relationship.

"And just what is it you have, Tanya?" Dad asked.

"Love, that's what. I have finally found a man who loves me just the way I am," I shot back.

"You have found a man with a wife and no backbone," he said. "You've found a worthless excuse for a man who has no respect for women. Not for his wife and not for you. My God, Tanya, you are pregnant with another man's child." And then he hung up.

About this time, Ben arrived to pick up Presley. It was a relief to have him there on one level. At least I didn't have to worry about our daughter being around if the wife caused any more trouble. But if Dad thought he could count on Ben to make a repeat performance of his fight with my band member, he was wrong. Ben had had his say, and he was finished with the whole thing. All he wanted was to see his child.

I got dressed and went down to the lobby with Tudy, and no sooner had we got off the elevator than I heard sirens. One of the guys rushed up to say that my boyfriend had been eating lunch with the rest of the band and had passed out again. His wife was nowhere to be seen. I later learned that she was up in her husband's room, phoning her parents in Phoenix.

I climbed into the ambulance with him and once again waited at a hospital while doctors tried to find out what was wrong. Once again, he said he didn't want to talk to his wife—either on the phone or in person. Right then, all I could think was that this man needed me and loved me. And maybe the needing was more important than the loving. Who knows? I couldn't think straight.

I went out in the hall to collect my thoughts, and a nurse stopped me. "His wife and her parents are here now. You'll have to leave now, because his family has asked to see him alone."

All I could do was go outside and wait for word about his condition. As the nurse made clear, I wasn't family, and I had no legal right to be there. I waited as long as I could, then I went back and did my show. His wife and her parents were gone by the next day, and when he checked out of the hospital, he told me not to worry, that he'd told her a divorce was the only answer. Since she was gone, I figured he was telling the truth. He also explained that the doctors believed what he was having were nervous attacks, but that they were nothing serious. I thought they sounded serious, though, and when we left Vegas, I kept worrying about his health. Any worries about my own I pushed aside.

We played a couple of shows in New York State and Pennsylvania, and then we headed back to Owensboro, Kentucky, to play a private show for a convention in the middle of June. I was wearing down, but I wouldn't admit it to anyone, not to my parents, not to Tudy, and not to myself. I was six months pregnant and spending my time being anxious that my guitar-player boyfriend might faint again. Owensboro is where it all came down, the final mess that ended my mess of a year.

He and I never shared a room out on the road. I always stayed in a suite with Tudy, or whoever came with me to help with Presley. After we checked into the rooms in Owensboro, I tried to call him, but his line was busy. I tried again in about half an hour, and then again in about fifteen minutes. I also checked in with Dad during this time, so I knew my boyfriend wasn't talking to him about band business. There could only be one other person occupying that much telephone time, and that was his wife. I went to his room and tried the door, which was locked. He was still on the phone, and he wouldn't answer the door. Tudy found a cleaning woman who opened the door for me, and I went straight over to where he sat on the bed and held my hand out for the phone.

"Give me that. I am going to tell her once and for all to give it up. She's going to have to accept this."

He shrunk back and clutched the phone to his chest. I think I realized then that much of what he'd been telling me had been bull. I grabbed the phone. I don't even know what I was going to say, maybe that the two of them deserved each other. He jerked the receiver back so hard that he hit himself in the face. He yelled something about his eye, but I stormed out and back to my suite. I crawled into bed and started to sob.

He knocked at my door in a few minutes, but I didn't want to talk to him yet. So he went across the hall to Tudy and Jerry's room and called my dad. Tudy says the conversation was fearsome. He was screaming at Dad, and Dad was screaming at him.

"You wanted me out of her life," he told Dad. "Well, you got your wish, because I'm gone."

While he was still on the phone to the musician, Dad got another call, the wife, also screaming. Since her husband had yelled about his eye, she figured I was beating him up. Unlikely, since I was so pregnant, but that's what she thought. I guess he didn't explain that he'd hit himself with that telephone. She told Dad that she was headed for Owensboro, and I'd better hope her husband was all right, because if there was a mark on him, she might kill me. And if she didn't kill me, it was going to cost $50,000 to keep it out of the press. How did we think it would look? she asked. Tanya Tucker, six months pregnant with Ben Reed's child and having an affair with a married man. Well, it wouldn't look real good. I saw that then, and I see it even more as I see it on this paper. It's not something I'm proud of having done.

Dad didn't care about it getting into the papers. All he cared about was that some woman had threatened his daughter and his unborn grandchild. Mother and Dad jumped in the car and somehow beat the woman to Owensboro. They came to my room, where I was still flat on my back in bed. I hadn't stopped crying since leaving the musician's room two and a half hours earlier.

Tudy and Jerry were standing in the lobby when the woman barged into the hotel. Jerry stood between her and the elevator, and he tried to reason with her. She wasn't in the mood.

"Tanya Tucker has been screwing my husband, and she's six months pregnant with another man's baby," she shrieked. "Now she's hit him in the face with a telephone, and if he's hurt, I'm gonna kill the bitch."

This hotel has a huge open staircase with lobby areas opening to each floor, so anything said on the main-floor lobby could be heard all the way to the top. Tudy says when the woman started yelling, the whole area turned silent. People on every floor who were waiting for elevators rushed to the railing to see what was going on. Most were probably conventioneers planning to attend my show that night.

She screamed at Jerry until he couldn't take it anymore, and then he physically picked her up, threw her over his shoulder, and carried her out of the hotel. Her husband was standing outside, so Jerry dumped her at his feet.

Picking this woman up was no small feat. She's not fat, but she's tall and athletic. She works out all the time and is probably almost as strong as Ben. Too bad she hadn't been there the night Ben roughed up her husband. It might have been a fight worth seeing.

The two left, and Jerry and Tudy came back up to my suite. They found Dad and Mother in the living room. Dad was positioned by the door, in case the woman tried to come in after me. I was behind the closed doors of my bedroom. Tudy looked in and saw that I was still crying. She went out and looked at my dad standing guard and said, "Mr. Tucker, I've never met you, so I may be speaking out of turn. But right now you have a daughter in there who needs your shoulder to cry on more than she needs your fists protecting her. I think she needs to hear that somebody loves her."

He came into my room and closed the door, then sat down beside me. "I'm so sorry about all this, baby," he said. "Your daddy loves you, I hope you know that."

Tears were still running down my face.

"You don't have to go on tonight," Dad said. "Let's just go home."

I don't know why, but it seemed like I had to play that show, swollen face, red eyes, and all. I went out and did it, knowing by then that half the people in the room had heard the yelling from the lobby and the other half had heard the story second-hand. I don't remember singing, but I do remember looking out through the crowd and seeing my parents standing alone at the back of the room.

I wasn't forty-one, but my daddy still called me baby. And I'll bet a lot of people were calling me crazy. Talk about singing a prophecy.

I sent Presley back to Nashville with Mother and Dad. Then I came home and sat on my back porch for three days. I let the phone ring off the hook. When my parents came over, I wouldn't talk. I wore the same sweat suit. I didn't comb my hair. I didn't take a bath. I couldn't eat anything or even keep water down. Within a week I was hospitalized for dehydration, and Dad canceled the rest of my summer concerts.

I spent the next few months trying to pull myself together. I knew I had to regain my health, if for no other reason than the fact that I was close to my due date. I couldn't allow myself to be a basket case when I brought this baby into the world. I'd have little private talks with myself about strength and staying tough and doing the right thing for all concerned. Sometimes I listened to myself, and sometimes not.

I really did love that band member at the time. Now I look back and wonder how I could have been so stupid. But I was, and that's that. I kept trying to tell myself that most women go through some bad relationships, but I wasn't sure. It seemed to me that I was batting zero in the men department. Capitol released my next album, *What Do I Do with Me,* that same month. The first single was a Paul Davis song titled "Down to My Last Teardrop." I was down to it, too.

※ ※ ※ ※

As the time drew closer for my baby to be born, I had one big decision to make. Ben had wanted to be in the delivery room when our child was born. He wanted to cut the umbilical cord and to be a part of everything from the first pain to the final push. But we were barely speaking after he roughed up my boyfriend, and I just couldn't allow him to be in there. It was a private time and something I had to do alone again. He was angry and hurt, but I had to tell him no. He came anyway. I didn't know at what cost until much later. He may have been an aspiring actor working as a waiter and doing construction, but he always tried to pay his own way. I never minded getting him a plane ticket to see his daughter, but it was a situation he tried to avoid as much as possible. He'd saved up money for the ticket to come for the baby's birth, plus an extra $1,500 for spending money for the weeks he'd be in Nashville. The day before he left town, he'd gotten a call to audition for a Coca-Cola commercial. He first picked up his ticket and the cash from the bank, and he had it in his briefcase. The audition was going to take fifteen minutes, so he shoved the case under the seat of his Blazer, locked the doors, and ran in to the reading. I'm sure he, too, felt like things were spinning out of control, and he wasn't thinking straight. When he got back his Blazer had been broken into. The stereo was gone as well as the briefcase with the ticket and the money. It killed him, but he had to call his parents and ask for a loan. I'd certainly have sprung for the ticket, but no way was he going to ask.

Both of us were in horrible moods when he finally got to Nashville several days before I was due. Ben stayed out at Hidden Valley, but I barely talked to him because Country Music Week 1991 was starting, and I was finally enough back to what passes for normal in my life that even though I was nine months along, I'd decided to head on over to some of the events.

FIFTY-ONE

I was at the October 1 BMI Awards ceremonies when I went into labor. BMI is Broadcast Music Incorporated, one of three performing rights societies that collect song royalties for artists. Without BMI, ASCAP, and SESAC, songwriters could be screwed out of a ton of money. Each year during Country Music Week these organizations have their own awards and honor songs and songwriters. I always try to go to those events to show support for the people who've given me material over the years, and to see people I haven't seen since the last awards show. They throw some of the best parties in town, too.

Shirley Porter and I had gone outside to smoke when the first contraction hit. During both my pregnancies I did try to be careful. I may like to have a good time, but I'm not stupid, and I cared very much about the health of those unborn babies. But every once in a while I'd just have to break down and light a cigarette.

As we were making our way outside, I had a selfish notion. I thought, "Man, everybody's having a great time partying and here I am, fixing to have a baby." When I got outside and sat down on one of the benches I could almost hear God shouting down to me: "Hey, Tanya, this baby was your choice!"

Then He added: "And by the way, here he comes!"

Shirley rushed me to Vanderbilt Hospital, where I checked in and phoned my parents. Then, as anyone who's been in labor knows, I waited for the baby to make his appearance. You forget the pain of labor, and I understand why, but in a way that's too bad, because once it's over you feel an incredible rush of personal power. It's like, "I did it. I've given birth. Now I can do anything, even be president if I want." Women ought to remember the beautiful, bittersweet feeling that occurs when they realize they've made it through the pain and brought a new human spirit into the world.

While I was waiting, I started thinking about a house we'd bought in Hendersonville some months earlier. It had been a hasty, unwise purchase, since I soon learned I couldn't keep horses on the property. My advice to young people looking at houses is this: Never, never let anyone hurry you into making a decision.

Suddenly I remembered that Clint Black and Lisa Hartman were thinking about buying a home in Nashville. I thought they might as well buy mine, and since I knew they were in town for the awards and they always stayed at the Vanderbilt Plaza Hotel, I phoned. It was around midnight.

Clint is one of the best guys in the business. I meant it that time when I was on *Oprah* with Lisa, and I told her she should get to know Clint if she was looking for a good one. He's a soft-spoken, kind individual who is never too busy to get involved in a good cause. Here's just one example that also began with a late-night phone call from me. It happened a couple of years ago. Instead of calling him from a hospital bed, I was asking him to visit one.

I was asleep one night, and the phone rang. It was La Costa, who told me that she'd just learned that a terminally ill teenage boy at Vanderbilt Hospital in Nashville had told someone that his two favorite singers were Tanya Tucker and Clint Black. Costa said he was in very bad shape that night. I rubbed my eyes and shook myself awake and said, "I'm on my way." But as I got dressed, I remembered Clint was in town, too. I called him and explained about the situation, and said how much greater it would be if we both came. I didn't have to ask twice. Clint just said, "I'll meet you there." He did, and when we walked into the room, we were lucky the young boy's heart didn't give out. I know mine almost did when I saw the stunned and happy look on the boy's face.

Clint's that kind of a guy. The sort who will get involved in good works whether he gets his name in the papers for it or not. And I'm the kind of woman who would call him up in the middle of the night to drag him off to a hospital or to sell him a house, no matter what emotional state I was in.

On October 1, or by now October 2, I was too late to make the sale. Clint and Lisa had already bought a house from Louise Mandrell. But we got to talking and I decided to tell Clint about Beau Grayson.

"I haven't told a soul this, Clint, but I'm naming this baby Beau, after my father," I said. "Beau Grayson." It had originally been my plan to name the baby Andrew Grayson and call him Drew. Ben had lobbied for Andrew since that's his father's name. And I've always loved the name Grayson. But Ben and I were no longer a couple by the time this baby was born, and I figured it was my call.

"You know, Presley's middle name is Tanita, after my mother and me," I said to Clint. "And I've been lying up here thinking about it all and decided my son should have his granddad's name."

"Well, that's so cool, Tanya," Clint said. "It's a great name."

"You're the only one I've told," I added, never thinking to mention that I'd decided to wait to tell my own family.

I have no idea why I confided in Clint. Maybe it's like the Jewish man who went to confession. He just had to tell *somebody*. And after all, who was Clint Black gonna tell?

Just before we hung up, Clint said, "I'm presenting the Female Vocalist Award with Roy Rogers tomorrow night. I sure hope I get to read off your name."

"You better do that," I said. "'Cause now I know where you live."

Ben and Presley and the rest of my family were at the hospital when Beau was born at 1:07 P.M. the next afternoon. Even though Ben wasn't present when his son was being born, he came into the delivery room right after the birth and was the first one to hold him.

After my family left, I was lying in bed watching the CMA show, still groggy, when suddenly, there's Roy Rogers and Clint Black on the screen and Clint is announcing to the world that I've had my baby and named him Beau Grayson in honor of my dad.

Who was Clint gonna tell? Everybody.

Daddy says he almost fell off the couch. I hadn't told him yet, and he couldn't believe it.

"Juanita," he said. "Did you hear that? Tanya's named that boy after me!"

Mom says she almost cried when she saw the look on Daddy's face.

Ben almost cried and fell off the couch, too.

Later, when they announced my name as the 1991 Country Music Female Vocalist, my parents sat there in shock. What an unbelievable day and night! It was a big night all around for Capitol Records. I'd won Female Vocalist, and Garth Brooks took home Entertainer of the Year, Single of the Year ("Friends in Low Places"), and Video of the Year ("The Thunder Rolls"). I had an additional thrill, too, because to top it all off, my pal Travis Tritt won the 1991 Horizon Award. He called and offered to bring my award to the hospital, but I knew the pain medicine would knock me out completely long before he could make it to the downtown area from the Opry House.

But as I said at the beginning of this book, I was so wrung out from the events of the past few months, the full impact of winning that award didn't hit me right away. When Beau Grayson and I arrived home two days later, I started to understand just how much a CMA Award meant to me, thanks to my fellow country music artists. The house was filled with flowers when we got there, and cards and letters kept pouring in. I never know what the public or my peers in the industry think of me and my image. This outpouring of support created a buffer from all the turmoil that seemed to be the order of the day for me.

I get nervous when too many people congratulate me; in fact, it's almost easier for me to take a cussing than a compliment. Maybe it's because I feel deep down that I deserve cussings more than compliments. And it's much easier for me to talk about the times I've messed up than the standing ovations or great reviews. But I do want to share some of the letters I received from other artists at a time when I was badly in need of support.

Barbara Mandrell wrote a note, saying: "I was so thrilled that you won Female Vocalist. You have deserved that forever, Tanya. You've had more big records and more big shows than anybody. I'm so proud." That made me feel wonderful, since Barbara has won so many awards herself. Ricky Van Shelton's note touched me as well: "In one of the best years yet for country music, one of the best things about it for me was you winning last Wednesday night. The CMA finally woke up."

A couple of weeks after the show, I received two letters that probably meant the most of all. One came from Conway Twitty and his wife, Dee, and the other from one of my idols, Tammy Wynette. The one from the Twittys said: "This is something Dee and I have never done, congratulated any artist on any award. Also, we purposefully waited for a while, so you'd know it wasn't just the 'heat of the moment,' although the moment they announced the Female Vocalist we almost fainted. Very seldom do these people 'do the right thing.' Somehow for once they got it right. We think you've deserved this award every year. You never fail vocally, and you consistently have great songs. You're good people, too, Tanya. Dee and I are big fans. We love you, CT and Dee. P.S. Tell little Beau hi for us."

That letter breaks my heart now, because even though he was one of the biggest charting artists in country music history, he never won one of those awards himself. That's a crying shame.

The letter from Tammy said: "I didn't want this to get lost in the shuffle. Thank God the CMA finally came to their senses. It was long overdue. Congratulations on the award, and the biggest award of all, your new baby boy."

Tammy, if I could hit your high notes, I'd cop all your licks.

*Just over a week after Grayson was born, we celebrated my birthday at the Creekwood Restaurant and Marina in Hendersonville. Mother and Dad ordered up steak, catfish, hush puppies, and all the trimmings, and although it was a small group of family and friends compared to my usual birthday blowouts, having both children made it one of the best. I don't know who was more anxious to show off Grayson, me or Presley. She loved her little brother so much. It was as if she had a live baby doll to play with, and she couldn't stay away from him. She called him her "baby brudder," and when she wasn't actually helping me out with Grayson, she was practicing on her dolls. One of the main things she wanted to master was burping the baby, so she'd hold her dolls and "burp" them for hours. When she finally got a real burp out of her brother, she couldn't believe it.

I kept telling my dad, "I need to come in off the road for a while. I don't want to miss a minute of these years with my babies." He kept saying, "We'll work it out. Right now, you've got to earn the money to support those babies."

While I stayed off the road longer after Grayson than I had with Presley, I did go to Fort Worth on December 13 to defend my Celebrity Cutting Championship. Mother and La Costa couldn't believe I was going to try to cut cattle that soon after childbirth, and they had fits. But I wanted to see if I could repeat my win. Christie Brinkley, Randy White, and Johnny Rutherford all returned for the event, along with others such as actress Linda Blair, *Northern Exposure* star Barry Corbin, and the Second Lady of the United States, Marilyn Quayle. Marilyn put in a good ride but didn't draw good cows. Afterward someone came up and told her that her cattle had all been picked by Democrats. I was again riding Mr. San Dancer, and we did fine on the first and second cows. Then I made a mistake I wasn't even aware of at the time. I accidentally touched the reins with both hands at once. There are all kinds of secrets to cutting. You have to ride with your rear down in the saddle almost like a bronc rider, and you have to keep your elbow right next to you, right in your gut. That keeps you from moving forward and losing points on form. And you don't ever touch the reins with both hands at once, like I did.

Christie Brinkley won the event. She got three great cows that moved around a lot and gave her a championship ride. I wasn't as disappointed as you might think, though. I was just glad to have made it through the cutting without feeling like I was doing my body any damage. I was also glad to be back in the world and coming out of the slump I'd been in throughout most of 1991.

The next event I was looking forward to was the 1992 Grammy Awards on February 23. I was up for Female Vocalist for "Down to My Last Teardrop," and I was to present the Male Vocalist Award with Chet Atkins. I wasn't going to get to perform, though. The Grammy Awards shows are packed with performers from all different kinds of music, and country often takes the backseat in on-camera performances and presentations. The artists receive their awards earlier in the day, long before the televised show begins. Then their names are announced, which gives them no opportunity to thank people on camera, or to take advantage of the nationwide visibility these shows offer. Still, I was excited when I left for New York that February. It was my first big event as the Country Music Association's Female Vocalist of the Year.

I'm always reading newspaper articles that claim to be insider reports on the behind-the-scenes doings at the Grammys or the Oscars or the Emmys. They usually concentrate on some funny comment or somebody's clothes. Well, I'm gonna give you an insider's report on the 1992 Grammy Awards. Keep in mind that I came there very proud to be representing Nashville and country music.

FIFTY-TWO

*C*het Atkins and I had been hanging around Radio City Music Hall a long time to rehearse, because Metallica was late. Finally they ran out onstage and delivered a big one-line opener for the benefit of the rest of the artists and industry people there.

"FUUUUUUCK!" one of them screamed.

Chet Atkins raised an eyebrow. "I only use that word in emergencies," he said.

Walking out and yelling the F-word seemed to be the same as saying, "Screw all of you jerks who had to wait."

In addition to presenting the Male Vocalist Award, Chet and I were to announce the winners of the Best Country Collaboration, Best Bluegrass Album, and Best Country Song, none of which would be awarded on camera. It was difficult to believe that the best song in country music didn't even deserve an on-air slot, but that's the way it was going to be done. For years, the Female Vocalist Award wasn't even presented during the telecast; in fact, I believe 1992 was the first year it happened. I think that change came about because Jimmy Bowen sent the Grammy committee a letter protesting its treatment of female country artists. I also heard that he was angry about some sound problems some country acts experienced, and he asked the Grammy people if it was mandatory that the sound men at the show take their dinner breaks when country acts walked onstage to perform.

Chet and I finally got to run through our part, and I went back up Sixth Avenue to my suite at the Hilton to get dressed and meet my girlfriend, Roe, who was flying in from Chicago to be my "date" for the show. When she arrived, I told her about Metallica and how mad I was that so few country awards were being presented during the televised portion of the show. Roe didn't say much, but she looked worried. She knows if I get pissed off, I'm not likely to keep my mouth shut about it.

When we got to Radio City Music Hall and went back to the dressing room area, I couldn't seem to find a door with my name on it. The dressing rooms at Radio City are tiny, and the halls are narrow, so the area was complete chaos. Artists and musicians and crew members had to literally fight their way through the mob scene. Everywhere we turned, people were pushing or pulling at you. I finally found my name. The sign on the dressing room door read: "Amy Grant's Backup Singers and Tanya Tucker." I don't like to think I have a swelled ego, but when I saw that doorplate I was furious. I didn't even get top billing. The reigning Country Music Association Female Vocalist was sharing a dressing room with Amy's backup singers. That spoke worlds to me about the Grammy's attitude toward country music. I took a deep breath and told myself to stay cool.

Roe and I had to squeeze our way in, because the backup singers were all getting dressed.

"Who are you?" one of them asked.

I introduced myself.

"Oh! I'm sorry," she apologized. "You're sharing the dressing room with us."

I had already figured that out.

I gritted my teeth and stayed completely professional while I retouched my makeup. I made small talk, complimented them on working for such a great artist as Amy Grant, and said I looked forward to their segment of the show. The girls were very nice and very Christian. They even stood in a circle and prayed while I was putting on my lipstick, although the one didn't have anything to do with the other.

Roe and I went on out and sat down in the theater. I was dressed in a gown I'd bought in Las Vegas specifically for the awards. It's a beautiful dress, backless, with a gold flowered pattern over sheer white. Roe and I sat down in the theater and the first thing I saw was an exact duplicate of the dress I was wearing.

"Well, shit," I said to Roe. "Wouldn't you know it." Before the night was over, I spotted another twin, or triplet. My first big event representing the Country Music Association as their Female Vocalist was not turning out to be as exciting as I'd hoped.

We sat back and watched the show. It had been widely predicted that Mary Chapin Carpenter would win Female Vocalist, so losing that award was neither much of a surprise nor a disappointment.

When it came our turn, Chet and I went up for our presentations.

Chet went first. "One of the happiest things that happened in the music business this year was the rise in popularity of country music."

"We always knew it was great, and now a large slice of the world population knows it, too." Even as I read the words from the TelePrompTer, I was thinking that the Grammy show producers didn't seem to be a part of that large slice that cared about country.

We then announced three of country's winners. The Best Country Collaboration Award went to Mark O'Connor and the New Nashville Cats, Steve Wariner, Ricky Skaggs, and Vince Gill, and the Best Bluegrass Album went to Carl Jackson and John Starling with the Nash Ramblers. The Best Country Song was "Love Can Build a Bridge," which Paul Overstreet and John Jarvis had written with Naomi Judd. I think that show could have added quite a bit of class by having fewer rockers and rappers onstage and more folks like Naomi Judd, Steve Wariner, Ricky Skaggs, and Vince Gill!

"Now it's time to pay attention to the boys . . . something I've done all my life." Of course, I didn't mention that my date that night was a girl. "For Best Country Vocal Performance, Male, the nominees are: Alan Jackson, Travis Tritt, Vince Gill, Garth Brooks, and Billy Dean."

Chet opened the envelope. "And the Grammy goes to Garth Brooks."

Garth wasn't there to accept the Grammy, so Chet and I thanked the Grammy committee on his behalf and went back to our seats.

After the show, Roe and I started weaving our way to the press area, where winners, performers, and presenters were each scheduled to answer questions from the media.

Suddenly a rough voice said, "You can't go in there," and a big hand grabbed me on the arm. I whirled around and saw a redneck security guard who was about six feet four and must have weighed 280 pounds.

"I most certainly can," I snapped.

At that moment, one of the women acting as an escort stepped in and said, "This is Tanya Tucker. She's supposed to be in there."

"Well, okay," he said. "But that one can't go in." He pointed to Roe.

"She's my friend, and she's going with me," I answered, getting angrier by the minute. I grabbed hold of Roe's arm and started past him. He grabbed my arm again, hard.

That did it.

"Listen, you fat SOB," I exploded, fists planted on the hips of my white gown. "I'm in the wrong mood to be screwed with. Let go of my arm or I'm gonna beat the shit out of you!"

I jerked away from him and dragged Roe right with me.

"Roe, I'm thinking about telling these Grammy people exactly how I feel. What do you think?"

Roe just grinned and said, "Well, I guess you'll tell it like it is."

We barely made it to the interview area when my name was called. I went up to the lectern and looked out at what appeared to be primarily the rock press. Very few of the country journalists I knew were there, so I felt that I was in enemy territory for what I was about to say.

Right away someone asked me in a very uppity tone of voice if I thought it was rude of Garth to be a no-show. I said Garth probably didn't want to get shoved around backstage. Then I took a deep breath and told them exactly what I and, I believe, most of the other country acts were really thinking.

"I'm gonna tell you people something. Country music is the greatest music in the world, and I'm proud to be a part of it. We come to these Grammy Awards and you all act like rock and roll is the only music in America. We come here as representatives of our music, and we get treated like redheaded stepchildren. I for one am getting pretty damn tired of it, and you can stick your awards up your butt."

Nobody said a word. I turned myself around and snapped

over my shoulder: "See this back? That's the last you're gonna see of me." Somebody took a picture of me talking over my shoulder.

I stomped down off the platform and walked by Alan Jackson, who was standing there next in line, shaking his cowboy-hatted head.

"Tanya," he drawled. "How am I gonna follow that?"

"Give 'em hell," I advised. Alan was too polite to give anybody hell, though.

The only two good things about that night happened while I was trying to make my escape. As I walked out, a hand reached out and took my arm once again. I turned and there stood Patti LaBelle. "Girl, your music is just awesome," she said. From the look on her face, I knew it wasn't just a music biz glad hand. "That's comin' right back attcha," I said, and hugged her. Then, Michael Bolton appeared out of nowhere and stopped me. "I'd like to talk to you sometime soon about doing a project together," he said. Well, those kinds of comments are a dime a dozen in show business, kind of like, "Let's do lunch" or "Have your people call my people." But they aren't bad to hear, anyway.

Then some rap group shoved Roe and me out of the way and snagged the limo we were getting ready to take back to the hotel. I couldn't believe it.

"Hell, we're practically across the street," I told Roe. "Why are we waiting for a limo, anyway?" I said. And we headed back to the hotel on foot.

I saw that picture of me turning my back on the Grammy Awards months later. It popped up in *People* when the magazine named me to its Ten Best Dressed of 1992 list. If that dress was what got *People*'s attention, there were at least two other women at the Grammy Awards who could have made the list, too.

FIFTY-THREE

We had an offer we couldn't refuse in '92. Black Velvet approached Dad about me becoming the new Black Velvet Lady and going on an extended tour sponsored by the liquor company. Dad was very concerned about this business arrangement, since I was known to drink more liquor than my share from time to time. I wasn't one of the first choices. Actually, Black Velvet considered approaching Alan Jackson about being a Black Velvet guy for a time. They finally decided not to break tradition and to keep the Black Velvet Lady theme. But when my name came up, the company questioned the fact that I wasn't always known for moderation when it came to a party. By the time they approached us, the company had decided my reputation wouldn't be detrimental to their image, and after talking with the company executives, Dad decided the liquor company wouldn't be detrimental to mine. What that means is that the company offered him enough money to take the chance.

What interested me was the company's plan to use this tour to raise money for multiple sclerosis. Dixie Pineda, a Dallas public relations executive who worked with Black Velvet, told me later that the company tried to come up with a charity that didn't get as much attention as some others did, as well as something that women in my age bracket would relate to. Donna Fargo, one of the women I most admire in country music, was diagnosed with MS years ago. In addition to admiring her as a writer/artist, I thought she showed unbelievable courage about having multiple sclerosis. She's an inspiration to anyone with a potentially debilitating condition, because she has kept a positive attitude and she seems to be winning her battle against MS, or at least staying even. She's still out there performing, too.

I began a series of meetings with Black Velvet, and we talked about how best to raise money for MS. One of the ideas I most liked was a dance contest for amateur two-steppers. Thus was born the "Smooth Steppin' Black Velvet Showdown," a series of regional dance contests that culminated in one national competition. Patsy Swayze was selected as the spokeswoman for the dance competition. Patsy is not only a nationally known dance choreographer but the mother of Patrick. She's the one who taught him to dance, for you *Dirty Dancing* fans. And if you ever wonder how Patrick kept his head on straight right after all the "sexiest man alive" talk that followed *Dirty Dancing*, I heard that one of the first things Patsy did was to sit her son down at the table and remind him that there was no room for "stars" in the family, just professionals. You gotta love that attitude.

So I was off on the Black Velvet Lady Tour, which meant I'd play over 250 dates over the next year. If I had any hopes of taking some time off to be with my kids, they'd have to be put on hold.

Yet another business opportunity presented itself in 1992. A friend of mine named Toni (T.C.) Carnicello brought some Mexican salsa out to my house and it was wonderful. I'm very particular about Mexican food, so when it passed the Tanya Test, it meant something. T.C. and I started experimenting with it, adding ingredients, fine-tuning the recipe, and finally we decided to try to market it. We enlisted the aid of my dad and started our new company.

The first thing I wanted to ensure was that this not be just a celebrity endorsement situation, where I didn't have any say-so. I knew that a lot of celebrity food lines didn't make it, and I'd wondered if it was because they got distanced from what they were selling. So I told Dad I wanted to be involved in everything, including absolutely any changes in the recipe that might be considered. If I was going to do this, I wanted to be a real player in the grocery market, with a full line of products developed in the coming years.

It took a couple of years, but Tanya Tucker Salsa became one of my ideas that not only happened but succeeded. We're now in over twenty states, with our biggest sales coming from markets like Denver, Phoenix, and Dallas/Fort Worth. Of course, Dad doesn't like to free up available cash to do the big marketing I'd like, so it's growing a little slower than it might, and you'll see me promoting the devil out of it at various events. But it's growing every day.

My goal is to be able to make money while I sleep. The fact that my entire family's livelihood depends on my ability to go out and work the road scares me. I'd like to own companies that generate income whether I'm standing on a stage with a microphone in my hand or not.

Another thing that caught my attention that year involved an unplanned encounter with an old beau out on the road. I was in Branson for a show that summer, and one of my performances coincided with one of Glen Campbell's. I decided to drop by his dressing room and say hello. He almost dropped his teeth when he saw me, and I could tell he was a little uncomfortable. But we talked a little about our tour schedule, our families and, well, who knows, maybe the weather. It wasn't exactly an intimate conversation. He did mention that his daughter, Debby, was with him and wanted to see my show. I immediately got butterflies in my stomach. Not because of any lust for Glen, but because he'd be out there watching my show. No matter what happened between us, he is one great performer, and I would never want him to see me do anything less than a great show.

Glen's autobiography was already at the publisher's, but he didn't say a word to me about it. I wish he'd given me a hint that it was coming, and that I was portrayed as such a jerk. All he would have had to say was, "Look, T, I've got this book coming out and neither of us come off looking very good."

But he didn't tell me anything about it. He just said he was anxious to see my show. "You watch," I told my assistant. "I'm gonna go out there and kick butt." I did, too. I kicked so much butt on that stage that the spaghetti strap of my dress broke. Luckily the dress had a built-in bra that held it up. After the show, Glen's daughter saw my assistant and told her what Glen had to say about it. He leaned over to her and said, "Do you have a safety pin?" She said she didn't, and he said: "Too bad, because if you did I'd go up there and pin that strap back myself."

I suppose in a lifetime, that's an insignificant incident, but any of you divorced women out there will understand the smirk I had on my face when I heard that's what had been said. We weren't ever married, but the split messed me up like a bad divorce, anyway.

If the Glen Campbell split didn't scare me about marriage, Shirley and Royce Porter's divorce did. I used to tell those two that if they ever split, then my faith in marriage would be completely shot. But sometime around the beginning of the 1990s, I could see the potential for a breakup. Shirley started asking me to come out to their lake house when Royce was away for days at a time either writing songs or off fishing with the guys. She said she was feeling more and more isolated from him and feared that the things that had made their marriage good—like trust and commitment—were rapidly fading. I was about the only person she could talk to, since so many of their friends were either songwriters or songwriters' wives. We were out on her boat one time when Royce was off on a writing binge, and she said, "I can't talk to people like Hank Cochran about what's going on. He'd just sit down and turn my concerns into a cliché hook line for his next country song. That's all it would mean to him."

In March of 1992, when Royce was away on a fishing trip, Shirley moved out. She didn't call me until after she'd done it, because she didn't want me to feel pulled between the two of them if things turned nasty. So she called Royce in Colorado, and then she called and told me. I'd seen it coming, but it was still a shock. She didn't ask for anything, either. I was proud of her as a woman and as a friend for walking away clean, even though she certainly would have deserved big-time alimony. She'd supported him while he wrote songs. But that's just not Squirrely Bird's style.

In fact, it was during this time that I offered her a job and she turned it down. She'd come to so many awards shows and television appearances and done my hair free that I thought maybe she should come on staff and we'd have the best of both worlds—friendship and our professional situation. I asked her if she could leave her present job for a hundred thousand a year. She said no, and I said, "Well, how much then?" Shirley just laughed and said, "Tanya, you don't have enough money to hire me. But I'll be your friend for nothing!" She just wanted to keep the friendship separate from any financial dealings. I respected her for it. And once again I was reminded of the importance of female friends in your life. You've got to protect those relationships fiercely. The men may come and go, but hopefully your girlfriends are there forever.

In August of '92 Shirley went to Fort Worth to visit a friend, and while she was there she met a guy she said seemed awfully nice. She hadn't gone out with him, though, but she said she might be just a little interested. At the time she called me about her potential new interest, I was embroiled in a very strange media confrontation with the vice president of the United States.

FIFTY-FOUR

*I*t's funny when you think about it. Glen and I once performed at the Republican National Convention, and we were wired the whole time we were there. As far as I know, our condition caused no ripples. The next time I came to the event I was a single mother, and they had people trying to get me kicked off the show, saying that I didn't fit into their idea of family values.

A statement released to the press when it was announced that I'd be performing at the 1992 Republican National Convention read: "If this is a convention of family values, I don't understand why Tanya Tucker was selected to sing the national anthem." That statement was made by one of the female delegates.

I am not generally a political person, and I don't usually get involved in public debates. I didn't set out to be the country singer raising hell at the Grammy Awards. I just said some things that I believed needed to be said. I do wish I were more politically aware, and I know I don't keep up with things like I should. But one thing I do feel strongly about is single mothers and what they have to face every day.

So when someone in the press mentioned that Vice President Dan Quayle had taken a shot at Candice Bergen's character, Murphy Brown, for her single motherhood, I said I'd like to talk

with him about it, and stated to the press: "Who is Dan Quayle
to go after single mothers? What in the world does he know of
what it's like to go through pregnancy and have a child with no
father who'll help take responsibility for the baby? Who is he to
be calling single mothers tramps?"

When I got to the '92 convention in Houston it was as if the
press wanted me to duke it out with the vice president. Every
time I turned around some journalist was wanting to talk about
it. I felt uncomfortable on one level, because I worried that it
looked like I was acting disrespectful. Lord knows my father had
drummed it into my head that you don't act disrespectful. But,
on the other hand, I felt I had something to say, and if I didn't
run into the vice president in person, I might as well make my
stand to the media.

What I said was that single mothers have a hard go, and Vice
President Quayle should educate himself about the difficulties. I
said I had good, strong family values and that my children were
certainly loved and cared for. I also said that I wasn't a typical
single mother, because I had a way to earn enough money to
give them whatever they needed and I had a strong family sur-
rounding me. My children also were lucky enough to have a
father who wanted to be actively involved with their upbringing. It's the women who get left by husbands who won't help
support their kids and the women who need job training that
are hurting. And it's men like the vice president who need to
reexamine their prejudices and do something to help these single mothers survive.

I also wanted one thing made clear. I never wanted to be held
up as an example, say, for teenage girls. A teenage pregnancy
can be such a tragedy. I waited until I was set financially to have
my children.

I've thought about that convention and the single mothers
issue a lot since that time. One of the things that irritates me
about this whole single mother versus family values concept is
the question of single fathers. Where are those guys in this mix?
I was lucky that Ben was there for his children. But too often
men disappear to leave the burden on the woman.

That is one of the things in this world that gripes my dad
more than anything. I told you about the time my folks tried to
elope when they were fifteen. There's a part of that story that
Mother and Dad didn't tell anyone for years. By the time they
discovered that no justice of the peace in Lovington, New

Mexico, would marry two fifteen-year-old kids, it was too late to drive back to Denver City, Texas. And since it was freezing cold, Dad suggested that they get a motel room. Well, my mother about flipped. No way was she going to spend a night in a motel with a man who wasn't yet her husband. Dad begged her. "Juanita, we're gonna freeze to death out here. We got to get us a room." When her lips turned blue from the wind whistling through the truck's broken window, Mother finally said okay.

They got the room, but Dad was so afraid she'd bolt out of there he slept on top of the bedspread, fully clothed. Nobody in Denver City ever knew about that night, but if they had, my mother's name would have been mud. People probably wouldn't have thought twice about Dad's involvement, just Mother's. Dad now tells this story to illustrate how unfair society is to females. All too often, the woman pays the price for what men and women do, innocent or not. To point an accusing finger at a single mother and never question the single father's involvement or responsibility is not just unfair, it's stupid.

Ironically, I had just made the video for my next single release, "Two Sparrows in a Hurricane," which I saw as a tribute to my own family values. Every so often in a singer's career, one song can take you to an entirely different level. "Two Sparrows in a Hurricane" was one of those songs. It was as much a pivotal point in my career as the so-called comeback in 1986. My asking price for shows increased, as did booking offers. When you think about what just one song can do, you start to understand why songwriters are such heroes around Nashville.

I was initially attracted to the song because it spoke of two young, very poor people getting married and making the marriage work despite their hard circumstances. Since it reminded me of my parents, I immediately knew I wanted to record it. I also knew I wanted to make a video that not only paid tribute to my folks but included Ben and our children. The song speaks of three stages of married life: the too-young newlywed couple, the young family, and the elderly couple. I asked Mae Axton to play the older woman, and she accepted. Ben and I and Presley and Grayson played the young family. Ben and I weren't a couple anymore, and my dad had to convince him to even appear in the video. In the end, he did it for the same two reasons I had: Presley and Grayson. No matter how things ended up between Ben and me, I wanted our children to have this film clip.

FIFTY-FIVE

I believe that the unresolved situations involving Ben and my band member during 1991, combined with events set in motion during 1992, led to 1993 being the saddest year of my life. It was a year filled with fear, pain, and despondency. The fear part of it started in the summer of '92 when my office began receiving letters from an overzealous fan who believed he and I should be married. He kept saying if I didn't marry him, he was going to find me and take me off in the woods to live with him. I should have just introduced him to my father, since Dad seems to be able to run off most of my suitors. As time went by, the letters turned threatening. The man knew my tour schedule and he also seemed to know my routine when I was in Nashville, so we hired some security guards to travel with me in case I was being stalked.

I first saw the man who'd been writing the letters at a '92 cutting event in Fort Worth. Dad had alerted security that I'd been receiving threats, so people were watching the crowd. I was waiting to ride when I noticed a man walking toward me. I noticed him right away, because in his T-shirt and baseball cap he didn't look like he belonged at a rodeo event where everybody was in cowboy hats and western shirts. When he got closer I could read what was written on his shirt: The Silver Assassin. The guards spotted him, too, because just about the time they announced my name and I rode into the arena, I saw them surround this guy and escort him out. All through the ride I kept thinking about him, and even before I finished and located my assistant and the security guards, I'd guessed that he was the one who'd been writing the letters. The guards had taken him back to his van, which had pictures of me plastered all over the inside. But since he hadn't done anything, or made any threatening advances, all they could do was tell him to leave the county. He left that day, and I didn't see him again until months later when I was in Nashville recording my next album, *Soon*.

The loss and sadness started with a phone call from my old friend Michael Tovar in Los Angeles. I've had bad news come over the phone lines before, but never like Tovar's bad news that September. "I've got AIDS, Tanya," Tovar told me. "I've known since March. But I just couldn't get the courage to tell you." I was numb when he spoke, although the thought that he could have AIDS had been in my mind a few months earlier when he'd flown to Las Vegas to do my hair and makeup for a show. I'd been requesting Tovar as my hair and makeup guy every chance I got. Back after Presley was born I'd lost touch with him for almost a year. During that period he had some bad financial times and lost his salon. By the time I learned about it, he was working on video shoots and whatever freelance work he could find. I hated the fact that he hadn't phoned me about the salon. Maybe I could have helped or put together a group of people to help. But Tovar was a proud man, and the only way he would take my help was to take assignments like the Las Vegas show.

When he arrived in Vegas, he tried to act as if nothing were wrong with him. He loved seeing my children, and on the surface, he was his usual upbeat self. But he appeared to have lost some weight, and he coughed a lot. I also noticed he kept wiping sweat from his face and neck. I asked if he'd been sick and he said no, just overworked and tired. Somewhere in the recesses of my mind, I wondered if he could possibly have AIDS. But the thought was so terrible, I immediately buried it. Even though I'd feared he was ill, I hadn't allowed myself to consider the reality. Now Tovar was confirming what I hadn't been able to face.

"I really thought I'd beaten it," he explained, and I understood. Tovar's motto had always been "accentuate the positive and eliminate the negative."

He hadn't been able to work and had been evicted from his apartment because he couldn't pay the rent. He was living with a psychologist friend named Wanda von Kleist who convinced him to begin calling his friends and allowing them time to say good-bye. I tried to stay positive during that initial conversation, telling him that people could live years with AIDS and that a cure might be just around the corner. Then I promised I'd come see him as soon as I could.

Wanda phoned me soon after Tovar gave me the news. I'd known her for some time, and through Tovar I had followed her life through graduate school and the time when she was setting up a practice in Los Angeles. She and I were both women who'd always wanted a lot out of life. And, also like me, she was a woman who tended to get very involved in the lives of her friends. He hadn't told me the whole story, and she knew I needed to know what was really going on. "He's already in the latter stages of the disease, Tanya," she told me. "He's refused medication that might prolong his life, and he may not have as much time as you think." I was in deep denial. Tovar was in his mid-thirties, and I could not accept the fact that he would die.

"I'm sure you have some questions about AIDS," Wanda went on. "You may not want to ask, but I know in the back of your mind you're probably worrying about personal contact with him. Don't be ashamed of feeling nervous about contact with him. It's a fair concern. AIDS is a deadly virus." I didn't want to admit it, but exactly how the disease might be transmitted was very much on my mind. Especially if I took the children to see him, which I wanted to do.

Wanda explained that AIDS is not transmittable by casual contact. She explained that you must have an exchange of bodily fluids such as blood or semen to contract AIDS. The chances of transmitting the disease through something like saliva are minuscule, practically nonexistent. She tried to prepare me for the realities of seeing Tovar for the first time since the disease had become full-blown. The changes would be more than physical, she explained. I'd need to prepare myself for some mental deterioration, too, since there were days when his memory lapsed. She also told me that although my denial was completely natural, it did not change the fact that Tovar was terminally ill. It was a reality I had to accept to move to a stage where, as his friend, I could help him face the rest of his life.

Soon after that call, Tovar moved from Wanda's into the Wayland Flowers Hospice, where he could receive round-the-clock care. The staff later told me Tovar brought a lot of life into the hospice. Even when he was sickest, he tried to be a positive force among the other patients.

When I called Tovar back, I said I was not only coming to visit as soon as possible, I was bringing my kids with me. "You don't have to do that," he said. "I understand if you're worried about them being around AIDS patients." Thanks to Wanda, I knew there was nothing to worry about.

When I got to Los Angeles and went to the hospice, I understood what Wanda had been talking about. Tovar was painfully thin. His skin, which had been so smooth and beautiful, had the texture of an old, old man's. I was happy to see that the hospice had a cheerful atmosphere. I couldn't have stood to see Tovar in some kind of dark, depressing place just waiting to die. He told me that many of his old customers had visited. Delta Burke came, as did Arsenio Hall. Barbara Carrera sent him a note that read: "You are a bright and shining light that never can be extinguished." He'd filled his room with photos of friends and former customers, too: me, Dolly Parton, Arsenio Hall, Barbara Carrera, and Hank Williams Jr.

Tovar loved to sit in the hospice yard, under an avocado tree, listening to "Two Sparrows in a Hurricane." He said that the song made him think of the two of us, tossed around in a crazy world just trying to get a firm footing. As we sat there under that avocado tree, Tovar showed me one of his most prized possessions, a gold ring with his name encrusted in diamonds. He slipped it on his thin finger, and it was nearly twice too large. "Look, Tanya," he said. "Look how bony I've gotten." I nodded in agreement, because there was no reason to lie. He looked skeletal. We talked about the old days a while. I remembered some of his wonderful fashion shows, which he painstakingly planned and choreographed. They were always slick and showy and well produced, with great music and special effects. He always said he loved to work under pressure, where you had one shot to get it right. Kind of like life, I guess. Then he told me that one thing he'd always wanted to do was to meet

Elizabeth Taylor. He absolutely worshipped her for her beauty and status as an entertainment icon. But even with all the celebrity events he'd attended or worked at, he'd never met the star. Tovar talked about how he admired Liz Taylor so much for her work on behalf of AIDS.

"She took a big gamble to speak out when she did," he said. "Elizabeth was trying to raise money for AIDS before it was fashionable. Some stars probably wondered what people would think if they got involved, but not her."

The minute I left him and got in the car that day I was on the cellular phone to my publicist in Nashville. "Find her," I instructed. "Do whatever it takes, but find Liz Taylor."

I headed back out on tour. I called Tovar almost every day but felt guilty about not being able to spend more time there with him. Thankfully, Wanda could visit on almost a daily basis, and I asked a friend of mine, Pam Hyatt, who worked for Arsenio Hall, to stop by as often as possible. Every time I came within a hundred miles of Los Angeles, I went to visit him, and it was painful to see the disease take its toll. With each visit he grew weaker and weaker. His night sweats increased and his cough worsened. But I never saw him feel sorry for himself or say "why me?" Tovar remained a gentleman to the end.

Tovar loved the "Two Sparrows in a Hurricane" video I'd made with Ben and the kids. So he was one of the first people I called when I learned that it had been nominated for Video of the Year by the Academy of Country Music.

"You're gonna be there with me, Tovar," I told him.

"I'll try," he said, but his voice sounded very weak.

"You'll do better than try," I said. "You'll be there."

The awards were scheduled for May 11, and on May 2 I had to go to the studio to begin recording my next album, *Soon*. I've never been in worse shape to record. When I made *Changes* I felt like partying around. When I made *Love Me Like You Used To*, I felt the sessions were interrupted because I was in and out of town so much on tour. With *Soon*, I felt like I was drowning.

It wasn't just Tovar's condition, either. Bad things happened in threes that spring. In addition to Tovar, I had a phone call from a good friend in Scottsdale, Arizona, Gilbert Ortega, who was having heart surgery. Even though he was going to recover, hearing about his health problems worried me. I'd met Gilbert through another one of those "celebrity events," an art opening that he threw at his gallery in Scottsdale a couple of years earlier. I first heard about it through Mae Axton, who already knew Gilbert and planned to attend. She called to tell me that Gilbert was a fan and would like to fly me to Scottsdale for a showing of Southwestern art. I'd hesitated at first, because my girlfriend Twila was flying in from Los Angeles for a visit, but Mama Mae convinced me.

So Presley and I picked up Twila at the airport and I told her to hang on, because we were headed for Scottsdale instead of the ranch. When we arrived, we were whisked off to a plush hotel room, pampered with facials, new hairstyles, and makeup jobs! The funny thing was, we didn't even see Gilbert for two days. Until the opening he remained a mystery. When we did meet him, he proved to be one of the most charming and knowledgeable men I'd ever met. He is one of the most important dealers of Native American art in the world, and among his friends in attendance that day was the renowned R. C. Gorman. We attended the opening and then went to Gilbert's beautiful house. Presley took one look at the picturesque grounds and big swimming pool and made herself right at home. She still loves going to Gilbert's, and if I ever book a show in Arizona, her ears perk up. Partly because of my friendship with Gilbert, my weakness is now art instead of fast cars!

Gilbert is one of the "rocks" in my life, a wonderfully stable person who seems eternal. So when I learned that Gilbert was going in for open heart surgery, it set me back.

On top of that news, I got a call from the promoter who'd hosted that trip I took to Hawaii in 1989 with Shirley Porter. He told me one of his partners, who'd seemed to me to be the original good-time Charlie, had killed himself. The suicide hit me hard. I felt that if I could have been there, or somebody could have been there, at the right time to give the person some encouragement, maybe that moment of despair might have come and gone. Like they say, it's a permanent solution to a temporary problem. And maybe that was part of what happened to me that year; everything seemed temporary, fleeting. Life, friendships—they could all vanish in a flash. That's the kind of thing you know on one level, but when it hits over and over you just can't deal with it. Or at least I couldn't.

We'd been recording for about a week, and I was scheduled to overdub vocals at Javalina Studio with the studio engineer, Warren Peterson. I absolutely didn't want to go sing. I was depressed and in no mood to perform, live or on tape. All I could think of was getting out to Los Angeles to see Tovar. I'd jump every time the phone rang, afraid it was the hospice calling to say he was dead. I thought that in the large picture, that session wasn't as important as my friend. I wanted to see him again before he died.

But I knew both the label and my dad would be furious if I didn't show up at the studio, so I went on over. It was early evening, around six or so, when I got there. Warren was busy setting up microphones. There was a guy in the control room who looked vaguely familiar and who seemed to know me. "Hello, Tanya," he said, in a familiar manner. So I thought he must be a musician friend of Warren's that I'd met at some earlier session. I said hello and sat down to wait for Warren to finish with his technical duties. The guy started talking to me, but none of what he said made any sense. It was as though he were speaking in riddles. He'd ask me what seemed to be nonsensical questions, then immediately have what seemed to be a nonsensical answer for them. I can't even say what any of the questions were. I was so down and distracted thinking about AIDS and heart surgery and suicide that I just sat there nodding my head like I knew exactly what he was talking about. Warren came out and told me to go on back to the vocal booth. I was just putting on my earphones when Warren came into the booth, shut the door, and asked me, "Who is that guy?"

I told him I didn't have any idea, that I had thought the man was a friend of his. By the time we both came out, he was gone. That was when it hit me. He was the man who'd written me the threatening letters, who'd been at the cutting in Texas driving the van papered with my pictures. I took that as an excuse to leave the session. I hadn't wanted to be there, anyway. So I went home, packed up myself and the kids, and headed for Los Angeles, Tovar, and the ACM Awards.

FIFTY-SIX

*T*ovar was with me, just like I promised him he'd be. The staff had told me that he wasn't well enough to attend the show, so Tovar and I had arranged that he'd visit with me at my hotel suite, watching it all on the television there in the room. The staff told me that Tovar nearly died several times during the winter, and that they honestly believed that anticipating the ACM Awards was what kept him going. I rented a suite at Universal City and sent a limo to the hospice to pick him up.

It broke my heart when I saw him. Tovar was always so handsome, such a natty dresser. The staff members must have known how important it was for him to look elegant when he stepped into what would probably be his last ride in a limousine. He had on a silk suit and an ascot, but his face was drawn and his eyes were sunken. We gossiped and talked about old times. He loved watching the kids in the suite, Presley running and Grayson toddling. I hugged his neck before I left for the show, and he wished me luck. I told him our friendship was all the luck I'd ever need. Before I walked out the door, he squeezed my hand and told me he thought this trip would be the last we'd ever see each other. As I said before, winning awards isn't what motivates me. But I did harbor the hope of winning something that night so I could be on camera and send Tovar a message on national television. I knew how much that would mean to him.

Kathy Mattea and actor James Brolin came out to present the video award, and when they announced that I'd won, I almost cried. I took a deep breath and walked up to the lectern. I told the audience how proud I was to have been a part of country music the past twenty years. I thanked Jerry Crutchfield and my record label. I thanked my father and my children. Then I said, "I'd especially like to accept this award for my friend Tovar, who is watching this show from my hotel room. This trip may be the last time I'll see him." There was more I wanted to say, but my throat closed up and I couldn't. When I got back to the suite, Tovar was still up and waiting to say good-night. He was very weak, but he was thrilled to have been a part of one success we could share. Taking him back to the hospice was one of the hardest things I'd done.

⚜ ⚜

I returned to Nashville and Javalina Studio the next night to try to finish recording *Soon*. When I got there, the record label's security men were everywhere. George Currey, who owned the private security company Capitol used, came over and showed me some items left behind the previous Sunday by the man I now thought of as the Silver Assassin. He'd somehow misplaced a baseball cap and his California driver's license. So we knew his name, but he was no longer at the address. In addition to the items he'd left by accident, he'd given a studio employee a map of Arkansas with a message printed on it. The message said if he couldn't have me, nobody else ever would. That is the kind of thing you see on television or read in paperback novels, and it sounds corny and comic unless it's directed at you.

The first thing I did was to call my house to make sure Presley, Grayson, and the nanny were all right. I didn't know enough about stalkers to know if they went after family members or if they were just interested in the person they'd targeted. The children were fine, and I told the nanny to lock themselves in tight and make sure the security system was activated. Then I asked George to call my father and to get some guards out to my house to make sure my kids stayed fine. I moved my Mercedes to a secluded spot behind the studio, where someone driving by wouldn't see it. Several guards stayed with me, and several headed for my house.

When I talked to Dad on the telephone, he asked me what I thought was a strange question.

"You haven't tried to hide that car, have you?"

I said of course I had.

"Well, get it back out there," he instructed. "Because this guy will come looking for you, and the security men can get him."

I moved my car to the front parking lot.

Sure enough, later that night he drove into the studio's parking lot and started to get out of his car. He'd ditched the Tanya-van and was driving a bronze Maverick. A security man approached him, and although he took off at a high speed, the guard got the license number. So now we at least knew what he was driving. The following afternoon a police cruiser spotted the car parked on Music Row, and they were able to arrest him before he took off again. He was carrying a large hunting knife and talked incoherently about me all the way to the jail.

I was mainly relieved because of the children. But again, I went home without finishing up my vocals. I just couldn't do it.

FIFTY-SEVEN

Several days later, when I woke up, I couldn't get out of bed. I was shaking and afraid, but I didn't know of what, I didn't even realize I was crying until my hair felt wet and I realized my tears had soaked the pillow. All I knew for sure was that I seemed to be falling apart. Thank God, Presley and Grayson were at Mother and Dad's house, because I couldn't function. The new assistant I'd hired to help Tudy, Becky Waymack, arrived that morning, and I couldn't even talk to her.

It was the beginning of the most terrifying time I've ever spent. When Tovar died several weeks later, I couldn't get up to fly out to his funeral. I wanted very much to be there, but I couldn't get myself out of bed. Wanda von Kleist described it to me and told me that per his request, my recording of "Two Sparrows in a Hurricane" was played at the service. She also told me that when word reached Elizabeth Taylor in Europe that Tovar's fondest wish was to meet her, although she couldn't come in person, she'd sent a very kind note, which he received before he died. And Wanda also told me that Tovar had named her executor of his estate, and there was something he'd wanted me to have: the ring with his name in diamonds.

I was a basket case for the next couple of months. My parents stepped in and kept my children many times. I'd pull it together long enough to see them every day or so, but I was feeling worthless as a parent right then. Mother and Dad would call and come by to see what they could do. Sometimes I could barely talk to them. Ben called to see if he could help. Sometimes I could talk to him, and sometimes not. Friends like Shirley Porter, T. Martin, Barb Shipley, Tracy Johnson—all the T-Birds—either called or came to try to help. No amount of sympathy, concern, or advice worked.

My family and friends wanted me to talk to a professional about my state of mind, but I balked. I still couldn't get past thinking that seeking help was a sign of weakness. People who were Tucker tough did not go to shrinks. I also didn't quite understand that depression is nothing to be embarrassed about or ashamed of. It's something that happens to people, and something that they can work through. But they usually can't do it alone. One of my problems was that I'd spent too many years thinking I could do everything on my own. So, on my own, I stayed Tucker tough and got worse.

If I couldn't get out of bed, I obviously couldn't perform. But there was one show at the end of May that I felt I had to play, and that was the Jimmie Rodgers Festival in Meridian, Mississippi. When my dad called and suggested I cancel, I knew I must be in bad shape. At our house you got to be sick two days, maximum, and that makes it pretty hard to fake an illness to get out of doing something. I remember once back in grade school when I had a boil right on my rear end, and after I'd stayed home for the second day, Dad told me that was all the school that I could miss. The next day, boil or no boil, I trotted to school, carrying a pillow to sit on.

But I knew I had to go to Meridian that year no matter what. Ever since I'd performed "Daddy and Home" on that Jimmie Rodgers tribute album, I'd felt a responsibility to the festival and tried to attend each year. If they lacked performers, the show's organizers always knew they could come to me and I'd make some calls. I couldn't let them down. Also, I'd committed to shooting a television special at the Festival. I'd met an independent television producer named Sheila Slaughter, who months earlier had asked if I would help her sell The Nashville Network on a series of shows about various country stars. She thought if her pilot featured someone who had a fairly high profile, the concept might fly. I said I'd do the interview, and she decided to shoot it while I was playing the Jimmie Rodgers Festival. I had given her my word. So on the twenty-ninth of May I was in Meridian.

I did my part of the show, and Sheila and I made the television special. I was in such a down state of mind that I didn't remember to put my showbiz face forward. I spilled my guts about some of the things that were weighing heavily on me. I talked about the huge responsibility I felt because my family depended on me, and about how very unhappy and depressed I was feeling. I talked about being so tired that I wanted to quit the road for a while and spend more time with my children. Sheila interviewed my brother Don, who was out on the road with me again, sometimes driving the bus and sometimes acting as bus manager, seeing to upkeep and repairs. He agreed that there comes a time in a person's career when family members can't take care of everything. Mother and Dad were along, but they didn't sit in on many of the actual interviews and didn't know exactly what the tone was going to be.

My God, when Dad saw it he flipped out. "What did you get paid for that?" he demanded. "It had better be a lot, because that show isn't going to do your public image any good."

He even went crazier when I admitted I hadn't been paid a dime. And I told him I didn't care what it did to my public image.

Not long after Meridian, I had a call from Travis Tritt. He didn't have any idea I was in such a bad state. He was calling to say he was going back to his girlfriend, a woman he'd broken up with several months earlier, and he wanted to know if I thought it was dumb to start up the relationship again. I didn't even know the particulars of their breakup in the first place, and it's always funny to me when people ask my opinion on relationships, considering my own track record. So I just said, "Travis, I don't care if you want to date redheaded Chihuahuas if it makes you happy."

We talked awhile and I told him how down I'd been, and how hard it was for me to get up, go out, and perform. I said I'd even thought about quitting. He had a fit and insisted I just needed a break. A couple of weeks later I received a letter from Marty Stuart, a good friend of mine who often tours with Travis. "Don't do it, T," he wrote. "Give yourself a rest, but don't quit. You're one of the good ones. An individual." Marty's one of the most spiritually uplifting people I know, and his words helped me through the rest of that dark time.

I went back to the studio and finished my vocals for *Soon*, though I don't know how. When you hear the sadness in songs like the title cut or "We Don't Have to Do This," just know that it was as gut-level real as anything I've ever done. One song, "Hangin' In, Hangin' Out & Hangin' On" I dedicated to the T-Birds, because they'd hung in there with me for all those years. Then I went on the road again. As much as I wanted a break, there didn't seem to be any way to do it without canceling concerts. During June of '93, I had only four days off.

I've always wished that I could make records on my own schedule, instead of this "block out two weeks in May" kind of concept. I'd love to record over a period of time, to go into the studio when I felt like I was really ready, instead of when the producer and the record label and the session musicians can book the time. In some ways it's the difference between when songwriters compose when the muse strikes them and when they clock in at an office and write songs from nine to five every day. I'd be willing to bet that most of the classic songs were penned according to the muse and not the time clock.

When my mental state didn't improve, I finally called Dr. Boehm, my OB-GYN, and told him I couldn't sleep or eat or stop crying. I admitted that I felt like I might be going crazy and I needed help. I think it was the first time in my life I'd ever asked for help for anything emotional. The counselors at Betty Ford would have applauded the move. Dr. Boehm explained that my mental state wasn't something for an OB-GYN to tackle, and he gave me the telephone number of a good psychiatrist.

It took all I had to make the call. But I did, and I went to see the man. It was a major breakthrough for me. He explained that I wasn't going crazy and that depression is not an uncommon state of mind. He also suggested that between the recording sessions, the stalker, and my road schedule, I wasn't giving myself time to grieve for Tovar. He explained that depression can often be caused by a chemical imbalance, and prescribed medication.

One of the most important things I've come to understand is that there's nothing wrong with seeking professional help when you're having problems. Actually, it's just plain stupid not to. The head of my record label, Scott Hendricks, says it's a shame when people hear the somewhat negative term "shrink" so often that they become turned off by the whole idea of counseling. He could be right, because as any writer will tell you, words can sway people whether they realize it or not.

I started to crawl out of the depression in late June, partly, I'm sure, because of the medication. Coming back from a depression doesn't happen overnight. One of the first things that changed was that I started sleeping better. Rest goes a long way toward helping recovery. Then my appetite started to return. Then I wanted to have my children with me, because I felt I was again capable of giving them the attention they needed.

I think another reason I started functioning better was because I was booked at one of the theaters at Opryland. Those are choice gigs for Nashville entertainers, because they give us an opportunity to be with our families, to see friends we'd never see out on the road, and to get some rest. The gig was a godsend for me, and the fog that had been clouding up my mind seemed to clear somewhat.

Presley's birthday was coming up on July 5, and that forced me out to go looking for birthday presents. That meant I was among people instead of on a bus or a stage or in my bed. I ended up buying not only for Presley but for my mother and for Ben. Dad says the amount I spend is often tied to how low I feel. If I'm down, I think I can buy my way up. And maybe he's right.

On the Fourth of July, Wanda von Kleist came to visit. She didn't say anything about Tovar's bequest when she arrived, and I didn't ask. I figured she wanted to give me the ring when the time was right. I didn't have to leave for Opryland until 4:30 that afternoon, so Wanda and I decided to take a ride around the ranch on my pink Harley. "It's Independence Day," Wanda said. "What better time to celebrate Tovar's freedom from pain?" We were dressed in little tank tops and shorts, and I drove us at breakneck speed through the Tennessee hills, our hair flying in the wind. Finally we stopped on the crest of a hill, got off the motorcycle, and stood there looking out onto the valley below.

"This could have been scripted by Tovar," Wanda said.

I agreed. Tovar would love the idea of two blondes on a pink Harley carrying out a mission he'd set up.

Wanda reached into her pocket. "Tovar wanted you to have

this," she said. "I think it meant more to him than almost any-thing he had." Tears started streaming down my face.

"Tovar saw inside your heart," Wanda went on. "You've had ups and downs in your life, the way he did. But, also like him, you are a good person, a loving person. You meant a great deal to him."

I couldn't respond. But I was thinking how lucky I was that in this Tovar-scripted scenario, one of the two blondes on the pink Harley had a Ph.D. in psychology.

Ben came in the next day for Presley's birthday. I don't know how to explain the relationship between Ben Reed and me. Sometimes I'll tell people that I kept giving it another try for the kids' sake. But that isn't entirely true, because I cared greatly for him and still do. We seem to fight a lot, and because we see each other only occasionally, we've grown apart. I do love the family feel when we're together with Presley and Grayson, though.

Presley's birthday was one of the best times Ben and I had had in six months, and in some ways it was like our current rela-tionship. We come together as a family for the kids, and we usu-ally have a great time. I long for these times when my entire family is together. Mother and Dad came over. La Costa and Don brought their kids. Ben cooked hot dogs and hamburgers on the grill. That day the theme seemed to be giving away vehicles. I gave Presley a Barbie Corvette, which she loved. So did Grayson, by the way! Then I brought out a Nostalgia Harley I'd bought for Ben and a new 500E Mercedes for Mother. Whatever my motivation, it was worth the money to see the looks on their faces. We didn't have long to enjoy the presents, though. Ben and I got to ride motorcycles for a little while, but I had to be in the studio by 6:00 P.M. to record "Already Gone" for Don Henley's Eagles tribute album to benefit his Walden Pond fund.

The next day I began filming *Tanya Tucker's Workout Video*. When I watch the video now, I can't believe how healthy and energetic I look. I wasn't completely out of my depression. But I think most entertainers learn how to put on a good face no matter what. We made the video over a two-day period, then I went back on the road and stayed with few breaks for the remainder of the year. I took Presley with me a lot. She loves being on the road with me, and I miss her so much when she's not. Grayson had turned into a grandpa's boy. So as often as not, Grayson preferred to stay behind and ride on the tractors or go with "Bo-Bo," as he calls Dad, on his daily ranch rounds, checking the horses and seeing to it fences weren't down.

I started planning the video for "Soon" while I was out on the road in late July. The story everybody got at the time was that I made that steamy video with Ben because I was uncomfortable about camera crews seeing me in bed with any other man. Actually, I tried to track down Kevin Costner before asking Ben. Why not? Wouldn't most women use making a video as an excuse to climb into bed with Kevin Costner? I sure would. Well, as luck would have it, I couldn't get Kevin, so I asked Ben. In case you haven't heard the song, "Soon" is about a woman whose married lover always tells her things will change, "soon." She finally gets the courage to tell him to kiss off. Of course, since the woman is singing about her lover, we had to include scenes of love-making.

I had a lot of fun making that video, in part because of my buddy Brian Edwards. Brian is a dear friend who used to be my jewelry connection for awards shows. He had an arrangement with a major jewelry store so they would let me wear their diamonds and rubies when I was on camera. A lot of the sparklers you see on celebrities are not actually owned by those people. They're borrowed.

Brian is gay, and even with the understanding of homosexuality I had from Tovar, I still sometimes can't help but think a gay guy just needs to be "saved." I once tried to "save" Brian. I was in San Francisco when Brian and my friend Pam Hyatt brought me some choices of costumes and jewelry for a show I was getting ready to do in L.A. The three of us sat around talking late that night. Brian had always been open about being gay, and I had never thought much about it. That night, all of a sudden, he says, "Well, of course, I've never had sex with anyone. Man or woman." My reaction was: "Then you don't know what you are! Here, let me change your attitude." Next I pulled my shirt up over my head and smothered his face in my boobs. I'm sure glad nobody from the record label was around, because it didn't fit my new classy lady image one bit. Brian was horrified, and he immediately fled to the extra bedroom in my suite. I started feeling terrible about what I'd done, and every fifteen minutes or so I'd go in to apologize. He'd be huddled there, too afraid to even take off his shoes. "Brian, are you okay?" I'd ask. "I'm sorry if I offended you."

"Just fine, Tanya," he'd whisper. "You don't have to keep checking." Translate that to: *"Please* go away!" He said later that he was afraid each time I came in that I was going to attack him. Luckily, he kept his sense of humor and we stayed friends.

Brian hadn't met Ben at that time. Months later, when we did the "Soon" video shoot, Brian and I were having some drinks at the hotel bar when Ben showed up to talk about the next day's shoot. Brian's eyes about popped out of his head when Ben Reed walked in the bar. Let's face it, Ben looks good. I grabbed Ben around the neck and kissed him, kicking Brian under the table all the while. The next day we shot the hottest video country music could even imagine. In fact, it was too hot for Country Music Television. Ben and I were in bed half the time, and although Ben had underwear on, it looked as though he were nude. We cleared the set for most of the scenes. Later, we had to re-edit a couple of scenes where they thought I showed too much skin. It all seemed fine to me. After all, Ben was the father of my two children.

I'd made it a point to invite Brian to watch the shoot, since he thought Ben was so hot, and he just hated the fact that we cleared the set. So, after we finished shooting, I snagged the underwear Ben had been wearing and had it sent to Brian's apartment as a present. I don't know who's going to be madder at me for telling that story, Ben Reed or Beau Tucker. Probably Ben Reed. Brian won't be mad. He's the one who insisted I tell it.

All this time Ben and I were going back and forth trying to figure out if we could make something work between us. I will say that sometimes when I was riding the bus or sitting in a hotel room, I thought I would die without him. Especially when he had the kids and I was alone. Even though I don't like to admit it now, all I have to do is read back over my diaries at the time, and I know I thought about him a good deal. I have friends who still believe Ben and I will one day work everything out. I'm just happy to report that we are good parents together. That's the most important thing.

But no matter how much we cared for the other, we seemed to argue all the time. Once we got into an argument over a dream I had about him and another woman. Then we got into an argument because he was up for a film role to play a homosexual, and the part required him to kiss another man. I told him he should take it, but Ben said he just couldn't do it. I couldn't believe he was that homophobic, and we ended up having a huge fight. I said he was missing an opportunity to get his career into high gear, and that started another argument. But then everything would be great and we'd forget what we were fighting about.

In the middle of trying to figure out my relationship with Ben, I moved once again. I was sitting on the bus one afternoon in late August when Dad phoned and said he'd booked me on a flight to Nashville the next morning. "I'm thinking of buying another ranch," he told me. "I want you to come and see it." Man, I thought, here we go again. I caught a plane, as he'd asked, and flew to Nashville where a car picked me up and took me to Deer Park Farms. We drove in and I about died. The property had this long, winding drive up to a three-story home with, I found out later, four thousand square feet of covered porches, balconies, and verandahs. Driving up, I saw a gazebo, a small private lake with a covered picnic pavilion, and a guest house that looked about the same size as the Song House.

The house itself was nearly thirty thousand square feet, and it had a master suite with a sitting area and a fireplace, his and hers walk-in closets, and his and hers bathrooms with heated marble floors. Walk through it? Try roller skate, because I had to get back and do a show that night. I couldn't believe the size of the place. It had ten-foot ceilings and ten—count 'em—wood-burning fireplaces. It also had a gourmet kitchen with four ovens and two warming ovens. The people who were living there had it beautifully decorated. I felt like I was walking through a palace. Then we went to the area I really cared about: the stock area. There was a nice house waiting for a stockman to move in, a six-stall barn, corrals, breaking pens, cattle pens, and a rodeo-size arena for team roping. That's all I had to see. "Looks good to me," I said. Then I headed back to the airport so I could fly back in time to make my show.

The next time I saw Deer Park Farms, Dad had bought it, and it was empty and felt like the world's biggest ghost town. I walked through the house with Tudy, and all I could do was shake my head and say, "Man, oh, man. How am I ever gonna fill this place up?"

Then, every time I'd pick up a decorating magazine or when the bus would roll into a city like Charleston, South Carolina, where they have so many old, gorgeous homes, I'd get excited about furnishing it. And I did pick up a few pieces on the road. I bought a table and chairs and a sideboard in Augusta, Georgia, and I made arrangements to have some of my old couches and chairs recovered. But every time I got back to Nashville and walked through that monstrosity of a house, all I could see was empty space and all I could hear was an echo.

In the end it didn't matter.

By the time I was back long enough to move in, the house had been decorated right down to the pictures on the wall. I do not blame my parents and my staff for doing it. Someone had bought the house at Hidden Valley, so I had to get moved to Deer Park and I wasn't there to oversee. But when I walked through the house and saw all this memorabilia that supposedly meant something to me and didn't, it didn't feel like home. I felt like a stranger in my own house. As usual, I went out on tour and pushed the house to the back of my mind. Sometimes when I'd come in off the road, I'd climb off the bus and not even go inside the house. I'd head straight to the barn and look at the horses. That is where it felt more like home.

FIFTY-EIGHT

The next year I was so busy with my career that "home" was my new bus anyway. As a matter of fact, it was the one home I planned myself, and the one in which I now travel. My Liberty Lady coach was built in Chicago, and traveling around in it is a far cry from that old Chrysler station wagon or the variety of buses we'd owned or leased through the years.

I first noticed this line of coaches earlier that year when I was playing at a big outdoor festival. Once I went inside one of them, I was sold. The bus manufacturers invited me to come to Chicago and pick out everything from the fabric for the furniture to floor coverings and window shades. Liberty Lady has a large front living section with two big couches, one of which folds out into a bed. I chose a color scheme of cream, black, lavender, and turquoise, and much of the glass throughout the bus is decorated with etchings of horses. The kitchen/dining area has a seating area, full-sized refrigerator, sink, microwave, and standard stove-top. There's an airdoor opening into the bathroom, which has a marble floor, full-sized shower, vanity, and commode. There's also a pantry with a washer and dryer.

Then another airdoor opens into my bedroom, which has enough closet space that I no longer have to carry my stage clothes on another bus. My wardrobe assistant and I usually go over the concert dates and bring enough costumes so I have several choices for each venue. If it's an outdoor festival or fair show, I'll probably wear something like a short leather overall outfit. If it's a big club, like in Vegas or Atlantic City, then I'll bring out the spangles.

There are two televisions and two stereo systems inside the main part of the bus and another underneath, just in case we should park and want to pipe music out for a picnic. Another great feature this bus has is a video security monitor, so I can tell who is knocking on the door of the bus even if I'm back in my bedroom. We can do business easily from the Liberty Lady's six phones and fax! And 1994 was a big year for doing business from that bus.

All four singles from *Soon* were hit records: the title cut, "We Don't Have to Do This," "Hangin' In," and "You Just Watch Me." Jimmy Bowen made good on his promise that my records would be gold and platinum. Sales were so strong, in fact, that the label decided to put together a boxed set that November. The collection included not only recent hits but also many of my early hits, which Jerry and I had rerecorded. The label said I was the youngest female recording artist to have her recordings collected in a boxed set, and although I don't know if that's true, it sure sounds great. Other highlights of that year were my Black Velvet Tour and the Smooth Steppin' Showdown dance contest, where we raised many thousands of dollars for multiple sclerosis. That was also the year I was inducted into the Hard Rock Cafe's "Walk of Fame."

I kicked off the year in January in Atlanta at the 1994 Super Bowl, Dallas playing Buffalo. (Sorry, couldn't resist that.) I went with Dixie Pineda, who had moved to Nashville to start her own public relations company. We'd worked so well on the Black Velvet campaign that I became her first client.

I will say that there is such a thing as having too good a press agent. Dixie had me booked solid for the two days prior to the Super Bowl. When we got to Atlanta, I didn't even want to get off the bus and face it all. I was about thirty minutes late to my first press conference. I got with the program fast, though, and spent the next two days in a flurry of interviews and photo opportunities. Just to make sure I was politically correct, one day I wore a Troy Aikman, Dallas

Cowboys, jersey to all the press events, and the next day my costume included a Jim Kelly, Buffalo Bills, shirt.

One of the best times we had in Atlanta was at the NFL Experience, where kids can play interactive football games, throw footballs through hoops, play passing games, and do other football-related activities. Most of the parents stood by and watched while their kids were having a big time in the play areas. In a lot of ways, I never felt like I was a kid, and in others, I feel like I still am. So I pulled off my shoes and jumped right in the ring with Presley to join in anything she wanted to play.

One day, right after we taped a CNN show, as Dixie and I were starting across the street, I opened a package of Lifesavers, offered one to Dixie, then popped another in my mouth. After a couple of steps, I realized that Dixie was no longer beside me. When I turned around to look for her, she was standing in the road, her eyes wide open, her hand at her throat. The security man walking with us just froze when he saw her face, but I knew right away what had happened. She was choking on the Lifesaver. People were standing around staring at us, but nobody made a move to do anything. For the third time in my life, I silently thanked my brother Don for saving my life and teaching me how to keep someone from choking. I grabbed her and quickly applied the Heimlich maneuver. The Lifesaver shot out onto the pavement, and I held Dixie while she stood there shaking and gagging. After she realized she was all right, Dixie was so embarrassed at having been seen spitting up on the streets of Atlanta that she was the one who wanted to hide out on the bus. But she, too, thanked her lucky stars for Don Tucker.

By the time the day of the show came, I'd almost forgotten why we were in Atlanta. There were four acts performing during halftime: me, Travis Tritt, Clint Black, and Wynonna Judd. I wore black leather pants decorated with gold sequins and a gold beaded tank top and jacket. After I sang "It's a Little Too Late" and came offstage, Dixie asked me what it had felt like to sing for such a huge television audience—to have millions of people tuning in and watching me. I thought a minute and told her honestly that the only face I could visualize watching me on any of those millions of television sets was my dad's. After all, as I admitted to Dixie, he's the one I've been trying to please all these years. I think most of us spend a good part of our lives trying to make our parents proud.

Not all my performances that year were spectacular. I appeared on a celebrity segment of *Wheel of Fortune*, with several entertainers, including Little Richard, with whom I'd just recorded "Somethin' Else" for *Rhythm, Country and Blues*, a 1994 album of collaborations between country and R&B artists. I love Little Richard, although he's the only man I've ever worked with who had a better makeup job than I did.

Little Richard and I might have cooked on "Somethin' Else," but we did not distinguish ourselves on *Wheel of Fortune*. Little Richard had brought down the house with one of his responses. When he was asked to "name a consonant," he thought about it and hemmed and hawed. Finally, he brightened up and announced, "Europe." Like everyone else, I nearly died laughing.

And as it turned out I had no right to have a chuckle at Little Richard, because I had the thing won and blew it. When I had some of the letters on the board for my phrase, "no _u_s, no _lo_ _," I decided I had it nailed and took a shot. "No nuts, no flowers," I proudly announced. Well, the phrase was "no guts, no glory," which must have been obvious to the audience, because they groaned even louder at my mistake than they'd laughed at Little Richard's European consonant.

Then William Morris got me the single biggest booking of my career, the opening spot at the opening ceremonies for the World Cup Soccer Games in Dallas. Paul Moore told me I'd be seen by 2 billion people! What a career boost!

I went to Dallas to rehearse for the show on Monday, June 13, 1994. Does that date ring any bells? I was in the dressing room watching television before rehearsals when a news bulletin came on that Nicole Simpson, former wife of football legend O.J. Simpson, had been murdered in Los Angeles. Nicole and O.J. were not just names from the newspapers to me. I knew them. We had many mutual friends, and we had even double-dated on occasion. The early reports were kind of fuzzy, and my first concern was for the kids. Were they being taken care of? Where was O.J.? It sounded like a nightmare, and it got worse as it started looking like O.J. was a suspect.

For the next couple of days, I stayed glued to the television set every minute I wasn't rehearsing or doing interviews. And when I did have an interview I was the first one to ask a question. Before the reporter could say anything, I'd want to know, "What's going on with O.J.? What do you hear?"

They had all heard that he was a suspect and might be arrested soon. I just couldn't accept it. I'd seen friction between Nicole and O.J., but I couldn't believe in a million years that he was capable of killing her. Midweek, I flew to Atlanta for one of the semifinals of the Smooth Steppin' Showdown. There, I did the same thing. Every time a reporter stuck a microphone in my face, I asked about the Simpson situation in Los Angeles.

On Friday I was back in Dallas for the World Cup Opening Ceremonies. As usual, I had the television on while I was getting ready, and I saw the news bulletin about O.J. being missing and wanted by the police. They almost had to drag me away from the television to go on stage and sing "Texas (When I Die)." I already had the feeling I was in the Twilight Zone. Then I walked out and saw the crowd. There were people from all over the world, of course, and from where I stood, it looked like most of them were Latin Americans. I hadn't thought about what to expect. Was country music big in Latin America? As I looked at the crowd, I began worrying that this evening was probably going to be the exact opposite of that time the deejays booed me at the Opry and "Texas (When I Die)" saved me. Thankfully, the crowd loved the song, and I loved bringing some good American country music to the rest of the world.

I didn't wait around to bask in the applause, though. A limo was scheduled to take me to the airport, where my friends Marvin and Barbara Autry were waiting with one of their jets to fly me to another show. As soon as I climbed in that limo I tried the television set. And that television was the first working one I've ever found in a limousine. This is the truth. They've all got 'em, but the ones I get never seem to work. This one flashed right on and there was a picture of a white Bronco carrying O.J. Simpson and Al Cowlings, being chased by what looked like every cop in California along the L.A. freeways. I think most Americans experienced that "sky is falling" feeling as we watched an American hero hunted down on network television. I kept waiting for the credits to roll and somebody to say it was a made-for-TV movie.

But also, in the back of my mind, I could just hear my booking agent, Paul Moore, cussing the Bronco chase that was probably keeping those 2 billion viewers from hearing his artist sing "Texas (When I Die)."

As the Simpson case continued to be covered and the subject of abused women came to the fore, I thought back on my time with Glen Campbell and realized that a lot of women have been abused and are being abused, and they either don't recognize it or won't admit it, even to themselves. I didn't. After seeing so many powerful television shows addressing this problem, I understand more than ever that too many women are in denial about abuse, and how dangerous that is.

I don't have any noteworthy comments on O.J.'s imprisonment, the trial, and the acquittal. I sent him a note in jail and promised to pray for him, which I did. But first I prayed for Nicole Brown and Ron Goldman.

FIFTY-NINE

*M*y next album, *Fire to Fire*, didn't do much, even though I felt it was good and solid. It was one of those times when upheaval at a record label affect artists and their projects, usually in an adverse way. When Jimmy Bowen was diagnosed with cancer that year, he resigned as president of the record label. Thankfully, he has since made a complete recovery. But at Capitol, by the time a new label head was in place, many records had been lost. That's just one of those things you get used to in the record business. Well, maybe you never really get used to it, but you know it can happen. And when you consider the fact that somebody beat cancer, it seems pretty irrelevant, anyway.

The man EMI eventually named president and CEO of Capitol Nashville was none other than Scott Hendricks, who had engineered so many of my records, including the one I made in the Bahamas in 1987. Scott had gone on to become one of the most successful record producers in country music. I was sure glad I'd treated him well back when he was an engineer! Here's a little lesson for anybody, whatever business you're in: Be careful whose toes you step on, because they may be attached to feet you'll have to kiss.

As I said earlier, executive changes at a record label are usually scary for an artist. This time was no exception, and it ultimately resulted in a producer change. I had been with Jerry Crutchfield for ten years, and the new regime believed a change was in order. So a new producer, Gregg Brown, was chosen. It felt the same way it had all those years ago when I moved from the security I'd felt with Billy Sherrill. I felt like I was fifteen years old and scared to death.

It was the idea of change that scared me, not the idea of Gregg Brown. He had produced Travis Tritt, and they'd certainly made great records. When I called Gregg's office to set up a meeting, I was told that he was out of town attending a Chris LeDoux concert in anticipation of Chris's upcoming sessions. Man, I thought, what a concept, a producer who actually goes out on the road and listens to his act play live. That was really reassuring. And when we did meet, I was impressed with how concentrated and focused Gregg was. I also loved the fact that he didn't have a barn full of artists.

I had time to think about the changes that were coming because I'd pulled back a little from the road. For most of 1995 I'd been telling my dad I had to take some time off. I tried to explain that I felt I was missing something. Never mind that I took Presley or Beau Grayson out on the tour with me whenever I could; I didn't know them the way I wanted to. I finally had what I wanted, a place where my kids could roam freely, a place big enough to keep all the horses I wanted, and a place where my dogs could run without getting hit by an eighteen-wheeler. And I was missing out on it.

So I put my foot down. That's something I'd never been sure I could do. From the time we started out, I had always felt like I was herded here and herded there and my role was to not make any waves. Back when I was a kid, it was natural to look to Dad during interviews when I was stuck for an answer. I still look to him for answers. But this time, I felt I had my own answers, and they gave me the strength to make some waves. Dad listened to me and pulled back on bookings.

Just when I was going to be home more, Shirley Porter moved to Dallas, and that about killed me. I hated the thought of her being so far away. Pat Burns, a guy she'd met a couple of years earlier, had become very important in her life, and she was planning on marrying him. "Please wait a year, Squirrely Bird," I asked. "You and Royce thought you had a perfect marriage. I know Pat is great, but please stay engaged for one year to make sure he's right for you." She agreed to do that for me.

In the meantime, I met a new guy. I hadn't been looking for a new relationship. I'd been so concerned with trying to look into the future and predict what might happen with Ben Reed and me that I was letting the present slip away. But at the same time, I had been listening to my housekeeper, Maydelle, talk about the guy who owned the landscaping service working on my ranch. "He's the best-looking guy I've ever seen," Maydelle kept saying. I hadn't paid much attention until one afternoon when Jonathan Cummings came into the kitchen to talk about some money my dad owed him for landscaping. Well, I had to take a second look if he was a bill collector. Especially because it was Daddy, not me, who owed him money. I loved that. We got to talking, and the more I listened to him, the more I liked him. I thought, "Well, I've always been a gambler." Maybe I'd try one more time.

Jonathan and I began dating and the press made a big deal about it, referring to him as the "gardener" or the "yard boy." Never mind that he owned his own business, and I was one of many clients. As a matter of fact, I've always preferred men who do some kind of manual labor, who enjoy hard physical work and aren't afraid of getting their hands dirty. Men like my dad.

Of course, Jonathan quickly learned that dating me means living in a fishbowl. But he's a very positive-minded individual. He's very secure within himself, which I think is the true mark of a person's worth. But that still doesn't make going around with me easy.

I try to fit in with everyone else wherever I go, and when people don't allow me to, I often wind up in trouble and in print. I'll tell you a fairly recent example. This is not a very important episode in my life, but it did make the wire services, so I think I should tell you what happened.

I love to go to Cody, Wyoming. It's one of my favorite places on this earth, and it's an area I sometimes fantasize about settling down in for good. The terrain is beautiful. The desert runs straight into the mountains, and the stark, wild-looking plateaus create a feeling that you're looking at the Old West before the land was chewed up. I dream of someday selling this huge house I live in and moving myself and my kids to a little place in Cody.

On one trip I made to the rodeo in Cody, the newspapers reported that a young lady had asked Jonathan to dance, and she and I got into a fight about it. Some papers suggested that we both had black eyes, and others said she'd thrown a drink on me. The whole thing started when Jonathan and I were in one of the local bars, a place packed with the rodeo crowd and assorted tourists. Jonathan had just shaken his head when we eased our way inside the crowded room. He hadn't wanted to go out, anyway. "We've got perfectly good cabins," he'd argued. But I wanted to see what was going on.

That's one trait of mine that will probably never change. I love to go out where the lights are bright and people are having fun. I like parties, even though they are neither as frequent nor as rowdy as in past years.

We found seats and had a couple of drinks. I was trying just to hang out like everyone else, so when people approached me for an autograph, I told them to write down their address on a piece of paper and I'd send them a signed photo when I got back to Nashville. Then I got interested in shooting a little pool, and I got a table. I'd just started playing when some guys walked over and told me that wasn't the way they played pool in Australia. Well, that was throwing down the gauntlet. I told 'em to pick up their cues and put down their bets.

One girl wouldn't stop pestering for an autograph. It was annoying, since my pool game with the Aussies had turned serious. The girl soon figured out that I was with Jonathan and she started hanging around where he was sitting. Pretty soon she was not just hanging around, she was hanging on. That didn't slip by me. Finally she walked over to me holding two shot glasses and said, "Hey, let's have a shot of tequila and make up."

I thought about that for about a second and said, "Hey, I don't even know you. There's nothing to make up *for*." She wouldn't let it alone, so finally I took the tequila and knocked it back. She offered to get another round, but I said no. If I was going to drink tequila, it would be with Jonathan and my pool-playing pals. When it was my turn again and I started to head back to the pool table, she deliberately bumped into me. I started to brush her aside. She shoved me. That naturally pissed me off, so I shoved her back. Right about then some people pulled us away from each other and Jonathan and I paid up and left the club. That was the extent of the big fight. She didn't ask Jonathan to dance, nor did she throw a drink on me. It was a pretty simple situation.

But then the next day there was a knock at the cabin door and when I opened it, there stood the law. The policeman acted a little embarrassed, but he said the girl from the previous evening had reported I'd hit her. All I could do was laugh. I said, "No, I didn't, but if you'll bring her around, I will." That should have been the end of it. But then someone, maybe the girl, turned it into a media event and there I was in all the papers again.

That kind of thing has happened so many times. Sometimes people use your name just to add a little excitement to their place. There was one club that told the folks and me that celebrities hung out there all the time. They mentioned the week's clientele, which included Tanya Tucker. I took my sunglasses off and said, "Are you sure Tanya Tucker was here last night?" She shook her head and said, "Well, I always worried that would happen when I started name-dropping!" That time I just laughed and said, "Aw, hell. Drop my name anytime if you think it'll help drag anybody in."

I remember a time when I was around eighteen; Mother and Dad and I were eating in a restaurant in Los Angeles. The waiter at the table behind us was being very entertaining as he waxed on and on about how he'd been partying the night before with that wild woman Tanya Tucker. When the young man came over to take our order, my dad decided to call him on it. I held my head down so he couldn't see who I was. Dad said, "Son, I'd like you to repeat your story about that party to Tanya, here. You're just fixin' to take her order." Then I looked up at the guy and he like to have died on the spot.

After Cody, Jonathan kept pointing out that I have a wonderful home and maybe I should appreciate it more and not head off to places where somebody wants to start something. In fact, most of the time Jonathan and I spend together has turned out to be at my ranch, and maybe the Cody, Wyoming, incident played into that decision. There's not a lot of hell-raising that goes on out here.

But I do still travel. Jonathan's mother, Sharon, invited me to join her on a trip to the Holy Land. That noncelebrity tour turned out to be one of the most wonderful experiences of my life. We went with a local church group led by a Hendersonville, Tennessee, minister, Dr. Rodney Cloud. I had wanted to visit the Holy Land for years, and my dad couldn't talk me out of going, even though he tried. Yitzhak Rabin had just been killed, and Dad was scared to death that fighting would break out in the Middle East and I'd be caught up in it.

So he gave me a million reasons I shouldn't go. He kept telling me how hard it was going to be, reminding me that I'd be hauling all my luggage around the Middle East with no assistants. I said if I couldn't make it two weeks hauling my own luggage, then I was seriously in need of an attitude adjustment. He reminded me about the 5:30 A.M. wake-up calls. "They're taking bets in Vegas you won't make it a week," he told me. "Well, don't you be betting against me," I warned him. I not only stuck to my guns about the trip, I took La Costa and Patsi Cox, my *Nickel Dreams* co-writer, with me. I also wanted to take Mother, but she decided she wanted to stay home with her grandchildren. Every time we stopped and visited another holy site, I wished again Mother had come along. One of these days I want us all to go, the entire family.

One reason I really wanted to take this trip was to learn more about the Bible. I've always thought I should know more about the time when Jesus lived and the land where He walked and taught. I also hoped that since I was trying to make some sense out of my life for this autobiography, maybe the Holy Land would be the place to do it. One of my friends asked me if I was sure I wasn't just trying to one-up Glen Campbell for being born again and using that as the climax in his book. Nah, I said, I've just been feeling Vacation Bible School calling me back.

We left on December 27, and for the next two weeks traveled through Israel and Egypt. Despite my father's warnings, I was never afraid or had any feeling of danger during the trip. In talking to the other travelers, I learned that none of us had felt any fear while we were there. I won't do a travelogue here, but I will tell you a few of the things that amazed me.

Jesus could be felt everywhere on the trip. We went to Nazareth and visited the church where the angel told Mary she would give birth to the son of God. In the church, I touched the water from the spring that had been running for thousands of years. We visited the River Jordan, where Jesus was baptized, and I saved a little of the water in a small jar to bring home with me. The river is much smaller than I expected, but there's a majesty to it that could only be described as spiritual. At the Sea of Galilee we saw an ancient fishing boat that very well could have been one that Peter cast his nets from. It was incredible to think that the Lord walked on that same water. To really feel the emotion of the places you see in the Holy Land, I believe some-times you have to get away from the group and sit alone. I tried to do that at many of these stops.

We spent New Year's at the Shalom Hotel in Jerusalem, and a group of us from the tour group went down to the hotel's lobby bar to ring in 1996. There were probably a hundred people from all over the world in the lobby area, and at midnight we all stood together and sang "Auld Lang Syne." It was incredibly uni-fying and probably a once-in-a-lifetime experience for me.

On New Year's day, we began our tour of Jerusalem in the old part of the city, at the Western Wall, once called the Wailing Wall. Our guide told us this story about the wall: "There once was a rabbi who visited the Wailing Wall. He stared at it for a long time. All of a sudden the rabbi began to laugh, and the men around him were horrified at such irreverence. One of them asked him what he found amusing about the Wailing Wall, the historic monument to mankind's suffering. The rabbi smiled and answered, 'I finally understand. This is as bad as it will ever be.'" There's a lesson in that for all of us.

We walked the path through Jerusalem that Jesus walked car-rying His cross, and we saw the spot where He rolled back the stone and rose again. There was a British guide at the tomb, and he said something that made me think. He said he was always glad to welcome the good Christians to the tomb, but he liked welcoming the less-than-perfect ones even more. I decided, well, that's me. I've done a lot of thinking about being less than per-fect. In the past I have prayed and I have cried about being a less-than-perfect Christian. But after visiting the places Jesus walked, I no longer believe there is any shame in sometimes failing before the Lord. There is shame in not trying, but not in failing.

All in all, I think the greatest thing I brought home from that trip was a renewed closeness with La Costa. We see each other here in Nashville, and we talk, but sometimes we don't express our love for each other very well. That's a big problem in our family, and I'm as guilty of it as any of us. Maybe more so. Don once said to me, "Tanya, you seem to be able to tell your dogs you love them easier than you can tell me." I do care desper-ately about my sister and brother, but I have been sloppy about simply assuming that they know it. I think after that trip La Costa understands just how much she means to me. Now I'll have to convince Don.

SIXTY

Almost as soon as I returned from the Holy Land, Jonathan and I started planning a wedding. A young woman named Stephanie Beck had come to work with me, and I enlisted her help, as well as that of other friends. We called up bridal consultants, bought piles of bride magazines, and I tried on wedding gowns. I started making some of my famous lists. I couldn't spend as much time on it as I wanted because my dad started sneaking in more concert dates. First one, then another. He'll do that. "I couldn't turn this one down, Tanya," he'll say. Then about the time I start for that one, he'll add a couple more.

One day when I was looking over wedding books and trying to figure out whether to have a big blowout with everyone in the world invited or just a small family and friends affair, I got a call from Shirley Porter. She said, "You know what, T? I'm gonna throw your request right back at you. I waited a year to get married, and now I know it's the right thing. I'd like you to do the same. Now that you've made this commitment, wait a year and see what happens."

"We've got all these plans started," I began protesting.

"Too bad," she shot back. "You've waited all these years to

make sure it was right, and I don't think you honestly know just yet."

I stared down at the bride books then back at the telephone receiver, and I knew in my heart I didn't know if this was right or not. So I said, "Well, Squirrely, I'll wait."

I explained to Jonathan, and I think he understood. This step has been so long in coming that when I do take it I want it to be in the right direction. Jonathan doesn't want to make a mistake, either. We'll just have to see what happens. In the meantime, all the bride's magazines and lists are filed under "Jonathan."

I love being at the ranch as much as I am now. It's a very peaceful environment out here. For the first time in the twenty-three years since I recorded "Delta Dawn," I can spend time doing things like cleaning the tack room in the barn, getting hooked on a soap opera, driving Presley to school, and helping Grayson learn to ride the horses. This is primarily an agricultural area. One of my neighbors is a blacksmith, another is a dairy farmer, and another a tobacco farmer. One family grows and supplies all the produce for the area grocery stores. On Sundays we go to a little country Baptist church, and at night sometimes the only man-made sounds you can hear are the trains whistling off in the distance.

We've got twelve horses now, and we're training two of them for cutting. We got a burro this winter and named him Poncho. Dad mentioned to me that he loved longhorns, so I bought thirteen of them for him to look after. George Jones gave me a yellow Labrador retriever, which I (of course) named Possum. We've got a Chesapeake Bay retriever who just had puppies, a Pomeranian who guards the back porch, and a cat who guards the barn. My dad comes over to check things out almost every day. He's much happier working on a tractor or feeding cattle than he is in an office working as a music manager. I wish he could give up all his management duties and just be a farmer, but until somebody comes along he trusts more than himself, he'll be at my side. Don is out here quite a bit helping Dad with the cattle or making sure the bus is in good shape. He's still my bus manager.

La Costa runs the Tanya Tucker fan club, and she has started her own company, La Costa Tucker's Country Chocolates and

Hard Rock Candy. She inherited our Grandma Tucker's candy-making abilities and entrepreneurial spirit. Fans ask about a CD of her wonderful songs all the time, and I'm hoping that Capitol Records will reissue some of her songs on CD this year. Her kids come over with her frequently to ride. Costa's daughter Kali is a beauty with long blonde hair, and one of the happiest dispositions I've ever seen. Zach, her son, is an honor student. They are both such well-mannered kids. La Costa has raised them wonderfully.

Don, too, has started a new company on the side. In addition to the work he does for me, he's an Amway dealer now. I love to see them both branching out, because they are both talented and intelligent people who have a lot to offer. Like La Costa, Don is a good parent. Don's daughters, Tyra and Alyssa, and his son, Lakon, are all great kids. Tyra is the more quiet of the girls, and she is just now getting into being a teenager. Alyssa is still a tomboy, and Presley and Grayson love to hang out with her. A rowdy older cousin who actually loves hanging out with the littler ones is kid paradise! Lakon just got married this year.

Presley and Grayson are both out-of-doors kids. They both gravitate toward the barnyard as much as their mother. And they are musical. Grayson has a set of drums he loves to play. He's a little handful. He's always going and doing, always busy. He'd like to be a ballplayer when he grows up, and he pesters anyone who comes around to play catch with him. He's started school this year and so far he loves it. Presley, now seven years old, is quite a singer, and every so often my dad will narrow his eyes and say, "Now, there's a superstar in the making." I'll tell him to see to it it's a long time in the making. I want her to do the other things she loves—read books, paint, play with her friends. She's a good little painter already.

Presley adores school, and I find it fun to work with her on her homework. I picked her up from school one day recently, and she was reading her homework assignment to me, and came to the word "hunch." She asked me what that meant, and it was wild, because you have to stop and think about what words really mean when it involves your child's schoolwork. My first thought was that it was something you felt you knew by instinct. Then I wondered if intuition was a better word. We talked about it until I could see she understood, and it was fun to see her face light up when she knew precisely what the concept meant. These are the kinds of day-to-day things I wanted to be home for and experience. And who knows, maybe if I try to work with Presley and Grayson all through their school years, I'll be ready to walk in and ace that GED test about the time they get out of high school! Maybe we'll all graduate together.

Both kids are strong-minded. They've got opinions and aren't afraid to voice them. Grayson's personality really started to emerge around the time he turned four. Up until then, he seemed mostly to follow Presley's lead. If I asked them what they wanted to eat for dinner, Grayson would go along with whatever Presley wanted. If she decided to play a certain game, it was fine with him. His independence started coming out slowly at first, with him hedging when she put in the dinner order or pulled out some kind of a game to play. And as the time went by, I saw more and more that he was wanting to assert himself. He had definite ideas about what he liked and didn't like, and his ideas were not necessarily those of his big sister.

For one thing, Grayson doesn't have the intense love of riding horses that Presley and I share. Presley is already an expert rider who sits the saddle better than I do. Grayson would much rather ride the burro or, better yet, the farm machinery with his Bo-Bo. We recently took a pack trip in the mountains, and Grayson absolutely did not want to get on one of those horses. I'd signed up for the trip thinking he could ride on the front of my saddle with me, but it turned out that each individual had to ride alone. But it wasn't long before he was feeling more comfortable sitting up there, and before the trip was over, he was waving away the man assigned to lead his horse. I hope that means he'll be out in the pasture riding horses with his mother and sister before long.

I still take them out on the road when it's possible, but the times are getting fewer these days. During their school year, of course, it's next to impossible. And I'm always worried about them when I take them on road trips. I don't care how many people are supposed to be watching them, those two can slip out of sight fast. They did it once in Las Vegas while we were shopping. I leaned down to look at something in a store window, and when I turned around, they were gone. I ran up and down the block hollering for them, and getting more frightened with every passing second. I finally spotted them standing in the doorway of a store where they couldn't be seen from the sidewalk. They were fine, but it took me a while to get rid of the knot in my stomach. That happened when I was with them, so you can imagine how paranoid I am about a nanny losing track of those two.

I don't want to miss my kids' youth. I'm already bad about looking at their baby pictures and tearing up as I remember some particular incident, whether I was directly involved or just heard about it from my parents. One day I want to send them out into the world with a pat on the back, not with me in hysterics over where the years have gone.

I'm thirty-eight now, and as I age and my parents age, I've started looking at them a little differently, too. I know I won't have them forever, and that is a frightening thought. I can't imagine life without Beau and Juanita Tucker. Thinking about their mortality causes me to consider my own. As I get closer to forty years old, I often think about age and being in my fifties, sixties, and seventies. Eighties and nineties, too. I guess my concern is that I not grow scared as I age. I've seen people start to lose their nerve as they get old. They start to fear death so much they forget to live, I guess. I don't want that to happen to me.

When I think about my own future, I sometimes wonder if I'll be on the road forever. A long time ago I read that Mick Jagger said he didn't want to be forty years old still singing "Satisfaction." Well, here he is at fifty-something, and still singing it. I'll probably be performing "Delta Dawn" until I drop, too. As long as anybody wants to listen, I'll be up there singing.

SIXTY-ONE

$\mathscr{T}$ had hoped to be completely off the road when it came
time to record my next album, but that didn't happen. My dad
was sneaking in dates as often as he could. If the money was
good, he signed the contracts. But this was to be my thirtieth
album, and I was nervous about it. For one thing, I'd taken some
time off. Few artists can do that without having a little uphill battle to fight when they get back. So I knew that this album had
to be as good as anything I'd ever done. I started thinking about
songs, and how I'd like to sing some different material, maybe
stretch a bit more than I'd been doing lately. My new producer,
Gregg Brown, agreed completely, and we did pick some edgy
songs, as I'd wanted. And some great, wonderful ballads. The
album's titled *Complicated*, and I'm really proud of it.

Now that the record is complete, I'm finishing up this segment
of my memoir. I say "this segment" because I ain't done living
yet! You never know what might happen and what I might have
to write about in Volume II. What's ahead? Well, I'm getting that
old list-making itch again. I keep writing down things I'd like to
accomplish. First of all, I'm putting together a new, innovative
show for my next year's tour. Because of this book, I've been
sorting through old photos and listening to the old songs, and I

hope to do a retrospective kind of concert and include a slide show. I'm excited about this year's tour more than any in recent times. Maybe taking a semibreak in 1996 was just what the doctor ordered, because I'm feeling energized and excited about 1997.

I'd still like to record an album of Merle Haggard songs. I'd also love to get together with some of my songwriting friends and write an entire album. If I could stay off the road long enough to focus myself on it, I sincerely believe I could do what Harlan Howard suggested all those years ago: let the songwriter side of me break free. I'd give anything to make another record with Billy Sherrill, too, but it would take a miracle to get him back in the studio. He relishes retirement and spends most of his time on his boat.

And I'd love to put together an album for a charity where artists produce the sides on each other. Dolly would pick someone to produce, Merle would pick someone. I think my choice to produce might be Jerry Lee Lewis, because he is truly unique. Part of what a producer does is try to harness all the dynamics at a recording session and focus them in one direction. I'd love to get some great honky-tonk pickers together with Jerry Lee and try to get that explosion of musical energy pointed down the same road. We'd pay the up-front costs on the album and give everything else to a charity.

While I was in the Holy Land it struck me harder than ever before that entertainers don't really contribute much to this world. We're not out there curing cancer or teaching school or anything. Maybe that's why we do those charity concerts. We know we're getting paid way more than some of the people who keep making the world a little better, individuals like teachers and social workers and nurses. I know that music does help people through bad times, though. Fans tell me stories about songs that have touched them all the time. So to make myself feel a little more consequential in the grand scheme of things, I just might start writing "music therapist" down as my occupation instead of "singer."

I wish I could end this book with a big revelation and tell you I discovered the secret of happiness. That's just not gonna happen. I don't believe life has easy or clear-cut answers, and because of that, I've been thinking a lot about the people who do make huge personal breakthroughs that change their lives. And thinking about the ways they were different from me made me remember an incident from when I was about fifteen and out on tour. The schedule was so close that I had to fly in a private plane from one venue to the next. There had been a quick storm just before we took off, and soon after we were airborne we saw a rainbow in the sky. We came closer and closer, until finally we flew right through the rainbow. It was one of the most incredible experiences I've ever had. I don't mean to overstate it, but it was like being touched by God or something; like seeing your child for the first time, or watching tears fill your parents' eyes when you've made them proud.

And I realized it makes a great ending for a book if somebody can talk about finding the end of the rainbow, but I honestly think folks who can are few and far between. Those of us who are still works in progress should just feel lucky to get a chance to fly through one once in a while.

TANYA TUCKER ALBUMS & SINGLES DISCOGRAPHY

10/72: *Delta Dawn*, Columbia (31742)
Produced by Billy Sherrill
"Delta Dawn"
"Love's the Answer"
"The Jamestown Ferry"

5/73: *What's Your Mama's Name*, Columbia (32272)
Produced by Billy Sherrill
"What's Your Mama's Name"
"Blood Red and Goin' Down"

3/74: *Would You Lay with Me,* Columbia (32744)
Produced by Billy Sherrill
"Would You Lay with Me (In a Field of Stone)"
"The Man That Turned My Mama On"
"I Believe the South Is Gonna Rise Again"

3/75: *Tanya Tucker's Greatest Hits*, Columbia (33355)

4/75: *Tanya Tucker,* MCA (2141)
Produced by Snuff Garrett
"Lizzie and the Rainman"
"San Antonio Stroll"

1/76: *Lovin' and Learnin',* MCA (2167)
Produced by Jerry Crutchfield
"Don't Believe My Heart Can Stand Another You"
"You've Got Me to Hold On To"

9/76: *Here's Some Love*, MCA (2213)
Produced by Jerry Crutchfield
"Here's Some Love"

2/77: *Ridin' Rainbows*, MCA (2253)
Produced by Jerry Crutchfield
"Ridin' Rainbows"
"It's a Cowboy Lovin' Night"
"Dancing the Night Away"

8/77: *You Are So Beautiful*, Columbia (34733)
Produced by Billy Sherrill
"Spring"
"You Are So Beautiful"

3/78: *Tanya Tucker's Greatest Hits*, MCA (3032)

10/78: *TNT*, MCA (3032)
Produced by Jerry Goldstein
"Texas (When I Die)"
"I'm the Singer, You're the Song"

10/79: *Tear Me Apart*, MCA (5106)
Produced by Mike Chapman

10/80: *Dreamlovers*, MCA (5140)
Produced by Jerry Crutchfield
"Dream Lover" (with Glen Campbell)
"Can I See You Tonight"
"Love Knows We Tried"

1981: *The Very Best of Tanya Tucker*, Columbia (15770)

7/81: *Should I Do It*, MCA (5228)
Produced by Gary Klein
"Should I Do It"
"Rodeo Girls"

5/82: *Live*, MCA (5299)
Produced by Snuff Garrett

1/83: *The Best of Tanya Tucker*, MCA (5357)

1/83: *Changes*, Arista (9596)
Produced by David Malloy

"Cry"
"Feel Right"
"Changes"
"Baby I'm Yours"

2/86: *Girls Like Me*, Capitol (12474)
Produced by Jerry Crutchfield
"One Love at a Time"
"Just Another Love"
"I'll Come Back As Another Woman"
"It's Only Over for You"
(*Girls Like Me* was originally released as an LP. In 1994 it was reissued in CD format: #29947.)

7/87: *Love Me Like You Used To*, Capitol (46870)
Produced by Jerry Crutchfield
"Love Me Like You Used To"
"I Won't Take Less Than Your Love" (with Paul Davis and Paul Overstreet)
"If It Don't Come Easy"

7/88: *Strong Enough to Bend*, Capitol (48865)
Produced by Jerry Crutchfield
"Strong Enough to Bend"
"Highway Robbery"
"Call on Me"
"Daddy and Home"

7/89: *Greatest Hits*, Capitol (91814)
Produced by Jerry Crutchfield
"My Arms Stay Open All Night"

5/90: *Tennessee Woman*, Capitol (91821)
Produced by Jerry Crutchfield
"Walking Shoes"
"Don't Go Out with Him" (with T. Graham Brown)
"It Won't Be Me"
"Oh, What It Did to Me"

8/90: *Greatest Hits Encore*, Capitol (94254)
Produced by Jerry Crutchfield
(early hits rerecorded)

6/91: *What Do I Do with Me,* Capitol (95562)
Produced by Jerry Crutchfield
"Down to My Last Teardrop"
"(Without You) What Do I Do with Me"
"Some Kind of Trouble"
"If Your Heart Ain't Busy Tonight"

9/92: *Can't Run from Yourself,* Liberty* (98987)
Produced by Jerry Crutchfield
"Two Sparrows in a Hurricane"
"It's a Little Too Late"
"Tell Me About It" (with Delbert McClinton)

4/93: *Greatest Hits 1990–1992,* Liberty (81367)
Produced by Jerry Crutchfield

10/93: *Soon,* Liberty (89048)
Produced by Jerry Crutchfield
"Soon"
"We Don't Have to Do This"
"Hangin' In"
"You Just Watch Me"

11/94: *Tanya Tucker,* Liberty (28822)
Box Set Collection Produced by Jerry Crutchfield
58-song set, "Delta Dawn" to "Soon"
(Originally released in CD format only. In 1995 the box set was
released in cassette format on Capitol Nashville #28822.)

3/95: *Fire to Fire,* Liberty (28943)
"Between the Two of Them"
"Find Out What's Happening"

11/96: *Complicated,* Capitol Nashville (36885)
Produced by Gregg Brown

---

*All product released under Liberty Records has since been changed in the EMI system
to Capitol.

Multi-Artist Albums

1/88: *Superstars Salute Jimmie Rodgers*, Step One (JRF-001)
Produced by Jerry Crutchfield
"Daddy and Home"

10/93: *Common Threads: The Songs of the Eagles*, Giant (24531)
Produced by Jerry Crutchfield
"Already Gone"

3/94: *Rhythm, Country & Blues*, MCA (10965)
Produced by Don Was
"Somethin' Else" (with Little Richard)

4/95: *Come Together: America Salutes the Beatles*, Liberty (31712)
Produced by Jerry Crutchfield
"Something"

2/96: *NASCAR: Hotter Than Asphalt*, Columbia (67510)
Produced by Blake Chancey
"Goin' Nowhere and Gettin' There Fast"

9/96: *The Best of Country Sing the Best of Disney*, Walt Disney
Records (60902)
Produced by Gary Burr and Tanya Tucker
"Someday My Prince Will Come"